INTEGRATING INSTRUCTION: LITERACY AND SCIENCE

TOOLS FOR TEACHING LITERACY

Donna Ogle and Camille Blachowicz, Series Editors

This highly practical series includes two kinds of books: (1) grade-specific titles for first-time teachers or those teaching a particular grade for the first time; (2) books on key literacy topics that cut across all grades, such as integrated instruction, English language learning, and comprehension. Written by outstanding educators who know what works based on extensive classroom experience, each research-based volume features hands-on activities, reproducibles, and best practices for promoting student achievement.

TEACHING LITERACY IN SIXTH GRADE
Karen Wood and Maryann Mraz

TEACHING LITERACY IN KINDERGARTEN
Lea M. McGee and Lesley Mandel Morrow

INTEGRATING INSTRUCTION: LITERACY AND SCIENCE
Judy McKee and Donna Ogle

TEACHING LITERACY IN SECOND GRADE
Jeanne R. Paratore and Rachel L. McCormack

TEACHING LITERACY IN FIRST GRADE
Diane Lapp, James Flood, Kelly Moore, and Maria Nichols

INTEGRATING INSTRUCTION

LITERACY AND SCIENCE

Judy McKee
Donna Ogle

Series Editors' Note by Donna Ogle and Camille Blachowicz

THE GUILFORD PRESS
New York   London

© 2005 The Guilford Press
A Division of Guilford Publications, Inc.
72 Spring Street, New York, NY 10012
www.guilford.com

Printed in the United States of America

This book is printed on acid-free paper.

Last digit is print number: 9   8   7   6   5   4   3   2   1

Library of Congress Cataloging-in-Publication Data

McKee, Judy.
   Integrating instruction : literacy and science / Judy McKee, Donna Ogle.
      p. cm. — (Tools for teaching literacy)
   Includes bibliographical references and index.
   ISBN 1-59385-156-1 (pbk.: alk. paper) — ISBN 1-59385-157-X (hardcover:
alk. paper)
   1. Language arts (Elementary)   2. Science—Study and teaching
(Elementary)   3. Language arts—Correlation with content subjects.   I. Ogle,
Donna.   II. Title.   III. Series.
   LB1576.M2485 2005
   372.6—dc22

                           2005004321

To the students who have stimulated our work

And to our husbands, who are committed to making this a better world and whose respect for teachers and schools is evident daily—and was especially evident during the time it took us to write this book

ABOUT THE AUTHORS

Judy McKee, MA, is a science consultant for Wilmette Public Schools in Wilmette, Illinois. As an award-winning educator, Ms. McKee has specialized in science education and in differentiating curriculum for students with special needs. She has presented workshops on science and integrated curriculum throughout the United States and for teachers in American schools in Latin America, and has taught numerous courses at National-Louis University and DePaul University. Currently affiliated with the Out of State and International Student Teaching Program at the University of Northern Iowa, Ms. McKee is active in professional organizations and has helped in staff development in many school districts. She has also authored several articles for professional education journals, and has contributed to books pertaining to integrating curriculum and science activities.

Donna Ogle, EdD, is Professor of Reading and Language at National-Louis University and past president of the International Reading Association. Dr. Ogle's extensive staff development experiences include working in Russia and other eastern European countries as part of the Reading and Writing for Critical Thinking Project, and ongoing projects in U.S. school districts, particularly in content reading and integrating curriculum. Her most recent books include *All Children Read,* coauthored with Charles Temple, Alan Crawford, and Penny Freppon; *Coming Together as Readers;* and *Reading Comprehension: Strategies for Independent Learners,* coauthored with Camille Blachowicz.

SERIES EDITORS' NOTE

This is an exciting time to be involved in literacy education. Across the United States, thoughtful practitioners and teacher educators are developing and fine-tuning their instructional practices to maximize learning opportunities for children. These cutting-edge practices deserve to be shared more broadly. Because of these changes, we have become aware of the need for a series of books for thoughtful practitioners who want a practical, research-based overview of current topics in literacy instruction. We also collaborate with staff developers and study group directors who want effective inservice materials that they can use with professionals and colleagues at many different levels that provide specific insights about literacy instruction. Thus the Tools for Teaching Literacy series was created.

This series is distinguished by having each volume written by outstanding educators who are noted for their knowledge and contributions to research, theory, and best practices in literacy education. They are also well-known staff developers who spend time in real classrooms working alongside teachers applying these insights. We think the series authors are unparalleled in these qualifications.

In this volume, Judy McKee and Donna Ogle share their passion for integrating literacy and science instruction. Both know how much children enjoy science content and how it develops their thinking and literacy skills during active, integrated explorations. The classroom examples they have included in this volume can heighten a teacher's understanding of ways to orchestrate the learning of science and literacy in the elementary grades.

DONNA OGLE
CAMILLE BLACHOWICZ

PREFACE

Judy McKee and Donna Ogle have collaborated for many years in exploring the connections between children's interests in science and their literacy development. Both were nudged into thinking deeply about how science might be a powerful context for literacy development by working with children. Judy recalls how she developed a deep commitment to integration of instruction:

"Those guys are really small!" exclaimed one of the boys as he peered into the large jar of pond water. "That's a cyclops!" I told him, handing over a magnifier. "If you look closely, you can see that she carries her eggs attached to her legs." "Yow!" was the response. The water was alive with other moving things, so I transferred a portion to a smaller container and gave another boy an eyedropper to capture one of the microorganisms for examination under a microscope. When the microscope was focused we could clearly see the daphnia, but I didn't immediately tell the children what it was. For that, we used a pond book to match the picture with what we saw in the scope. It was the early 1960s, and I was working with three 7-year-olds assigned to my second grade. They were there before school so that I could help them with their reading.

Yes, I said *reading* because somehow those boys perceived that reading is a chore offering little pleasure. I was determined to change that perception. We embarked on spending some extra time together studying pond water I had brought into the school from a nearby park. A pile of books was used to arm the boys with facts and information qualifying them as class "experts" for that ministudy.

During structured reading group, held every morning, we covered the perfectly acceptable basal reader and many of the accompanying lessons from the teacher's manual required by the school district. I tried to make those lessons as productive as possible. However, as the year progressed it was obvious that the students I had concerns about were much more interested in our afternoon science lessons. I could see them using books to learn the facts and master information. Eager faces and enthusiastic comments showed me that I should capitalize on this.

Slowly, they made progress as I provided books of real interest to them, incorporating teachings from morning reading group and ushering them into the world of bugs, spiders, pond animals, and earthworms. We observed and examined these creatures. Then we read and wrote about them.

The district reading consultant came into my room to "help" me, a new teacher with struggling readers. She asked what I was doing to promote their success. I explained that I often spent time before school with these children and proudly told her that at these times and during afternoon science lessons the boys "turned on." I added that they seemed to be much more interested in reading about science topics than reading the required text. The consultant's eyes grew wide, making her disapproval clear. She promised to be back later with a schedule so that I could use classroom time to "put reading instruction first." Two days later she presented me with a new afternoon timetable and a few books from a new basal series. She was adamant that I scratch my science extras: "After all, your most important job is to teach these boys how to read!"

I refrained from telling her that I thought I was doing just that, but instead meekly took the plan. For a while afterward I tried having an afternoon reading group, using the second set of books, but it seemed like drudgery for all of us. Soon I quietly revived my former activities. I have never been sorry. By motivating with a subject of genuine interest to struggling readers, by gearing lessons to student needs for feeling important and "in the know," and by reinforcing strategies taught during more formal reading instruction, I was sure I was onto something. The other students in the class profited from my approach as well. The enthusiasm shown for our science studies and for reading and writing about them was reward enough. However, a few years later when my class was used as an experimental group in my school district to see if students exposed to hands-on, activity-oriented science integrated with literacy instruction would fare better than other classes on achievement tests, I was pleased to learn that my hunches were right. My class did perform better on the tests, including the reading tests. I was also told that my students performed better on questions involving reasoning.

For Donna, who had begun as a social studies teacher and continues to explore ways to link content learning with literacy development, the science connection began when she was a graduate student working in the Reading Clinic at the University of Virginia. In contrast to the reading specialist whose limited vision Judy had first encountered, Donna's mentors always sought connections to content and students' interests. She recalls:

As the graduate tutors designed programs individually for children, one boy in particular stood out. The only subject entry we could find for him was science; the tutor constructed one science activity after another, which then became the content for his language experience stories and for his word study. We would all gather around the station where the tutor and boy engaged in active learning. Both were highly engrossed in their activities, and the rest of us could learn vicariously from their intensity and joy of exploration. That experience and all the subsequent years working with teachers and children have reinforced the importance of linking literacy to highly engaging and personally motivating study of the real world.

Judy and Donna began collaborating around their common commitment to children's learning. This book is a compilation of their experiences and a reflection on what is possible. It is also a celebration of the great teaching and learning alive in our schools.

ACKNOWLEDGMENTS

This book developed as a result of the exciting instruction occurring in classrooms in Wilmette, Winnetka, Evanston, Glenview, and Palatine, Illinois. We are deeply appreciative of the opportunities to visit and participate in the ongoing explorations created by these excellent teachers. We also know that the work of these teachers is possible because of the commitment the school districts have to excellent instruction in science and literacy.

We particularly thank the teachers: Judy Sawdey, Marj Steiner, Ann Retzinger, Jim Tingey, Susan Dennison, Meridith Frost, Linda Garcia, Kate Miller, Pam McNish, Sally Williams, Lisa McMahon, Carol Skalindar, Debbie Gurvitz, and the TREE team at Pleasant Ridge School: Jan Hinton, Kathy Pattengale, and Deanna Sainati. Many of the examples of student work and the pictures and descriptions of children actively engaged in learning come from these teachers' classrooms. Matt Fuller, Director of Technology and Media Services in Wilmette District 39, was invaluable in helping us with the technology chapter. We also thank Mary Stitt, former principal of Olive School in Arlington Heights, Illinois, who has been influential to many teachers throughout her career, helping them to realize the value of integration.

CONTENTS

INTEGRATING INSTRUCTION:
LITERACY AND SCIENCE

CHAPTER 1

LANGUAGE LITERACY/ SCIENCE LITERACY

It was time for "Read and Relax" in Tory's fourth-grade classroom. After a frustrating search, he finally located an old science textbook and in desperation took it to his teacher. "Is it okay if I read this?" Tory, like many boys who want to read about the real world, often finds himself in a classroom devoid of the books and magazines he would love to read (Allington, 2001; Smith & Wilhelm, 2002). Most science textbooks won't hold such students' attention for long. However, when interesting science trade books and magazines are available, both boys and girls often lose themselves in the pictures and texts and don't want to stop reading when independent reading time is over. Children's interest in science is an important foundation for this book.

Research also provides a strong argument that the active study of science helps children develop logical thinking, language, and reading competencies (Guthrie & Ozgungor, 2002; Topping & McManus, 2002). In addition, reading and writing about science help develop and reinforce desired science concepts (Yore, 2003; Palincsar & Magnussen, 2001; Thier, 2002). Upon examination, it is clear that scientific literacy and language literacy have much in common (Alvermann, 2004; Baker, 2004; Casteel & Isom, 1994). They work together in strengthening skills and strategies in both curricular areas. As Marlene Thier (2002) explains, "Good science—and effective teaching and learning in science—is dependent upon strong language skills. Indeed, science and language are inextricably linked in the pursuit, determination and communication of meaning in the context of the physical world" (p. 8).

This book is written for teachers of students in elementary grades 1–6. It is highly practical and represents a synthesis of our work in literacy and science. We know many elementary school teachers who already integrate language arts and science and understand that when reading and writing fit naturally into the science curriculum, the results are deeper and richer experiences for their students in each area. Other teachers are attempting to do the same, but would like to know and do more because they can see the many advantages. They want to learn the rationale behind such integration and seek guidelines for implementation; moreover, they want and need encouragement to move ahead. We hope that the information offered in this book will prove useful and practical and that the many strategies and activities presented will be compelling enough to invite teachers to try them. We also hope that this "experimentation" will stimulate new applications and tailor-made lessons that work for them and their students.

DEFINING OUR TERMS

When we discuss language literacy, we mean the ability to use reading and writing, speaking and listening sufficiently well to engage in thinking and to communicate ideas clearly. We further extend the definition to include the ability to critically analyze and evaluate information available through the media and technology. As educators, we hope to create capable, confident readers and effective communicators through oral and written language. We hope to nurture students who will come to make informed decisions for themselves and to contribute wisely to society. Foundational to all language acquisition is that students develop the ability to think.

Teachers are also responsible for helping our students develop science literacy through experiences designed to achieve an effective grasp of the skills and concepts needed to understand our scientific world. The National Science Education Standards (National Research Council, 1996) "are designed to guide our nation toward a scientifically literate society," in part because "Americans are confronted increasingly with questions in their lives that require scientific information and scientific ways of thinking for informed decision making."

As research and advances in technology continually change our understanding of the world, we realize that the collective knowledge in science does not remain static. Students will experience this firsthand when guided by teachers to develop the practices of real scientists through process skills. They will be learning through inquiry, with discovery being the key. Inquiry-based science is activity based and process oriented, leading to continued and expanded curiosity and further questions for investigation. For pragmatic reasons, especially time limitations and the lack of sophisticated supplies in the classroom, an elementary teacher is, unfortunately, often forced to move on before all of the students' questions about a particular topic can be answered. The inquiry process can then be transferred to students' individual exploration through reading trade books and magazines. Their wondering and questioning can continue to stimulate deeper, richer understandings. Questions like "Were we correct in thinking that?" after a hands-on exploration, or

"Can we find out the answer to that by listening to this book read aloud?" promote inquiry. As students gain experience in both reading and science, they begin to form metacognitive practices, allowing them to independently generate their own questions to explore ideas and concepts. This inquiry approach is based on activity-oriented science but encourages reading as a natural extension.

COMPARISONS

A few years ago, while preparing for a teacher workshop on "Reading, Writing, and the Science Connection," Judy's co-presenter, Carol Koretz, remarked, "Isn't it interesting that science and reading are so similar?" They then thought about how the acquisition of the two literacies uses reciprocal sets of processes and skills that complement and strengthen each other. They began to look for research to support their ideas on the matter.

In fact, they soon discovered that the acquisition of both language literacy and science literacy is dependent on the students' ability to think critically in similar ways. Yore, Craig, and Maguire (1995) also assert that the reading process corresponds to the process of scientific inquiry. Both require skills in setting purposes, questioning, predicting, analyzing evidence and drawing conclusions, and communicating results.

In reading, students are asked to predict the outcome of a story before they read it. In science, they are asked to predict the outcome of an investigation. Students in literature are asked to interpret the stories they read, and in science they are asked to interpret the results of observations and experiments. In language arts, students are asked to communicate by writing and speaking. This is also true in science.

Ruth Wellman's (1978) early work "Science: A Basic Language and Reading Development" noted that in science activities and experiments students must use all of their senses to promote their perceptual and logical skills, and these skills then contribute to the development not only of science concepts, but also of vocabulary and oral language skills necessary for learning to read and write. To develop an accurate understanding of observations and experiences in the natural world or during science investigations, students need to be able to precisely articulate what they see and think.

There is a similar need to develop the ability to ask purposeful questions for both language and science lessons. To foster this ability, teachers need to continually ask relevant questions, at the right time, that become an invitation to a closer look rather than a demand for the correct answer. Questions like "Have you seen?" or "Do you notice?" help focus attention where it is needed. Problem-oriented questions such as "How can we tell if a mealworm responds to light?" encourage students to think and develop a process to permit further investigation. Finding a solution will involve making predictions, forming hypotheses, and deciding how to test them. It also requires interpreting findings and reaching conclusions.

The right questions are crucial to reading lessons as well. Questions such as "What was important about that?" or "Why do you think that happened?" will help fine-tune understanding. "What would happen if?" is a question that encourages students to think and investigate further. As in science, an inquiry approach to reading material will facilitate deeper reflection and richer meaning.

Writing is also an important part of science, as it is in language arts. Throughout the process of scientific investigation students need to make notes and record their observations. Keeping journals or diaries of their work establishes the scientific habit of tracking ideas and questions during investigations. If students are reading to confirm information or answer questions, they also need to make notes and share these with others. Sharing the conclusions of scientific activity is important as well; students have to learn to write reports that can be shared with others either in print or in electronic formats. Writing is a way of slowing thinking and making it visible. Writing is a powerful thinking tool across the disciplines. Don Murray, a writer and teacher of writing, explained, "I write so I can see what I think."

An important part of thinking and learning is being able to share ideas and ask questions. Listening and speaking can develop quite naturally when students work together on science projects. However studies of student collaboration in both reading and science (Palincsar & Magnussen, 2001; Johnson & Johnson, 1999) indicate that students need direction in learning how to work together—to elicit each other's ideas and build on the group's contributions. The high motivation that comes from investigating science in the classroom can provide a context for teachers to provide needed instruction. Inquiry and problem solving are social skills dependent on good oral communication.

Finally, effective questioning during science and reading can be useful as a formative assessment. Answers to well-posed questions, with many of them open-ended, can indicate how well concepts are understood or misunderstood in science or how students comprehend or fail to understand what is being read. Not only is it important that students in both curricular areas answer questions and solve problems posed by the teacher, but it is also important that they generate their own questions and problems. We need to help students develop the skills required for an active, self-directed search for understandings and knowledge.

There is one obvious and major difference between teaching reading and teaching science. Students can learn to read by reading, but they cannot learn science by merely reading about it. The nature of science demands and compels them to be active participants. They catch and observe insects and earthworms and gather population data on them; they investigate sound, magnets, and prisms; they experiment with solids, liquids, and gases. These experiences help students to form concepts so that they will be able to comprehend what they are reading when these subjects are presented in text form.

RATIONALE FOR INTEGRATION

For a long time now, more and more has been expected of teachers. Not only has the curriculum been expanded, but responsibilities normally reserved for parents or the larger community have been assigned to educators. Added to an already overburdened schedule, the pressure for high-stakes standardized testing in math and reading has forced teachers and administrators to reduce the time spent on science. However, this situation is changing in some states because science is being added to the list of subjects tested that students must pass if they are to graduate from high school. Thus, there is further pressure on teachers, who are told that they must be responsible for student learning in science as well as the 3 R's, along with everything else. The federal No Child Left Behind Act requires that students in grades 3–8 be tested in science every year beginning in 2007. But there is a way out. If teachers teach science with literacy links, it would not only help to strengthen literacy but would also help to solve the problem of time limitations. The time available would be well spent in helping to achieve the goals of both scientific and language literacies.

Guthrie, Schafer, and Huang (2001) have examined the effects of integrated reading instruction on reading achievement in the upper elementary grades (4–5). They found that when students had more chances to read because teachers integrated literacy instruction into the content areas, the result was increased reading comprehension, stronger conceptual development and problem-solving skills in science, and heightened motivation to read in general. The Center for Excellence in Literacy Achievement (CELA) study of exemplary fourth-grade teachers (Allington & Johnston, 2002) concluded that integration was a key to these teachers' being able to create authentic learning experiences and elicit real inquiry and challenging thinking in their classrooms. Johnson and Georgis (2001) also found that reading in the content areas motivates students to read. Opportunities to reinforce desired strategies for reading and vocabulary development, as well as related written responses, were natural extensions of lessons.

Reading in scientific materials is motivating for many students. In fact, a sizeable proportion of young readers prefer to read informational materials, especially about the real world. Unfortunately, many elementary teachers don't share this interest and have focused most of their reading instruction on fictional texts. Duke's (2000) findings are captured in the title of one of her research articles, "3.5 Minutes a Day: The Volume of Informational Reading in First Grade Classrooms."

The need to teach students to read informational materials is clear. Most of the reading students do in school is in informational texts, in textbooks and in searching the Internet. Likewise, adults in our contemporary world do most of their reading in informational materials. Even pleasure reading is divided into those who prefer fiction and a growing number who read the ever-increasing array of nonfiction books and magazines available. The need to improve students' familiarity with informational texts has been recognized by the state and national standards and assessments. In many states the reading assessments have an equal number of fiction and informational passages. Therefore, integrating reading instruction with science and encouraging independent reading of science books and magazines can help teachers develop well-rounded readers.

However, in schools most of the informational material students receive comes from textbooks. Despite the publisher's efforts, these books are often so heavily loaded with information required by national standards and state mandates that they include little elaboration to make them comprehensible to some children, given the range of reading abilities of students in many schools. "Textbooks—they're boring!" is a frequent lament of students. Unfortunately, many elementary teachers in the United States are still spending an hour or so a week on textbook instruction, with little or no active science to go along with it. Even the textbook companies these days don't approve. They know that students need experiences doing science, not merely reading about it, so kits and activity-oriented lessons are often included with textbooks. Still, students often must wait until they are in a junior high lab to have hands-on science experiences. Experts agree that buying new textbooks and requiring more minutes of instruction won't help students' growth in either language literacy or science literacy. What does work is reading for various purposes about science or during science lessons. Students must learn how to search for new information, they must be able to read directions, and they need to be able to express themselves orally and in writing about what they think and learn during their science experiences.

Chittenden, Salinger, and Bussis (2001) encourage integrated instruction beginning in the lower grades. They contend that in the early grades there is little expectation for students to read to gather information, even though learning to read is a major focus. In their study they found that beginning readers can and do extend their knowledge by reading from meaningful books: "If children do not encounter meaningful content in books until the 3rd or 4th grade, the major message they may be learning in the meantime is that reading lacks purpose" (p. 72).

Both science and reading can be taught in a manner that is tedious and dull or one that is active and inviting. One way to turn off a student's interest in any subject is to reduce it to reading about it, looking up vocabulary words, and answering a few questions afterward. Instead, when students have a practical motivation to answer questions that originate from their personal wonderings and investigations, they are more likely to master language as a tool that can help build a memory bank of pertinent information and experience.

Students learn science better when they write about what they are thinking. The act of writing forces them to synthesize new ideas with prior knowledge and to reflect on what they don't know as they organize their thoughts. This may lead to asking new questions and designing new experiences or recreating previous ones for further reflection.

Narrative and expository pieces written in connection with science lessons can be helpful in assessing students' science learning and thought processes. Teachers can then better evaluate the success of their lessons and adjust their plans for more productive outcomes.

The ability to read and write profoundly affects a student's achievement in most areas of a curriculum. When used in content lessons such as science, this ability works in two ways: reading and writing to learn, and learning to read and write. It makes such good sense to link literacy skills to science in order to strengthen each area that, fortunately, more and more elementary school teachers are doing it.

MAINTAINING INTEGRITY OF BOTH LITERACIES

All teachers need to be aware of best practices and current data on the acquisition of language and scientific literacies. National and state standards were crafted to establish the objectives for each grade level for the purpose of achieving optimum student learning. The national standards, and those in most states, include reading across different texts, reading critically, and reading that enables students to synthesize and represent ideas. Reading processes are stressed, in addition to various strategies to be used with a wide range of text structures. The standards emphasize reading for a purpose and the critical evaluation of ideas. Standards for writing often include developing a plan, organizing ideas, writing paragraphs, understanding and developing style, editing, and using technology. Standards in oral language ask that students be able to communicate clearly for a variety of audiences and that students know how to listen actively. The use of technology to locate and process information and report findings of investigations is also required in both science and language arts. See Table 1.1 for the National Science Education Content Standards of the National Research Council and Table 1.2 for the Standards for the English Language Arts of the National Council of Teachers of English (NCTE) and the International Reading Association (IRA).

Even with good classroom instruction and effective remedial interventions, many students struggle with textbooks and the one-size-fits-all approach implicit in their use. If they are struggling with reading in science, students are unable to learn much from textbooks. Therefore, many teachers today find that they must use methods and reading materials other than those dictated by their science curriculums. They may rewrite the curriculum, often spending their own money on appropriate trade books to accompany it.

For teachers to teach science effectively in the elementary school, they incorporate active inquiry-based experiences into their lessons. They also include reading, writing, and vocabulary development. Students benefit when the focus is on

TABLE 1.1. National Science Education Content Standards

Grades K–4

Content Standard A (Science as Inquiry)
   As a result of activities in grades K–4, all students should develop:
   1. abilities necessary to do scientific inquiry
   2. understanding about scientific inquiry

Content Standard B (Physical Science)
   As a result of activities in grades K–4, all students should develop an understanding of:
   1. properties of objects and materials
   2. position and motion of objects
   3. light, heat, electricity, and magnetism

Content Standard C (Life Science)
   As a result of activities in grades K–4, all students should develop an understanding of:
   1. the characteristics of organisms
   2. life cycles of organisms
   3. organisms and environments

Content Standard D (Earth and Space Science)
   As a result of activities in grades K–4, all students should develop an understanding of:
   1. properties of earth materials
   2. objects in the sky
   3. changes in earth and sky

Content Standard E (Science and Technology)
   As a result of activities in grades K–4, all students should develop:
   1. abilities of technological design
   2. understanding about science and technology
   3. abilities to distinguish between natural objects and objects made by humans

Content Standard F (Science in Personal and Social Perspectives)
   As a result of activities in grades K–4, all students should develop an understanding of:
   1. personal health
   2. characteristics and changes in populations
   3. types of resources
   4. changes in environments
   5. science and technology in local challenges

Content Standard G (History and Nature of Science)
   As a result of activities in grades K–4, all students should develop an understanding of:
   1. science as a human endeavor

(continued)

TABLE 1.1. *(continued)*

Grades 5–8

Content Standard A (Science as Inquiry)
   As a result of activities in grades 5–8, all students should develop:
   1. abilities necessary to do scientific inquiry
   2. understanding about scientific inquiry

Content Standard B (Physical Science)
   As a result of activities in grades 5–8, all students should develop an understanding of:
   1. properties and changes of properties in matter
   2. motions and forces
   3. transfer of energy

Content Standard C (Life Science)
   As a result of activities in grades 5–8, all students should develop an understanding of:
   1. structure and function in living systems
   2. reproduction and heredity
   3. regulation and behavior
   4. populations and ecosystems
   5. diversity and adaptations of organisms

Content Standard D (Earth and Space Science)
   As a result of activities in grades 5–8, all students should develop an understanding of:
   1. structure of the earth system
   2. earth's history
   3. earth in the solar system

Content Standard E (Science and Technology)
   As a result of activities in grades 5–8, all students should develop:
   1. abilities of technological design
   2. understanding about science and technology

Content Standard F (Science in Personal and Social Perspectives)
   As a result of activities in grades 5–8, all students should develop an understanding of:
   1. personal health
   2. populations, resources, and environments
   3. natural hazards
   4. risks and benefits
   5. science and technology in society

Content Standard G (History and Nature of Science)
   As a result of activities in grades 5–8, all students should develop an understanding of:
   1. science as a human endeavor
   2. nature of science
   3. history of science

Note. From National Research Council (1996).

TABLE 1.2. The 12 Standards for the English Language Arts of the NCTE and the IRA

The vision guiding these standards is that all students must have the opportunities and resources to develop the language skills they need to pursue life's goals and to participate fully as informed, productive members of society. These standards assume that literacy growth begins before children enter school as they experience and experiment with literacy activities—reading and writing, and associating spoken words with their graphic representations. Recognizing this fact, these standards encourage the development of curriculum and instruction that make productive use of the emerging literacy abilities that children bring to school. Furthermore, the standards provide ample room for the innovation and creativity essential to teaching and learning. They are not prescriptions for particular curriculum or instruction.

Although we present these standards as a list, we want to emphasize that they are not distinct and separable; they are, in fact, interrelated and should be considered as a whole.

1. Students read a wide range of print and nonprint texts to build an understanding of texts, of themselves, and of the cultures of the United States and the world; to acquire new information; to respond to the needs and demands of society and the workplace; and for personal fulfillment. Among these texts are fiction and nonfiction, classic and contemporary works.
2. Students read a wide range of literature from many periods in many genres to build an understanding of the many dimensions (e.g., philosophical, ethical, aesthetic) of human experience.
3. Students apply a wide range of strategies to comprehend, interpret, evaluate, and appreciate texts. They draw on their prior experience, their interactions with other readers and writers, their knowledge of word meaning and of other texts, their word identification strategies, and their understanding of textual features (e.g., sound–letter correspondence, sentence structure, context, graphics).
4. Students adjust their use of spoken, written, and visual language (e.g., conventions, style, vocabulary) to communicate effectively with a variety of audiences and for different purposes.
5. Students employ a wide range of strategies as they write and use different writing process elements appropriately to communicate with different audiences for a variety of purposes.
6. Students apply knowledge of language structure, language conventions (e.g., spelling and punctuation), media techniques, figurative language, and genre to create, critique, and discuss print and nonprint texts.
7. Students conduct research on issues and interests by generating ideas and questions, and by posing problems. They gather, evaluate, and synthesize data from a variety of sources (e.g., print and nonprint texts, artifacts, people) to communicate their discoveries in ways that suit their purpose and audience.
8. Students use a variety of technological and information resources (e.g., libraries, databases, computer networks, video) to gather and synthesize information and to create and communicate knowledge.
9. Students develop an understanding of and respect for diversity in language use, patterns, and dialects across cultures, ethnic groups, geographic regions, and social roles.
10. Students whose first language is not English make use of their first language to develop competency in the English language arts and to develop understanding of content across the curriculum.
11. Students participate as knowledgeable, reflective, creative, and critical members of a variety of literacy communities.
12. Students use spoken, written, and visual language to accomplish their own purposes (e.g., for learning, enjoyment, persuasion, and the exchange of information).

Note. From National Council of Teachers of English and International Reading Association (1996). Copyright 1996 by IRA. Reprinted by permission.

depth rather than breadth, which increases opportunities for their reading and writing. It is important that students have time for investigation to learn concepts, that they know enough to formulate questions independently, and that they can problem solve. Continuing curiosity motivates inquiry. The students want to learn more. This approach takes time, allowing students to dig deeper and reflect on what they have learned.

As students move through a unit of study, they may develop a number of open-ended questions so that as time goes on, these questions may eventually be answered through experience or by reading. Questions such as "Will it ever be possible to travel outside our solar system?" "Is there life on Mars?" "What are all the factors contributing to monarch butterfly migration?" or "What does a baby firefly look like?" can motivate long-term inquiry. Some of these questions, especially those concerning astronomy, remain unanswered even for the experts.

As adults, we also have many questions that intrigue us and for which there are often no answers. A few years ago, Judy McKee had the privilege of going to Michoacán, Mexico, to visit the overwintering grounds of millions and millions of monarch butterflies from North America. On return, she commented, "The experience was so awe-inspiring that from now on I will conduct an informal ongoing search in newspapers and periodicals for new information gleaned from the research that continues on these astonishing creatures. How and why they have continued this age-old seasonal migration, defying all odds, to wind up thousands of miles from their starting point, remains one of the most intriguing of natural phenomena."

Teachers need to teach and guide specific daily language literacy experiences. Many teachers use guided reading groups, literature circles, writers' workshop, and other methods that help them vary instruction and create contexts for students' active, constructive learning. As stated earlier, there can and should be clear expectations for carryover to other subjects. Students should be accountable for key language skills that are necessary for science learning. When students are aware that what they learn in language arts is meant to be used both in and outside school, they don't complain, "Why do we have to spell correctly or use paragraphs in science?" The use of skills that have been taught and reinforced well during language arts lessons (such as the use of capital letters and periods in second grade) can be expected. Elementary school students can be responsible for the correct spelling of unit-specific vocabulary words in a list of words prominently displayed, or for common spelling words that they should have mastered during spelling lessons. The teacher needs to be the judge. However, it is important to keep in mind that the focus should be, first, on concepts and, second, on the way they are represented when science is integrated with writing.

Students will have to be taught specific strategies to get the most out of informational text. They must be taught how to engage in the process of inquiry and how to use the many kinds of informational texts at their disposal, ranging from encyclopedias to the Internet, to magazines and trade books.

We don't want to overlook the importance of having classroom libraries full of all types of reading materials. There should be books at various reading levels on a wide variety of science subjects. Science magazines and newsletters on display attract students with contemporary issues and explorations. There should also be room for students to bring books and artifacts from home, too, to keep an open-ended collection.

CONCLUSION

Language literacy and science literacy can easily be linked to enable teachers to better achieve their goals and to adhere to standards within the time frame they have available. With such an integrated approach, teachers have endless opportunities to develop students' language and reading strategies. Inquiry-based science experiences provide the context in which students learn to think critically and develop understanding from concrete activities and print materials. The natural culmination of this type of learning is that children learn to share their discoveries in written and oral form.

CHAPTER 2

ORGANIZING FOR INTEGRATED INSTRUCTION

Teachers know that being well organized is a key to a successful year. This means creating a classroom that is inviting to children and arranged so they can access resources and work together. It also means having in mind a clear design for using time effectively each day and a clear routine of activities so students can engage comfortably in all the teacher wants to do. In this chapter we share some frameworks for classroom organization and for the ongoing routines that bring literacy and science together in meaningful learning.

PREPARING A LEARNING ENVIRONMENT: A GOOD PLACE TO LEARN REFLECTS A WELL-DEFINED PHILOSOPHY

Anyone who walks into Ann Retzinger's classroom is astonished. Like a fine work of art, it invites the viewer's eye from focal point to focal point as he or she takes in the welcoming space. Preservice teachers are sent to Ann's room to take notes on the arrangement of furniture, materials, displays, centers, and student samples and to query Ann on her rationale for how the room is set up.

The congruence between Ann's philosophy of teaching and the classroom she has designed is apparent. She strives for a setting that promotes feelings of community and comfort. It is obvious that student curiosity, experimentation, and a desire to learn are fostered by her classroom design. Her philosophy supports individual differences and learning styles, multiple intelligences and interests.

That Ann runs a student-centered classroom is evident at first glance. Her desk is located in a far corner of the room. She never sits there. Like many teachers, she uses it as a repository for paperwork, memos, and piles of this and that. Student work is abundantly displayed in an artful, well-organized manner. This work is respected, never left dangling or displayed so long that it looks sun bleached, dusty, or tired. Displays are changed often so that each learner will have his or her work featured several times throughout the year.

A Brief Overview

Attractive and frequently changing centers offer the students diverse opportunities to read, to experiment, to discover, and to think. The experiences Ann plans for her students in the centers complement science and social studies units, as well as topics in math. Interest in the Discovery Center is stimulated by colorful displays of books organized by topic, games, microscopes, science projects, and myriad other supplies and props, some brought from home by students. The Art and Creative Writing Center is set up with a variety of materials for creative endeavors. Interactive bulletin boards, informational charts, and posters enhance the area as well. Print is everywhere: in labels, in directions for activities featured, and in questions to ponder. Specially selected books are highlighted for students to peruse.

Even the configuration of the desks in the room changes from time to time. Ann sometimes arranges them in the shapes of letters. For instance, one morning the students may come in to find the desks arranged in the shape of a capital E. "Why do you think they are in that shape?" she might ask them. The students then brainstorm words that begin with an E, putting them in sentence context such as "Eager—We are eager to start our new unit on earthworms." "Explore—We will explore our school playground habitat." "Enthusiastic—We are enthusiastic to learn about everything." When these are written on the overhead for the students, they note that other words in the sentences also begin with E. Ann might use the configuration to introduce a unit of study this way. For instance, Earthworm Environments are studied during the unit on habitats.

Ann knows that the environment she creates can dramatically affect her students' attitudes toward learning. Creating such an environment entails arranging a practical physical layout, making materials and supplies accessible, and encouraging students to have a sense of belonging and ownership. The students are taught how to pick up group clutter, to be responsible for straightening their own belongings, and to take pride in a neat classroom.

The artistry with which she visually arranges her room makes it feel organized. Colorful bulletin boards, posters, and other print materials help distinguish the centers. Whenever the class is working through a social studies or science unit, the whole room turns into an interactive children's exploratorium, yet everything is orderly and easily accessible.

When people come into Ann's classroom to view it and listen to Ann talk, they are gleaning information from a consummate educator who doesn't leave a stone unturned in thinking about her students and what she wants to accomplish throughout the year. After careful consideration of her goals and objectives for the year, which are based on what she knows of her incoming class, their special needs and other considerations, and the powerful curriculum she will be directing, Ann begins to set up her classroom.

Design Considerations

Here are the main components Ann uses when creating an environment that is organized, stimulating, and comfortable in order for her students to learn effectively:

Rationale

➢ The room reflects a match between the teacher and the learning goals and objectives to be accomplished.

Flexibility for small-group work

➢ Furniture and space can be rearranged to accommodate a variety of instructional approaches, including individualized, partner, small-group, and whole class.

Whole-group area

➢ The area is large enough to comfortably allow for read-alouds, direct instruction, informal discussions, and student presentations.

➢ For a primary-grade classroom, a rug can be used to designate the area.

➢ Older students may be uncomfortable on the floor if they are there for very long. Desks will most likely define their whole-group area. Arranging desks in a circle promotes discussions, and small clusters of desks can double as small collaborative group areas.

➢ Students have an unrestricted view of the chalkboard.

Centers

➢ The centers in the room are conveniently located, attractive, and well organized. Worthwhile activities are featured, with materials and directions available. Students can work in the centers independently without distracting others.

Climate

➢ The setting evokes a feeling of comfort and a sense of community.

➢ It stimulates curiosity and invites students to investigate, experiment, explore ideas, imagine, and think.

➢ One can discern responsiveness to student differences, such as those between struggling learners and advanced learners.

➢ Activities, displays, and materials represent an appeal to multiple intelligences and to the gender and cultural differences of students.

> There are attempts to meet the needs of students who speak English as a second language.

> Areas are designated for the display of student work.

Practical considerations

> Students and teacher are clearly visible to each other.

> The teacher's desk is out of the way, but students are clearly visible if the teacher uses it during class time.

> Posters and other necessary visual aids are posted for easy viewing.

> People are able to move easily from place to place in the classroom.

> Space is available for the personal belongings of all.

> Materials for daily student use are readily accessible, and other supplies are located conveniently elsewhere.

> An off-limits zone is provided for teacher records and supplies.

> Organization is apparent.

> Student safety has been considered.

Figure 2.1 depicts the layout of Ann's classroom.

More Ideas

Jim Tingey's fourth-grade classroom is well organized and attractive, while including a large assortment of supplies and books in well-designated nooks and crannies. It runs smoothly with as much responsibility as possible given to the students. For instance, the students care for the animals in the Critter Center. All Theme Tables have displays that pique curiosity, with elements inviting the students to look, touch, and explore. Jim's method for checking out books and videos is addressed in Chapter 8.

Judy Nelson, a second-grade classroom teacher, believes in providing students with comfortable spots that invite them to explore and read the many books in her class. Outfitted with a colorful rug and several pillows and surrounded by shelves and tubs of books selected for independent reading, the Cozy Corner is a favorite place, roomy enough for two or three students to enjoy perusing and reading books. In addition, several Cozy Mini-Areas for one or two students, outfitted with rugs and pillows, are located under tables throughout the room. Four plastic-covered cushions that line one wall are used for reading. During daily silent reading, each of these areas, providing space for as many as 12 students, are sought-after retreats for classroom readers. In addition, the areas are often used for partner or small-group work.

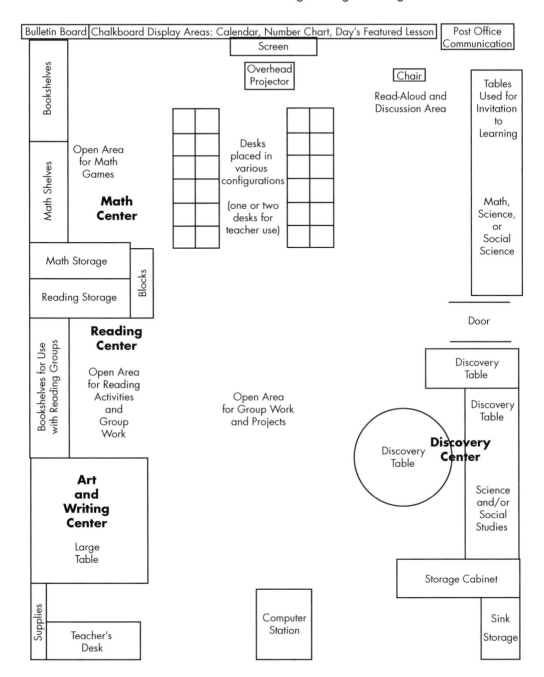

FIGURE 2.1. Room plan of Ann Retzinger's classroom.

Judy also has a Listening Station in her room, which consists of a tape recorder, headphones, and a station junction so that several students can listen at once. Students can listen to tapes and follow along in matching books selected from a series of see-through bags. Tapes of songs, poems, books, and stories, some of them recorded by the students at the center, are also available.

Learning Centers: Boon or Bust?

Many teachers would like to try learning centers in their classrooms if only they knew how to set them up with appropriate and inexpensive materials and supplies. Another concern is how to manage them so that student involvement remains productive. They worry that things may get too chaotic and that student accountability may be missing. Those teachers who use learning centers establish them slowly and thoughtfully, keeping in mind their goals for the students.

Goals of Learning Centers

➤ Learning centers should provide opportunities for students to grow toward important learning objectives set by the teacher.

➤ Activities should focus on the mastery or reinforcement of specific skills or on extended exploration of topics of study in the class.

➤ Learning centers should offer students options appropriate to their interests, reading levels, learning styles, and varying cultural backgrounds.

➤ Worthwhile activities should vary from simple to complex and from concrete to abstract.

➤ Students will increase their independent work skills when centers include clear directions and expectations.

Starting Small with Learning Centers

In using learning centers to integrate science and language literacies think about setting up a reading center, a writing center, or a science center first. Then, as the year progresses, you can add more learning centers to fit the class's evolving needs.

The physical layout of the room will indicate the best placement of centers. Bookshelves are necessary for both a science and a reading/language arts center. Portable shelves can also isolate areas. Using walls for displaying posters and student work, and the tops of shelving for books and supplies, can save space.

Reading and Writing Centers

A Reading Center and a Writing Center can be combined into one Language Arts/ Reading Center, but it may be so popular that it may be best to find a separate place for each. These centers should be separated from areas of higher activity because the students working in them will usually need quiet.

The center(s) will need the following:

Reading Center
➢ Comfortable chairs or seating. The seating can be merely a rug and some throw pillows or an old couch.
➢ Shelves or containers with several genres of leveled reading materials on various subjects.

Writing Center
➢ Appropriately sized table and chairs that can be used at times for student collaboration. If these items aren't available, some clipboards and an expanse of rug will do.
➢ A variety of papers for writing.
➢ Pencils and other writing utensils.
➢ Word wall or chart of frequently misspelled words and/or words designated for mastery.
➢ Dictionary and thesaurus.

The Writing Center might be located near a current or future Communication Area (for older students) or a Post Office Area (for younger students), an area with slots for students and teacher to exchange suggestions and notes. It would be advantageous to have a word processor and printer in the center as well.

Science Center

➢ A table or other space for experiments, supplies, and student displays.
➢ A selection of books with both illustrations and text.
➢ A kid-friendly microscope.
➢ Various types of magnifiers: magnifying glasses, tripod magnifiers, small and large magnifying boxes for live specimens.
➢ Shelves or containers with science trade books, general and specific to units of study.
➢ Shelves or containers with construction paper, graph paper, and other supplies for creating signs for displays and writing simple explanations.
➢ Containers for student nonfiction writing relating to science.
➢ A comfortable space for group work or reading.
➢ A tape recorder and tapes containing information on topics included in the center.

Activities at a classroom Science Center are usually open-ended and can relate to a current unit. They may provide enrichment or reinforce desired concepts. When group work is allowed, increased opportunities for English language learners and students who need to increase their verbal skills are presented in a nonthreatening way. In addition, listening to tapes can provide auditory reviews of topics, can be helpful for students who are less fluent in English, and can help to sharpen listening comprehension.

Student Responsibilities

To build ownership, some teachers ask for student input when deciding where the centers should go and what should go in them. Students can also help define what behavior is appropriate for each learning center. Younger students may need to role-play to practice how to use the centers. At first, only one center should be opened. When that one is running smoothly, another can follow.

Written directions at centers should be kept to a minimum and very easy to follow; otherwise, they defeat the goal of self-regulation. A plan for what to do if help is needed should be in place. Sometimes a teacher can assign students to be "assistants" for a center as long as that responsibility doesn't interfere with those students' ability to complete their own work. Materials should be readily available. Students will also need to know what to do with the center assignment when it is completed.

Built into every classroom design should be a maintenance plan that includes the students in as many ways as possible. Students must not only be responsible for their own materials, but for those of the community as well. One successful teacher divides the class into committees responsible for various areas of the room. Duties within the committees can be assigned as in cooperative groups, with one dependable person serving as "overseer" to make sure that everything is put in its place. If the students select the overseer for their group, the committee may be more likely to follow gentle directives from that person, even though each person should be encouraged to be "his or her own boss."

A Reminder

The teachers we have described know how to capture interest through an engaging classroom environment that provides reasons for people to want to step into that classroom. It all takes time, planning, and a willingness to change things if they aren't working or if student needs and interests shift.

Providing ample opportunity for student responsibility will not only free the teacher to spend time on other important things, but will also create a sense of ownership in the students. With ownership comes pride and a desire to keep things organized, help the classroom run smoothly, and create and maintain an attractive classroom in which all students are free to learn to the best of their ability.

YEARLY PLANS AND DAILY SCHEDULES

Armed with your curriculum and a calendar, you begin the first job in planning for the year: blocking out times for science and social studies units to be undertaken in the months ahead. Knowing that these time frames can't be written in stone if you take into consideration student needs and interests, it helps to know that you have made a plan. It also helps to know that you have worked through goals, objectives, skills, and standards to ensure that students will receive a full complement of learning during the year. The next sections address designing specific science units integrating language and science literacies.

A daily schedule that is developmentally appropriate for the students in your care is the next challenge. Carefully planned days will provide the structure and necessary blocks of time for learning in all curricular areas.

Classroom Themes

In planning for a teaching/learning year, many teachers use themes or "big ideas" to organize the curriculum in hope of fostering connections the students will understand. These are different from *thematic units*, which are discussed in Chapter 3. During the year students often refer to the themes, allowing for more in-depth connections and understanding of what they are studying.

Pam McNish, a fourth-grade teacher, uses the theme "biomes," generated from her district science curriculum. During the year students are introduced to major biomes on Earth, the life zones of plant and animal communities determined by the climate, temperature, and precipitation. Throughout the year she combines science and geography by focusing on location, geology, ecological systems, natural resources, history, and human interaction within the following biomes: oceans, deserts, rainforests, grasslands, and tundra. Each corner of the classroom holds maps, posters, pictures, learning games, and CD-ROMs. Science activities and exhibits are changed frequently to help students become familiar with the selected biomes. Numerous nonfiction and fiction resources are available for students to use for inquiry and personal reading. Written products are often the result of information gathering and student reflections.

There are periods during the year when one of the biomes is studied thoroughly. At that time still more materials and activities are available in the center. For example, a study of Illinois history, also in Pam's district curriculum, connects to the Grassland Biome Center, exploring the prairie that once covered 40% of Illinois. How native people and pioneers adapted to this unique ecosystem is an important focus of the study. The school garden, with its patch of prairie plants, enriches the study. Later a unit on oceanology will bring students to the Ocean Biome Center, where information for map study, ocean geology, ecology, conservation, and an in-depth concentration on fascinating sea creatures like whales, will be located. During the Rainforest, Desert, and Tundra Units, these regions are also compared and contrasted with the other biomes to bring deeper understandings by providing order and structure to the study of each unit.

Referring to the class biome centers can assist students in synthesizing information and applying it in meaningful ways. For example, knowledge of class pen pals in Egypt is enhanced because students are somewhat familiar with the desert biome, which provides information about the place where their new friends live. They have learned about deserts through maps and studies of climate and landforms, and even something about desert peoples. The students then find it easier to formulate meaningful questions when writing to their pen pals. Communication with these new friends broadens their understanding of the biome, and knowing something about the lives of their Egyptian pen pals has helped them better understand what living in the desert is like.

When current events are discussed in class, maps and other information can be accessed in the biome centers for clearer understandings and associations. Pam states, "We are a global community with access to information from around the world, so our students are very aware of what is happening in the news. Our study of the Earth's biomes helps them understand current events in meaningful contexts. It also provides a perfect marriage of science and geography and readily offers opportunities for language arts extensions."

There are many other possible themes that can work well. Life cycles, seasons, phases of the moon, day and night, beginnings and endings are examples of *cycles*. The science associations are obvious, but the idea can be used to encourage other connections. Moving through a school year from beginning to end and then starting over the next year can be explored, including emotional issues and various types of growth that are inherent in such cycles. The theme of *change* can encompass these kinds of personal issues, as well as how natural and human-made things change over time. Seasons, geology, and astronomy also fit into the theme of change. These examples can easily incorporate the goals and objectives of science, math, reading, and writing, as well as those of other curricular areas.

Daily Schedules

With more and more responsibility on the shoulders of teachers, finding time is always an issue. There are many suggestions supported by research that will improve education for all children. Decisions like reducing school size, creating small schools within larger schools, or reducing class size to fewer than 20 students in lower elementary grades are, unfortunately, out of the teachers' hands. Scheduling the day to accommodate student and curricular needs is sometimes beyond the teacher's control as well. A chopped-up day, with students coming and going to specials like art, music, and physical education, does not allow for the larger blocks of time needed for teaching, learning, and reflection. Of course, these areas of the curriculum are important and necessary, but we hope that, eventually, administrators, who, admittedly, have their own set of demands, will be able to better accommodate the learning needs of students by arranging for reasonable blocks of classroom time in class schedules.

Nevertheless, there are many ideas that can be incorporated into the school day to assist in working with integrated curriculum to include science literacy and language literacy. Keep in mind that the success of the students is paramount. How we use our time will reflect our respect for and understanding of our students. It also will indicate the commitment we have to curricular goals and objectives.

There must be a natural flow to the school day, with a balance of group times and individual practice times, as well as active times and calm times. The pacing of activities can make or break the ability of students to absorb and reflect on their learnings. Proceeding at a breakneck speed for hours dampens student (as well as teacher) enthusiasm for a day at school.

The following is one teacher's daily schedule, which provides well for the students' needs and reflects the expectations for the students' achievement.

1. *Greeting time.* This teacher believes that each student should be greeted at the door with a smile and a personal acknowledgment. It is quite possible that this will be the only time during the busy day that the student will be warmly and directly spoken to by the teacher. Each person in the room needs to feel a sense of belonging, and this small act can make the difference.

2. *Getting ready.* Each student is responsible for checking in, turning in homework, and making sure that pencils are sharpened and materials are ready for work.

3. *Morning mini.* Each morning arriving students are expected to complete a short assignment. It can be a quick review, a brainteaser, a short reading passage and a question requiring a written answer, earlier work to be corrected, anything that can be done independently. This establishes a quiet, structured start to the day.

4. *Group openers.* A community time with a set routine is important at the beginning of the day. Routine procedures such as the Pledge of Allegiance, attendance, and lunch counts are assigned to various students. This is the time for sharing educational items brought from home that pertain to the various areas of study. The daily schedule is also noted at this time.

5. *Language arts block I.* Writing and/or writers' workshop, spelling, and word work are featured.

Break. Recess, or if outdoor recess isn't allowed, a time for rest and relaxation (R & R).

6. *Read-aloud.* This is a time for a teacher read-aloud. The teacher uses this time to help the students learn. Read-alouds are discussed further in Chapter 4.

7. *Language arts block II.* Reading instruction in small groups is conducted while the remaining students work independently on the application of skills, research, math practice, and integrated curriculum projects such as those detailed in Chapter 3. The students may engage in these activities at their seats or at the learning centers in the room.

Break. Lunch and recess or a time for R & R.

8. *Class meeting.* After a recess period is a good time to talk about problems facing the students. In a safe environment, students and teacher can attempt to resolve issues that come up in class or on the playground. Potential solutions are generated. At later class meetings, feedback is given on the success of the suggestions and alternative possibilities are offered. These meetings are important because they allow the students to feel a sense of responsibility and ownership for problems encountered by the group while developing problem-solving and interpersonal skills in resolving more personal types of issues.

9. *Sustained silent reading or read-aloud.* The students enjoy 20–30 minutes of silent reading with books that they choose from shelves or containers organized according to genre and subjects. Partner reading is an option at this time too.

10. *Math.* Math concepts are taught and applied. At times opportunities for science–math connections are offered.

Short break.

11. *Science or social studies.* Various units are emphasized during the year. Though this period of the day is generally reserved for science or social studies, much of the work generated during the rest of the day is related to the current unit of study. Science experiments and investigations may be done at this time.

12. *Cleanup.* Each child is responsible for his or her own area, as well as for a task contributing to the general neatness and organization of the room. This not only fosters responsibility in the students, but also makes less work for the teacher later so that more time can be spent on more worthwhile teacher tasks. One of the more reliable students can be the director, who gently makes sure that all tasks have been completed.

13. *Closure.* The teacher strives to have a positive, reflective ending to the day, encouraging students to think over the day's events. The teacher might review an important idea for the students to carry away with them and attempt to end on a positive note. It is good for the teacher to stand at the door at the end of the day, just as it was at the beginning of the day, to give a brief good-bye to each student.

Other Tips for Success

It is common knowledge that the days don't usually run smoothly at the beginning of the school year. In fact, veteran teachers know that it is wise to go slower then, taking care to establish clear expectations and standards.

Building in student responsibility in as many ways as possible goes a long way toward making things easier on the teacher. Ann Retzinger, our master educator, often reminds her students, "Your desk is your space and the room is our space." She expects the students to keep their own areas organized so that the class won't have to wait for them to "get ready" for the next lesson or project. Students are also reminded that their things shouldn't get in the way of other people. Community areas, such as centers and open work space on the floor or on a table, are joint responsibility areas, and those who work there must be responsible for tidying up after themselves.

Make sure the students have a sense of pride and ownership in their classroom. The best way to engender ownership is to enable them to feel enthusiastic and successful in a school environment that is nonthreatening and inviting. Many teachers allow the students to give their parents a "walk through" during the year to show off what's happening in the room.

Sometimes, no matter what the schedule, it's good to just go with the flow for a while. To thoroughly complete science experiences as well as integrate reading and language, the usual schedule may have to be dropped. Also keep in mind that some of the best teaching goes on when student interest is piqued and it just doesn't make sense to stop an activity and wait until tomorrow to continue it. When students are enthusiastically ready for more and you stay with the subject at hand, you are valuing their interests, their questions, and their timing. Naturally, because of the many curricular demands and schedules to be honored, it can't be done all the time, but the results can be rewarding on those occasions when enough time is allowed to thoroughly explore an experience, reflect on it, and make language connections while it is still fresh.

In the busy hubbub of most American classrooms, students should be allowed, if at all possible, a time for reflection each day. This can sometimes be done during the class meeting or at the end of the day. It can be a time when students reflect on their own strengths and weaknesses, on accomplishments and new information, and on what they want to share with their parents at home.

Conclusion

Blocking out times during the year for teaching units and carefully developing a feasible daily schedule will assist in the accomplishment of goals and objectives throughout a day and over the course of the year. In addition, the classroom's arrangement of furniture that allows for individual and group work; learning centers that invite students to explore, think, and learn; and the general attractiveness of the classroom setting are all important components of a successful school environment. When the classroom is set up for inquiry-based learning and flexible plans are put into place, then integration of curricular areas can proceed easily and naturally.

CHAPTER 3

INTEGRATING SCIENCE AND LANGUAGE IN SCIENCE UNITS

"There's just too much to teach and too little time in the day to get in all that I am expected to cover!" This complaint is common among teachers who feel responsible for preparing their students with the knowledge and skills outlined in the national and state standards. The result of this increased pressure for accountability is that many teachers either shortchange some curriculum areas, especially science and social studies, or are learning to become more effective in combining their content teaching through thematic or integrated instructional units. In a review of case studies of teachers involved in integrating instruction, Ogle and McMahon (2001) found three basic approaches to integration. Some teachers begin integration by concentrating on one area of the curriculum, conceptualize how they want to teach that topic or area, and then see if they can add standards or content from other areas. Other teachers begin with a theme or topic and then try to find what they can incorporate from two or three content curriculum standards. Yet others begin with activities or projects they want to teach and then look for links to the appropriate skills or standards.

A report on elementary science and literacy integration from Australia found similar patterns. Bruce Waldrip (2001) reported that some teachers and schools began with themes and then tried to integrate as many curriculum areas as possible into those themes. Others used what Waldrip calls "a superficial" integration, in which skills were taught but the students didn't engage in real science learning or thinking. Another teacher in the report was able to truly integrate literacy with science, keeping the development of scientific thinking and knowledge as her goals.

Both of these studies point to a common finding. Teachers don't have a common approach to integration. There are several ways in which teachers use elements of curriculum integration in their teaching. In this book we provide examples of integration based on science concepts and standards. We know there are other ways to create an integrated curriculum, but this approach is sound and ensures that scientific processes and concepts are taught and learned. Once the scientific objectives are clear, then we ask about the language and literacy skills and strategies that are basic to the thinking and learning students will do. What materials are going to be used? What types of writing and reading are naturally needed for learning? Then we look at the expectations for students at the particular grade level and determine what can be reinforced from prior teaching, and what needs introduction for the first time, for students to be successful learners.

Bringing the best practices for science learning into the classroom is imperative, as teachers feel increasing pressure to improve student achievement in science. Students should be grounded in experiences that enable them to see the meaning of what they are doing, how the information they have gleaned fits into a meaningful whole, and how it fits into real-world situations. If they don't develop a basic conceptual context or see the meaning of what they are doing, they will have a problem in retaining information and will be unable to apply what they have experienced (Shepard, 1992, p. 303).

Adequate time to teach the expected concepts in each unit, as well as opportunities to reinforce learning with language arts objectives based on the needs, skills, and experiences of students, must be taken into consideration. Thus, it is clear that planning ahead of time for good science teaching throughout the year is critical.

FRAMEWORK FOR PLANNING UNITS

There are many factors to consider when planning a science unit that will assist students in constructing their own knowledge in science and science-related areas. First of all, students need ample opportunity to be actively engaged in the learning process. Because science is a dynamic undertaking based on questioning, investigation, and thinking, teachers need to carefully provide active, engaging opportunities for students to experience and explore the concepts being studied. Schools with activity-based science programs have these as a starting point. Schools that use textbook-based science instruction can use the many activities and experiments suggested by the books' authors.

Appropriate activities are essential in science so that students have frequent opportunities to practice science—observing, recording data, making notes of interpretations, and reading about what others have learned.

As teachers plan for the range of students in their charge, it is also important to incorporate as wide a variety of teaching approaches and multiple resources as feasible to reach more students. Methods must vary in order to deal with the range of learning styles, multiple intelligences of students, and differentiation for differing intellectual needs. Some students will become fully engaged in the "hands-on" aspects of scientific investigation. We can think of a bilingual student who loved to observe and record the eating and activity patterns of the hamster in his classroom. This child was precise and persistent in making careful observations, so the whole class benefited. Yet he was not a good reader and was appreciative of the way the teacher partnered him with a student who helped extend his knowledge by reading from articles on hamsters. Another member of their team was a good illustrator, and the teacher made sure that this strength was also elicited and used well as the students studied the life pattern and habits of their hamster.

With increasing numbers of bilingual students in our classrooms, attention must be given to ways in which ideas and strategies can be implemented in a bilingual classroom. There should be a balance of science reading and experiential learning. For bilingual students more focus on the language of science, both in general terms of investigation and in introducing the specific words that are central to the content, is essential. Many schools are now using science units to help bridge oral languages for bilingual students. Making sure there is lots of talk, as well as many scaffolded activities with concepts in print and lots of reading material that is accessible to the students, can make a significant difference in their learning and feelings of self-esteem within the school. Innovative teaching methods such as peer teaching in small groups, role-playing, and visualization techniques can assist bilingual students in understanding concepts.

UNIFYING CONCEPTS

When the National Science Standards were formulated, conceptual and procedural schemes were offered to unify the science disciplines so that students could better understand the natural world. Powerful ideas or, as many call them, "big ideas," help link concepts and processes, integrating all knowledge and connecting with other disciplines as well as science experiences across the grades. These concepts help students to organize their thinking about science and construct a holistic understanding of it. Unifying concepts and processes include:

➢ Systems
➢ Evidence, models, and explanation
➢ Change and constancy
➢ Evolution and equilibrium
➢ Form and function

Elaboration of these concepts is available at www.nap.edu.

Language arts standards have also been developed by the International Reading Association (IRA) and the National Council of Teachers of English (NCTE). (See Chapter 1.) They emphasize the importance of students reading a wide range of reading materials for a variety of purposes. Students are expected to know and apply a wide array of strategies as they read and write. Among the 12 standards, those most directly related to science learning include the following:

1. Students read a wide range of print and nonprint texts to build an understanding of texts, of themselves, and of the cultures of the United States and the world; to acquire new information; to respond to the needs and demands of society and the workplace; and for personal fulfillment. Among these texts are fiction and nonfiction, classic and contemporary works.
7. Students conduct research on issues and interests by generating ideas and questions, and by posing problems. They gather, evaluate, and synthesize data from a variety of sources (e.g., print and nonprint texts, artifacts, people) to communicate their discoveries in ways that suit their purpose and audience.
8. Students use a variety of technological and information resources (e.g., libraries, databases, computer networks, video) to gather and synthesize information and to create and communicate knowledge.
12. Students use spoken, written, and visual language to accomplish their own purposes (e.g., for learning, enjoyment, persuasion, and the exchange of information).

Most states in the United States have also developed more specific standards appropriate to particular grade levels. These state standards generally reflect the importance of students' ability to read informational text, organize ideas, and create reports of written communication that demonstrate research and inquiry.

PROCESS SKILLS FOR ELEMENTARY SCIENCE

Teaching science as inquiry involves moving away from traditional methods and allowing students to investigate and discover the facts, concepts, and laws of science firsthand. This approach focuses more on logical thinking in the acquisition of new knowledge and less on rote memorization of information. Real scientists use certain processes to make discoveries and to "know" about our world. These same skills should be specifically taught to our students. Knowing and using them will foster learning by enabling students to think and act in specific ways so that they can construct their own knowledge base.

The following process skills should be considered when designing a unit. Students will then come to have deeper understandings of concepts when reasonable portions of the planned science experiences emphasize them.

1. *Observing.* Students determine properties of an object or describe an event by using their five senses. *Caution*: Tasting during science by elementary school students is not recommended! Scientific tools can be used.

2. *Communicating.* Students report findings, using oral and written vocabulary, diagrams, maps, graphs, equations, and visual demonstrations.

3. *Classifying.* Students sort or group objects or events according to their properties.

4. *Interpreting data.* Students collect and organize data to make it meaningful, and suggest possibilities for further inquiry.

5. *Predicting.* Students anticipate outcomes and draw conclusions, using the results of prior experiments.

6. *Inferring.* Students draw conclusions or make "educated guesses" about a specific event, based on past experiences.

7. *Identifying and controlling variables.* Students begin to understand variables as conditions or factors in an experiment, that variables can be manipulated, and that a controlled variable in an experiment remains constant.

8. *Measuring.* Students can use standard and nonstandard tools to measure different variables, such as length, area, volume, weight, temperature, time, force, and velocity.

9. *Making hypotheses.* Students propose an explanation for an observation or event or realize a possible solution to a problem that must then be verified or disproved through experiments or testing.

10. *Experimenting.* Students design an investigation and test hypotheses for verification.

RELATED LANGUAGE ARTS COMPETENCIES AND ACTIVITIES FOR SCIENCE UNITS

In the following portion of this chapter we illustrate ways to successfully integrate literacy into science units. In the interest of space, we cannot include an entire unit but, for the most part, concentrate on literacy connections. The examples depicted lend themselves well to other science units. Titles of trade books and literature connections are listed at the end of this book in the "Children's Literature" section.

Over the years we have tried many avenues for integrating language literacy into science units. In addition, we have observed teachers use a variety of techniques and have seen many student samples. Here is a list of ideas that can focus thinking on ways to integrate your units.

1. *Collect trade books, related fiction, CD-ROMs, and website URLs.* Students will have access to a variety of materials to help them develop understanding. They learn that any one author may not be able to match their levels of knowledge. They also know that sometimes authors oversimplify concepts when they try to explain ideas to children. Therefore, it is always good to use multiple sources of information. Teachers may use books for read-alouds and reading instruction, and students may use the resources for independent or partner reading and research.

2. *Activate prior knowledge.* Students learn that in reading or initiating new learning activities, it is important to think about what is already known about the topic or theme. Brainstorming as part of a group activity is a natural way to start a new inquiry. Strategies like using a "what we already know, what we want to find out, what we have learned" (KWL chart; Ogle, 1986) or semantic mapping of ideas make this initial thinking concrete.

3. *Generate ongoing vocabulary awareness.* A key to content learning is using the precise terms that identify ideas or phenomena. Teachers introduce specific vocabulary that is used in the books. Students then develop independence by learning to preview materials to see what terms are used by the authors, taking notes on what words are important, and using various strategies to learn them. In activity-based experiences they need help from teachers in identifying the terms scientists use to design experiments, interpret information, and identify key ideas.

4. *Practice text inquiry.* While students are learning, they need to be active participants by predicting, forming questions, and charting and constructing meaning. They test ideas by looking at different sources of information—observations, written notes, and other books and materials by authorities (some on the Internet or on CD-ROMs).

5. *Conduct research after scientific investigations.* Good research starts when students have questions about something they are studying. Scientific investigations provide a great opportunity for students to learn to engage in research by asking questions and seeking various perspectives on the answers. Their own research, combined with information from authorities, is important. Strategies to make and combine notes from various sources, and then come to conclusions and share them appropriately, can develop over time.

6. *Compare information and check out contradictions through reading and writing.* A key to good critical thinking and reading is checking sources of information and verifying ideas. For students to come to their own conclusions about their investigations, they need to use their skills in consulting multiple sources to confirm their findings.

7. *Discuss and list major concepts learned through scientific investigations, reading, or using technology.* Students reinforce new learning by discussing, generating, and organizing lists of new information and important concepts. These can be displayed in a prominent place, allowing for ideas to be considered and concepts strengthened. Information can be used in written assignments and discussion.

8. *Keep journals.* Writing is an important way to learn. Students can understand the value of writing journal entries when they make notes during scientific inquiries. Learning to use the scientific terms associated with each unit is made easier when students can individually use them in writing. Chapter 7 provides many examples of how students develop their understanding as they write about their learning by recording concepts, facts, and information related to science experiences in individual journals.

9. *Share information.* An important way for students to gain confidence in themselves as learners is to share what they learn. A key to language arts is knowing how to communicate in oral, written, and visual forms. Science is a natural context in which students can be motivated to learn to communicate well. Just as scientists are part of a scientific community and share their findings with others regularly, students can share information during class discussions through written assignments and through class newsletters or family news flashes.

10. *Create original stories, poems, and cartoons.* A focus of language arts is the importance of students' being able to construct literary pieces—stories, poems, graphics, and cartoons. Works like *Poems for Two Voices* and the Magic School Bus books are examples of professional authors' creations derived from science concepts. Students, too, can incorporate new information in original ways.

CREATING UNITS AROUND SCIENCE

We have found that some science units are based on investigations; thus, students develop concepts as they explore phenomena like light, photosynthesis, metamorphosis, and life cycles. Others depend heavily on texts that provide information on various concepts, like units on astronomy or oceanography. Examples from both types of units are provided here; however, in all units there are a variety of types of activities and learning experiences. Though as many hands-on experiential activities as possible should always be included, some units naturally lend themselves to text inquiry. In the following sections we present many options for utilizing both approaches to create units that fully integrate language arts with science investigations, offering opportunities for reinforcement and deeper knowledge of content and concepts.

There are several ways to create integrated instruction. We suggest starting with a content focus that is rich enough to engage students in inquiry over an extended period of time—from 2–4 weeks.

1. Identify the key learning *standards and/or benchmarks* that are part of your science curriculum.

2. Think of ways students can be *actively engaged* in exploring the topic to develop concepts and a deep understanding.

3. Before deciding whether you will teach the unit, be sure to check with teachers at other grade levels to be sure they haven't developed and taught similar units.

4. Check to be sure that there are *varied learning resources and written materials* available for the study. Are there hands-on experiences for students?

5. Are there *multiple levels of materials* students can read and study? Are materials available at a variety of reading and conceptual levels? Do they represent different points of view? Are there people who can be called on to make the study even more concrete and personal? Are there websites that can be bookmarked for the students' use?

6. Think about the *reading, writing, and oral language* opportunities within the unit. Consult the standards and benchmarks in language arts for your grade level. What opportunities does the unit provide for introducing new skills and strategies? How can you model and teach these new processes? Which of their developed skills and strategies will students apply? How will you assess their use? Specific areas to consider include the following:

➤ Are there text features that students haven't used before that can be high-lighted (i.e., maps, graphs, inserts, or diagrams)?

➤ Are there text structures that students haven't used frequently that can be highlighted and that students can use for their own writing?

➤ How can vocabulary important to the content be identified? How can students be helped to internalize and use it?

➤ Can students use some new form of note taking and writing?

➤ Can students be asked to think critically and identify aspects of perspective or point of view?

➤ Can some reading across texts and Internet sites be structured?

➤ Can the culmination of the unit involve writing and sharing orally so students develop new skills in communicating?

7. Then envision the ways you can *assess students'* developing understanding as they participate in the unit. What can you do initially to assess entry knowledge? What are the learning points along the way that can help you adjust instruction and meet students' needs? In what ways can you and your students make a final assessment of the accomplishment of goals? Developing a model of the work you would like to see at the end of the unit is another good way of ensuring that the students and you are on the same path. Rubrics of what excellent work should look like are also very helpful.

8. Plan a *sequence of activities* that involves students actively anticipating, building knowledge, and consolidating their learning.

Anticipation stage

➢ Establish students' interest and connection to the unit content.

➢ Identify what they know related to the topic of study and the vocabulary they have that will be available to them as they learn.

➢ Help them develop their own purposes and questions to guide their inquiry.

➢ Introduce the activities and materials they will be using: science journals, graphs of changes they will observe, Amazing Fact notes that they will make, observations and experiments, and so forth.

Building knowledge stage

➢ Organize series of activities and experiences for students.

➢ Develop mini-lessons.

➢ Provide for whole-group, small-group, and individual activities.

➢ Engage students in reading, writing, and talking about their learning.

➢ Encourage students to continue to ask deeper questions.

➢ Create visual and graphic records of what students are learning.

Consolidation and sharing stage

➢ Create activities that permit students to consolidate their learning.

➢ Provide ways to share the learning with others.

➢ Celebrate the students' accomplishments.

BAT UNIT (TARGETED GRADES: 2–4)

Because of bats' unsavory reputation as creepy, scary creatures of the night, they can be absolutely fascinating to most students. Therefore, they are excellent subjects for motivating students' text research. Intriguing facts about these animals abound in recently published books for children. Sleuthing out information is not only a compelling activity, but can help to give a sense of mastery over something that might be frightening to many students. In addition, as the myths about bats are dispelled, students will begin to understand the importance of these unique mammals.

NATIONAL SCIENCE EDUCATION CONTENT STANDARD C (LIFE SCIENCE)

As a result of activities in grades K–4, all students should develop an understanding of:

1. The characteristics of organisms
2. Life cycles of organisms
3. Organisms and environments

Unifying Concepts: Form and Function, Change and Constancy, Systems

Literacy Objectives

The following are derived from the IRA and NCTE national and state standards listed in Table 1.2:

7. Students gather, evaluate, and synthesize data from a variety of sources.
   ➢ Learn to use table of contents and index.
   ➢ Make note cards of important information.
   ➢ Use information presented in simple tables, maps, and charts.
   ➢ Identify text organization (description, compare/contrast, life cycle).
   ➢ Comprehend unfamiliar words using context clues and prior knowledge.
   ➢ Create a written and/or visual summary from information gathered.

Reading and Language Arts Activities

Whole Group

Anticipation stage

1. Activate prior knowledge—semantic map.
2. Generate questions.
3. Initiate vocabulary list.
4. Collect and introduce trade books to class.

Building knowledge stage

5. Read aloud and discuss *Bat Loves the Night*.
6. Plan for teacher or student nonfiction read-aloud periods.
7. Add information to large semantic map.
8. Continue to generate questions.
9. Discuss findings on questions posed.

Small Group or Independent

10. Generate Kinds of Bats in the World list.
11. Generate What Do Bats Do? list.

Partner or Independent

12. Conduct Amazing Fact searches.

13. Draw or construct bats and write descriptions of physical features and adaptations.

14. Compose expository paragraphs using information developed from research.

Consolidation and sharing stage

15. Create a *Save the Bats* brochure.

16. Write and illustrate stories and poems about bats to share.

Science Activities

Whole Group

Building knowledge stage

1. Make echoes against a brick wall on the school playground.

Partner or Independent

2. Construct ears using various materials that will enhance hearing and compare them with those of bats.

3. Compare the anatomy and physiology of bats and humans.

4. Design and construct bat masks with bat ears and nose leaves.

Independent

5. Practice making progressively larger scale drawings on grids of the world's largest bat, as a prelude to painting a life-sized bat on the playground or sidewalk.

Consolidation and sharing stage

6. Recreate the world's largest bat, with a 6-foot (1.8-meter) wingspan, on the school playground.

Assessment

1. Assess entry knowledge by initiating a semantic map.

2. Use a rubric for fact-finding.

3. Use a rubric for paragraph writing.

4. Use an informal evaluation of student interest and participation in achieving learning objectives.

Activities Described

Semantic Map and Associated Vocabulary List

In Chapter 4 we detail the way a semantic map can be used to initiate a unit on bats. This not only provides a starting point for our study, in this case a short one, but the map sparks a list of vocabulary words that are written on chart paper and kept in prominent view. As the Bat Unit progresses, new words are added. A student may embellish the list with illustrations to assist other students in knowing the meaning of some of the words.

At this stage students often come up with myths and misconceptions about bats, which can be included along with other comments. As the students immerse themselves in "bat awareness," the map is updated by adding new information and the items that students learn are not true are deleted. Because the map can become fairly extensive, using the class chalkboard works well. Curiosity often motivates the students to continue to find new information.

During read-aloud times, trade books can be read by the teacher or students while all students listen for (1) new information to add to the semantic map and (2) new words to add to the vocabulary list.

Questions and More Questions: Beginning Inquiry

A natural extension of the semantic map is the generation of a list of questions for research on chart paper. At first the list might look something like this:

How do vampire bats suck blood?

Where do bats live?

What do bats eat?

How do bats teach their babies to fly?

A space is left beneath each question so that students can record answers as they find them. They should write the answers in their own words and in legible writing. They can add illustrations to accompany their findings. Older students can use index cards for note taking and organize them so that they can be used for later projects.

As the students gather information, additional questions will be raised. Individual students can continue the process independently.

Lists Using Simple Research

An easy way for younger students to do research is to list "What Do Bats Do?" on chart paper. With the paper secured to a spot where students can easily write, they can add interesting facts as they find them. Students take great pride in writing carefully so that other students can read the information later.

The following is an example of a list generated in early second grade:

1. Bats hang by their toes.
2. Bats hang by their thumbs, too.
3. Bats help us. They help us get food.
4. Bats fly with their hands.
5. Bats are nocturnal.
6. Bats use echolocation.

The following is an example of a list generated in third grade:

1. Bats help pollinate thousands of plants that give us fruits, spices, and other things.
2. We might not have koalas if we didn't have bats because they help pollinate eucalyptus trees in Australia.
3. Bats help keep rain forests growing through seed dispersal.
4. A big colony of bats can eat 45 kg of insects in one night.
5. Bats spend a lot of time cleaning themselves.
6. Bats usually roost upside-down but when they go to the bathroom they swing themselves right-side-up so they won't get dirty.
7. Bats may live over 30 years.

Limit students to recording each fact only once on the list; this rule ensures that they will read and reread to ascertain that they are adding new information.

A second-grade class became fascinated with the idea that there were more than 1,000 different kinds of bats in the world, making up nearly one-fourth of the world's mammal species. Enthusiasm for listing all 1,000 species spread through a small group of boys. They decided to pursue this project with a vengeance, even staying in at recess to get the job done.

First they got books on bats from the resource center and from the classroom science shelves. Then, on a large piece of paper labeled "Kinds of Bats in the

World," they began to make their list. They soon learned that the names of bat species were found in the indexes at the back of the books they were using. That, in itself, was an important discovery and one that would serve them well in future attempts at research. Taking turns, the boys listed as many names as they could on the chart paper. The number of names on the list reached 67 when they realized that there were scientific names and general names in the books, and for that reason they might sometimes have listed a single species twice. This was an advanced concept for second graders and another useful piece of knowledge. Because the project was self-generated, and they were missing several recess times, the boys did not reach 1,000 names. They were proud to fill three full pages of large paper and happy to report what they had learned to the class and to present the final product displaying their research.

The following is an example of a "Kinds of Bats in the World" list (partial):

1. Little brown bat
2. Red bat
3. Slit-faced bat
4. Spear-nosed bat
5. Mexican free-tailed bat
6. Moustached bat
7. Horseshoe bat
8. Hollow-faced bat

Some of the names sparked increased interest in learning more about bats through independent research.

Amazing Fact Searches

Several times during the unit students were asked to engage in an Amazing Fact search to find facts that had not yet been uncovered (see Chapter 5). The facts were written on fact sheets designed specifically for the project, which could then be used to add to the semantic map, to answer questions posed, or to add to the Things Bats Do list.

Writing Paragraphs

The Amazing Facts could also be used to reinforce paragraph writing: main idea, supporting details, and concluding statement.

The following are examples of "Batty Paragraphs" written by third-grade partners:

> Bats are very busy animals. They are responsible for most of the new growth of plants in rainforests. Groups of bats can scatter 60,000 seeds a night. The largest groups of insect eating bats can eat 500,000 pounds a night. Although these wonderful sources of life are very busy at the listed things, they also have a large nursery population to take care of. They know their own baby among thousands. What we have told you is amazing but if you go and learn more details the most amazing may be yet to come.
>
> By Janey and Susan

> Bats are weird but wonderful. Bats are the only mammals that can fly. One kind of bat's skin is so oily and thick that its folds are the perfect home for earwigs. Bats use echolocation using nose leaves and ears to navigate in the dark and find food. These are only some of the weird things we learned about bats.
> Bats eat weird things in weird ways. For instance, some bats can make bugs come with a special call. Other bats can dine on small lizards and toads. Some bats even eat smaller bats. Some bats can fish with their claws. Afterwards some bats use their claws instead of a toothbrush. As you can see bats are weird but wonderful.
>
> By Steve and Jordan

For more detailed information on using fact-finding to encourage paragraph writing, see Chapter 5.

Save the Bats Brochure

One reading group made a brochure for all the other second graders in the school and to take home to their families. The brochure emphasized the importance of bats and included a flag bearing the message "Just Say No to Killing Bats!"

Bat Drawings to Scale

One teacher used the following directions to guide students in drawing bats to scale: Compare the largest bat in the world—the Malayan flying fox from Asia, with a wingspan of nearly 6 feet (1.8 meters)—with a Kitti's hog-nosed bat from Thailand, which is only 1 inch (3 centimeters) long (McKee, 1992).

Have each student copy a flying fox bat on graph paper from a numbered depiction of it on a small grid (see Figure 3.1). Enlarge the bat on a piece of larger graph paper. Repeat several times, with the bat getting progressively bigger and students becoming comfortable with the process. Finally, using masking tape, create a grid on the school blacktop or cement so that students can use chalk to draw a life-sized replica of the largest bat in the world. The bat can then be painted with tempera paints. (The painting will be visible for about 6 weeks in climates with moderate precipitation.) If there is enough room, a colony of these bats can be painted, allowing small groups of students to each have a turn with sketching and painting.

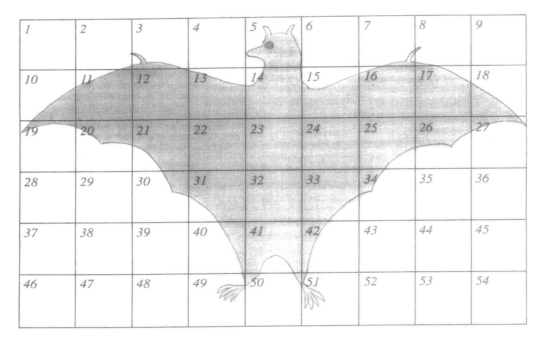

FIGURE 3.1. A sample grid for creating a life-sized flying fox. Each square should measure 20 centimeters on each side. The bat's wingspan is 6 feet (1.8 meters).

ELECTRICITY UNIT (TARGETED GRADES: 4–6)

If they are lucky enough to have been allowed to do it, students will always remember the first time they discovered how to make a bulb light up using a battery, wire, and a bulb. This hands-on experience is one of many engaging experiments in a well-developed Electricity Unit. Although this science unit consists mainly of experiment-oriented inquiry, appropriate text can assist students in understanding the subject's breadth. Understanding static electricity, electricity in circuits, batteries, conductors and insulators, electricity and magnetism needs reinforcement with trade books.

NATIONAL SCIENCE EDUCATION CONTENT STANDARD A (SCIENCE AS INQUIRY)

As a result of activities in grades K–8, all students should develop:

1. Abilities necessary to do scientific inquiry.
2. Understanding about scientific inquiry.

NATIONAL SCIENCE EDUCATION CONTENT STANDARD B (PHYSICAL SCIENCE)

As a result of activities in grades 5–8, all students should develop an understanding of:

1. Transfer of energy.

Unifying Concept: Systems

Literacy Objectives

The following are derived from the IRA and NCTE national and state standards listed in Table 1.2:

7. Students conduct research on issues and interests by generating ideas and questions, and by posing problems. They gather, evaluate, and synthesize data from a variety of sources (e.g., print and nonprint texts, artifacts, people) to communicate their discoveries in ways that suit their purpose and audience.

   ➤ Establish purposes and be able to formulate questions for inquiry.
   ➤ Use writing to report observations and hypotheses.
   ➤ Select and organize information from various sources.
   ➤ Locate information in a variety of resources.
   ➤ Clarify meanings of new vocabulary.
   ➤ Use glossaries and dictionaries where appropriate.
   ➤ Combine information from experiments and reading.
   ➤ Use new content vocabulary in discussion and writing.
   ➤ Keep notes of information and ideas that are developed during the learning process.
   ➤ Actively participate in the development of new understandings through experiments and reading.

Language Arts Activities

Whole Group

Anticipation stage
1. Initiate a KWL chart.
2. Begin reading *Ben and Me* by Robert Lawson.
3. Develop questions for scientific inquiry.
4. Initiate a vocabulary list.

Building knowledge stage
5. Discuss and list uses of electricity.
6. Listen to a guest speaker/scientist present information.

Partner or Independent

7. Read trade books to find answers to questions posed in a KWL chart.

Independent

8. Record and illustrate findings in a lab journal.

Science Activities

Whole Group

1. Design experiments that will allow students to answer questions posed in the KWL chart.

Partner

2. Experiment with static electricity by doing hands-on activities.
3. Discover how to make a simple circuit.
4. Sort conductors and insulators.
5. Assemble a switch.
6. Make a simple machine using a motor.
7. Construct an electromagnet.
8. Build a series circuit.

Whole Group

Consolidation and sharing stage

9. The class goes through a whole day without using electricity; record and share reflections of the experience.

Assessment

1. Make an informal evaluation of student interest and participation in achieving learning objectives.
2. Use a rubric for nonfiction text inquiry and organization of facts.
3. Use a rubric for written responses.
4. Use a rubric for lab journal entries.

Activities Described

Vocabulary List

Here is a list of vocabulary words generated from the unit before, during, and after several hands-on experiences:

I'm bright!

safety	current electricity
switch	static electricity
shock	conductor
outlet	insulator
plug	simple circuit
power plant	series circuit
battery	positive
bulb	negative
atoms	electrons
positive charges	negative charges
electromagnet	generator
transformer	voltage

Nonfiction Text Inquiry

Trade books can be used to answer questions generated in the KWL discussions, such as the following:

> What is static electricity?
> How does a simple circuit work?
> Why are some things conductors and other things insulators?
> What is a power station?
> How does using electricity affect the environment?
> What is alternative energy?

The answers to these questions can be recorded by each student in his or her own words and discussed in class. A written product created by the whole class, such as an informational pamphlet, may be undertaken.

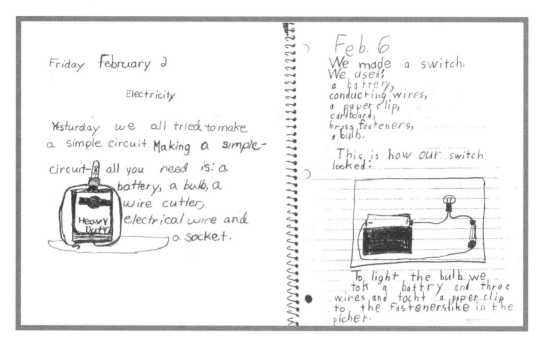

FIGURE 3.2. Second-grade journal entries.

Lab Journal

Students can reinforce what they learn from the results of their experiments by writing about them. They should be encouraged to provide careful illustrations of what was done to complete some of the questions in their KWL that the students wanted to explore: How can I make static electricity? How can I get a light bulb to light? What things are insulators and what things are conductors? How can I make a switch? How can I make an electromagnet work?

One teacher encourages the students to make a list of materials needed and to provide details about the successful procedure. Combined with a careful illustration, this information can serve as a guide in case a student wants to redo the work later. Most students are enthusiastic about this activity, as they are eager to repeat the experiments. Note that most materials can be purchased at a hardware store. See student samples in Figure 3.2.

RAINFOREST UNIT (TARGETED GRADES: 3–5)

Science can't be a dry subject when you're learning about a rainforest. A study of the majestic, mysterious tropical rainforest will seem like a venture into another world to most students, offering numerous possibilities for inquiry and discovery. Opportunities for integrating curriculum abound.

NATIONAL SCIENCE EDUCATION CONTENT STANDARD C (LIFE SCIENCE)

As a result of activities in grades K–4, all students should develop an understanding of:

1. The characteristics of organisms.
2. Life cycles of organisms.
3. Organisms and environments.

Unifying Concepts: Form and Function, Change and Constancy, Systems

Literacy Objectives

The following are part of the 12 standards of the IRA and NCTE listed in Table 1.2:

1. Students read a wide range of print and nonprint texts to build understanding of texts, of themselves, and of the cultures of the United States and the world; to acquire new information; to respond to the needs and demands of society and the workplace; and for personal fulfillment. Among these texts are fiction and nonfiction, classic and contemporary works.

   ➢ Compare the text structure of books read.
   ➢ Create a graphic organizer of the text.
   ➢ Compare and contrast authors' points of view.

2. Students read a wide range of literature from many periods in many genres to build an understanding of the many dimensions (e.g., philosophical, ethical, aesthetic) of human experiences.

4. Students adjust their use of spoken, written, and visual language (e.g., conventions, style, vocabulary) to communicate effectively with a variety of audiences and for different purposes.

   ➢ Participate in a play.
   ➢ Read orally with expression.

5. Students employ a wide range of strategies as they write and use different writing process elements appropriately to communicate with different audiences for a variety of purposes.

   ➢ Prepare a descriptive report.
   ➢ Prepare a compare/contrast essay.
   ➢ Engage in creative writing about the rainforest (stories, poems, or raps).

7. Students conduct research on issues and interests by generating ideas and questions, and by posing problems. They gather, evaluate, and synthesize data from a variety of sources (e.g., print and nonprint texts, artifacts, people) to communicate their discoveries in ways that suit their purpose and audience.

8. Students use a variety of technological and information resources (e.g., libraries, databases, computer networks, video) to gather and synthesize information and to create and communicate knowledge.

Reading and Language Arts Activities

Whole Group

Anticipation stage

1. Activate prior knowledge—KWL chart.
2. Generate questions for the KWL chart.
3. Initiate a vocabulary list.
4. Collect and introduce trade books to class.
5. Show students how to use rainforest software.

Building knowledge stage

6. Read aloud and discuss *A Walk through the Rainforest* by Kristin Joy Pratt.
7. Teacher or student nonfiction read-aloud periods.
8. Add information to the KWL chart.
9. Continue to generate questions.
10. Compare rainforests with temperate forests.
    - Location on world map
    - Rainfall
    - Stratification of layers
    - Biodiversity

11. Generate lists of animals according to animal families, such as the following:
    - Primates
    - Felines
    - Insects

12. Read about people of the rainforests.

Small Group or Independent

13. Prepare a play using the book *The Great Kapok Tree* by Lynne Cherry.

14. Read and discuss *One Day in the Tropical Rainforest* by Jean Craighead George.

15. Read *The Shaman's Apprentice* by Lynne Cherry and Mark Plotkin.

> ➢ Discuss how the lives of various native people of the rainforest differ. How are they the same?

Note: The books cited in this list, and others, can be used in literature circles.

Partner or Independent

16. Select an animal and research facts about it.

17. Prepare a report about the selected animal.

18. Compose expository paragraphs using information gained from research.

> ➢ Compare temperate rainforests and tropical rainforests.
> ➢ Compare our state forests with tropical rainforests.
> ➢ Compare our lives with those of people who live in rainforests.

19. Write and illustrate stories, poems, and raps about tropical rainforests.

Whole Group

Consolidation and sharing stage

20. Compile creative writings for publication in a class book.

21. Write a letter to an influential person regarding rainforest conservation issues.

22. Create a "Save the Rainforests" brochure.

Science Activities

Whole Group

Building knowledge stage

1. Mark off the height of the tallest tropical rainforest trees on the school playground.

2. Set up a display of potted plants originating from rainforests.

> ➢ Examine them to analyze their adaptations to their environment.
> ➢ Use eyedroppers to see how the plants have developed drip-tip leaves.

3. Set up a hydrological rainforest bottle with a rain cycle chart.

4. Make a rainforest terrarium.

5. Visit a conservatory, a zoo, or a museum.

6. Set up a display of "gifts" from the rainforest (products we use that come from the rainforests of the world).

7. Sort the gifts into things that help sustain the forest and those that are a problem for the forests if we continue to use them.

8. Create a classroom rainforest, making it as authentic as possible (McKee, 1991).

Partner or Independent

9. Construct plants and animals for the class rainforest. Place animals in appropriate layers of the classroom rainforest to show where they would live, make examples of their food, and include their life cycles.

Independent

10. Continue to construct plants and animals and place them in the rainforest.

Consolidation and sharing stage

11. Invite families to the class to view the forest.

Assessment

1. Assess entry knowledge with a KWL chart.

2. Use a rubric for fact-finding.

3. Use a rubric for paragraph writing.

4. Use informal evaluation of student interest and participation in achieving learning objectives.

5. Check for content by asking students to write a simple paragraph about why rainforests are important.

Activities Described

To plan appropriate activities for this and other comprehensive units, some teachers find that using *Bloom's Taxonomy* helps them to cover their goals, including differentiation for the various abilities within the classroom.

In 1948 a group of educators embarked on the task of classifying educational goals and objectives. Work on the part of the taxonomy dealing with cognitive domain was completed in 1956 and is commonly referred to as *Bloom's Taxonomy of the Cognitive Domain*. The taxonomy includes competencies educators want students to achieve arranged in a hierarchy ranging from simple to more complex thinking:

- ➤ Knowledge
- ➤ Comprehension
- ➤ Application
- ➤ Analysis
- ➤ Synthesis
- ➤ Evaluation

A grid displaying ideas for a Rainforest Unit generated by using *Bloom's Taxonomy* is featured in Figure 3.3. It should be noted that the activities are those in which most students can participate to some degree, bringing to the assignments whatever abilities they have.

Tic-Tac-Toe

It is good to allow students choices in how they will accomplish required goals and objectives. To provide options for students, a classroom tic-tac-toe format such as the one shown in Figure 3.4 can be useful in organizing a selection of unit-related seatwork and independent activities. A tic-tac-toe sheet with a number of activities filling the squares can be distributed to each student. Each activity includes some kind of product, such as a short report, kept by the students in work folders in their desks to serve as proof of accomplishment. Students check off tasks as completed, striving to get "Tic-Tac-Toe" (three activities completed), "Super Tic-Tac-Toe" (six activities completed), or "Super Duper Tic-Tac-Toe" (nine activities completed).

A Tic-Tac-Toe Center can be set up with all the necessary supplies, worksheets, and books to complete the work. Each student should keep a Tic-Tac-Toe folder in his or her desk to keep this work separate from other work. Depending on the students' abilities, they may be responsible for keeping the work organized and then turning it in all at once with the Tic-Tac-Toe sheet.

With the Tic-Tac-Toe Center available, students always have something to do during their free time. They are allowed to make decisions and work independently. They value the opportunity to engage in the Tic-Tac-Toe activities they have selected. However, teachers who have used this strategy caution that the novelty can wear off if it is used for every unit.

These activities are meaty and help students to think more deeply about the content and to work independently. The ability to make choices helps to increase students' motivation to do careful and thoughtful work. Notice that the assignments are taken from the *Bloom's Taxonomy* planning grid. For examples of student work, see Figures 3.5 and 3.6.

	SCIENCE	READING	WRITING
Evaluation	Collect "gifts" of the rainforest (chocolate, pictures of mahogany, vanilla, etc.) Decide whether using the "gift" sustains the forest or depletes it.	Read information about rainforest conservation. Discuss issues: the impact on native people, the impact on us.	Compose a letter to an influential person regarding rainforest conservation issues.
Synthesis	Create a large classroom rainforest on walls of the room. Make it as authentic as possible. Show life cycles, relationships, and adaptations. Add birds that migrate from the United States to tropical rainforests.	Read *Welcome to the Green House* by Jane Yolen. Do a choral reading with the whole class. Accompany it with appropriate rainforest sounds.	Write a story, poem, or rap about life in the rainforest, using as much factual information as possible. Or write a letter to a child who lives in a rainforest. Ask significant questions.
Analysis	Make a rainforest terrarium using small rainforest plants. Observe the water cycle inside the terrarium that keeps it alive.	Read and discuss how the native people use plants for medicinal purposes. Compare these plants with plants used by Native Americans.	Compare tropical rainforests with temperate ones. Or compare the lives of people in the rainforest with our lives.
Application	Design a rainforest leaf from waxed paper that will easily shed water.	Read and compare the information in two rainforest books. Are there discrepancies? Using a map, locate the rainforests discussed in the books.	Write reviews of two or more rainforest books. Record discrepancies. Tell whether or not you would recommend the books to others, and why.
Comprehension	Collect and observe potted plants from the rainforest. Decide how each plant adapts to the environment.	Read about adaptations of plants and animals that help them survive in the rainforest. Read about birds that migrate from the United States to tropical rainforests.	Select a plant and/or animal and write about its adaptations for a class book or newspaper.
Knowledge	Measure out the height of the tallest tropical rainforest trees on the school playground (250 feet).	Read trade books to gather information about rainforests and the plants and animals that live in them.	List important facts about rainforests of the world. List rainforest "gifts."

FIGURE 3.3. Grid for using *Bloom's Taxonomy* to plan integrated Rainforest Unit.

From *Integrating Instruction: Literacy and Science* by Judy McKee and Donna Ogle. Copyright 2005 by The Guilford Press. Permission to photocopy this figure is granted to purchasers of this book for personal use only (see copyright page for details).

Choose at least three activities to do during the Rainforest Unit.
Everyone must do the one in the middle.
Put a check in the corner of the square when you complete the activity.

View the following items under a microscope: 1. Butterfly wing 2. Feather 3. Insect or spider Draw what you see on the sheet provided. Show detail.	Read *The Great Kapok Tree* by Lynne Cherry. Decide which animal has the best reason for saving the tree. Write a paragraph about it.	Illustrate the water cycle in a rainforest. Explain it in writing.
Make a paper doll representing a person who lives in a rainforest. Be able to tell about the person's life.	Make an authentic animal to add to the class rainforest. Make certain that it has its food displayed, too. Show how it protects itself. Be able to tell interesting facts about the animal.	Read about birds that winter over in the tropics and raise their young in temperate zones. List them on the sheet provided.
Read and compare two nonfiction books. Rate them on a scale of 1–10 and write whether or not you would recommend them on a sheet of paper. Tell why you rated them the way you did.	Compare your state forest with a rainforest. Use the sheet provided.	Create a rainforest rap or poem.

Three in a row = Tic-Tac-Toe

Twice three in a row = Super Tic-Tac-Toe

All nine activities = Super Duper Tic-Tac-Toe

_____ I kept my papers organized.

_____ I did my part to put things away.

_____
signature

FIGURE 3.4. Classroom Tic-Tac-Toe.

Compare Illinois forests with rainforests

Illinois	Rainforests
-Different plants and animals	-More plants and animals
- Native people live in towns. and cities	-Native people live there
- Season	- Tropical
- less rain	-Same temperatures
	-up to 400 inches of rain a year!
	- Grows in layers
- lots of soil	- Less soil
- Protected	- Endangered
	-Different cultures
	- some natives only see their tribe
-We know a lot about the world and its people (tv and travel)	-No one knows more about the forest than the natives who live there.

FIGURE 3.5. Student-generated list comparing rainforests with forests in Illinois.

There's the bugs and the bees
And the cocoa trees
Where the temperature
Is always 80 degrees.

It's a place for you
And a place for me,
A place for wild things
And native people to be!

The trees can grow 200 feet tall.
It's nice to hear the raindrops fall.
The sound of birds is everywhere,
You might see a sloth with long, green hair!

There's the Scarlet Macaw and the Cock-of the Rock.
The chopper bugs go chop, chop, chop!
The Harpy Eagle looks down for its prey.
All the monkeys do is play, play, play!

You can hear bees buzz in the tall, tall trees.
It's good to feel the tropical breeze!
So let's say it again, our rainforest rap.
And keep up the rhythm and keep up the tap.

There's the bugs and the bees
And the cocoa trees
Where the temperature
Is always 80 degrees.
It's a place for you
And a place for me,
A place for wild things
And native people to be.

FIGURE 3.6. Rainforest rap by fourth-grade girls (to be recited rhythmically with corresponding body movements).

Microscope Observations

Learning to use scientific tools such as magnifiers can open up a new world of understanding for students. Figure 3.7 was prepared to be used with Classroom Tic-Tac-Toe.

Look carefully at an object through the class microscope or another magnifier.
Draw what you observed in the squares below.
Label your work.

1.

2.

3.

4.

5.

6.

FIGURE 3.7. Microscope observation sheet.

CHAPTER 4

VOCABULARY EXPANSION THROUGH EXPERIENCES

A goal in every classroom should be to help students develop a desire to discover new words, learn new meanings, and understand their broad range of uses. Fortified with ongoing enthusiasm and curiosity about words and their use, students are better equipped to develop concepts and understand nuances of meaning. This is necessary to navigate the school world, as well as life outside and beyond it. Therefore, enhancing one's vocabulary should ideally become a lifetime quest.

The current research on reading comprehension also confirms how important vocabulary is to understanding. In their review of instructional research, Blachowicz and Fisher (2002) concluded that students need teachers who create an interest in words, provide both direct and incidental instruction, and teach core content vocabulary directly. Students need to see, hear, and use new terms in many contexts to develop a deep understanding of them. This attention to words pays off for students.

Compiling a list of the content-specific vocabulary needed to understand units in science is a graphic way for teachers to realize the central role of vocabulary in science. Emphasis must be placed on helping students develop their understanding of concepts over time. Struggling readers often do not know the words they encounter in new material so that when they are reading, their attention is focused on decoding new terms, leaving little opportunity to think about meanings (Allington, 2001). The extensive vocabulary involved creates challenges for teachers who want to help students make full use of textbooks and trade publications in science. That's why vocabulary demands our attention as we plan for science teaching.

Specific vocabulary instruction is needed in all subjects, of course, but one of the important components of a strong science program is attention to the wealth of words and terms that describe scientific concepts and have specific, technical meanings. Teachers need to help students identify key terms that must be learned and to differentiate common uses of many terms from their more specific scientific meanings. For example, the word *cycle*, which is well known to children in relation to bikes, takes on a special meaning in science as it describes recurring processes and events like "the water cycle." Or consider the word *class*, used in so many familiar ways, but referring to a particular part of the classification system, under kingdom and phylum. The list goes on and on; students need to be attentive to specialized meanings all the time. Both these specialized meanings and new scientific terms that the students won't have encountered elsewhere must be learned.

With the increasing numbers of English language learners (ELLs) in classrooms across this country, it is important that teachers be particularly sensitive to the problems our vocabulary can create for these students. They can easily become confused by the multiple meanings for terms they are just learning. Careful attention, so that students can see key terms written and then have their different meanings clarified, can make science learning much more rewarding. We have also found that many key scientific terms are similar to cognates in other languages since many derive from Greek roots. Therefore, putting some terms on the board and asking for the same concepts in the first languages of your students can be an interesting activity and may help everyone to identify connections between languages. For example, when a class was studying earth formations, they made a list of key terms in English and then in Spanish. There were many easily connected terms, which relieved the ELL group and helped all students gain respect for how languages borrow and grow.

Smart teachers capitalize on the importance of vocabulary as they move through formal and informal units of study with their students. Inquiry-based science experiences and related reading provide many opportunities for extending word knowledge and developing new ideas. In turn, sound vocabulary development helps to ensure an accurate, vivid recollection and understanding of science concepts and related written text. Teachers who both encourage students to attend to new words and provide a structured approach to vocabulary development can help students build their interest and knowledge.

As the students progress through the grades, they are exposed to ever more varied and complex reading material as part of science. Therefore, vocabulary development becomes even more essential to success. The students must not only understand related print in science texts and trade books, but they need to understand how to follow directions when doing science experiments and must be able to report results by writing and talking. They need to keep expanding their understanding of scientific terminology so that they move from recognition of terms to full ownership of them. The richness and diversity of language is palpable when teachers create meaning-rich contexts for discovery and then draw on students' shared experiences to increase understanding. Real experiences and opportunities for students to talk together about their science topics encourages, enhances, and extends effective communication.

In this chapter, you will be given many ideas to assist students in becoming familiar with and competent in using the vocabulary necessary to perform adequately during science lessons and related activities. The students must have many experiences with and easy access to the words they need for thinking, learning, and communicating so that using science vocabulary becomes a natural part of their school experience. We begin by describing the general classroom climate that stimulates interest in words and then provide strategies that help students focus on important terms, build expanded meanings for these terms, and use them in reading, writing, and speaking.

BUILDING A CLASSROOM CLIMATE FOR WORD AWARENESS

Classrooms in which students are actively engaged in science are those in which students enjoy words and are encouraged to try out new words as they are learning. Teachers who help focus students' vocabulary development in language arts can build on this foundation. Many elementary teachers now have "Word Walls," where the words the students are learning in literacy instruction are listed. In the primary grades these are often alphabetized, and new words are added as the students are learning them. Teachers regularly read books about words and language to the children, including the *Amelia Bedelia* series and joke books that play on words. Upper-level teachers often introduce a Word of the Day to help students expand their vocabularies, and many encourage students to keep vocabulary notebooks so that new words can be rehearsed and used independently. Most reading programs give some attention to words that derive from other languages, especially Greek and Latin. All of these activities can be linked to learning vocabulary for science.

The Language of Lepidoptera

Starting the year off right can send a clear message to students that language learning is fun. There are many ways this can be done. In the following section, Judy McKee provides an example of how she built students' expectations and enjoyment. She also explains her ways of highlighting the language of science.

As a second-grade teacher I began each year with a study of butterflies, capitalizing on the readily available opportunity offered by these lovely creatures that were abundant on the school grounds. My initial activity was to introduce vocabulary during the time-tested Word of the Day exercise every morning. The first word was *lepidoptera*, which means "insects with scaled wings."

The word was placed on the chalkboard under the heading "Word of the Day." As one of the activities for the first day, I printed the word on the overhead projec-

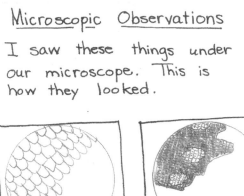

FIGURE 4.1. Student illustrations of observations using a microscope.

tor. I first pronounced the word and defined it for the students, placing it in the context of their upcoming study of butterflies. Then I asked them to relate some of the things they already knew about butterflies. I informed them that they would be learning some "big words during this unit" and that "*lepidoptera* is one of them." Next, I helped the students chunk the word into pieces (syllables), enabling them to read it using this important decoding strategy. To reinforce the word, one of the assignments given the students that day was to copy the word neatly on lined paper and then illustrate its meaning. The students were encouraged to show their parents this work later and to explain the meaning of the word.

A butterfly wing, with its scales clearly visible using a small microscope, was placed in the classroom science center next to a sign clearly labeled "Lepidoptera = Butterflies and Moths." (See Figure 4.1 with an illustration of what the students would see under the microscope.)

Every child was expected to examine this and/or the other examples of butterfly and moth wings collected in a small container and left in the science center. A large selection of nonfiction books was also available, with posters and photos completing the display. Space remained in the science center for students to add illustrations and written work on the subject.

Labeling the parts of a butterfly provided a simple but productive method for learning about lepidoptera early in the unit. Again, I first allowed each child to examine real butterflies I had collected over the years and exhibited in a small display case. Then I moved on to discuss charts I bought or designed myself, talking about them to connect and expand on what the students knew or had observed earlier. Next, the students either cut and pasted or printed the vocabulary words onto their own charts. Although in some situations students may be asked to label things without really understanding their meanings, in this case the pictures helped to build concepts, the goal of science learning. Drawing and labeling this early in their school career also established an important way for students to think about and learn new words.

Throughout the following days, as the Life Cycle of Butterflies and Moths Unit unfolded, students learned the power of words, bandying about "lepidoptera" and other terms such as "metamorphosis," "chrysalis," and "pupa." The words came to life every year when students observed metamorphosis firsthand by raising their own butterflies from caterpillar to pupa to adult. Their parents often commented on the new awareness of words their children exhibited and on how proud the children were to know vocabulary that even parents might not know or use.

Teachers Set the Tone

It is important that classroom teachers further word knowledge by modeling their own interest and delight in language. For example, a fourth-grade teacher might exclaim, "Did you hear the way the author used that word? Let's listen to that again!" Another time he might focus on an entire passage, telling his students to discuss why it was well written and to comment on the author's use of vocabulary. After discussing the qualities of good word choices, his students worked in cooperative groups to search for well-written passages and carefully selected words in the writing of fine authors. Later they shared their findings during small-group or whole-class discussions.

Teachers of younger grades can do the same thing, but they can extend the experience by asking each group to illustrate a page for a class book called simply "Passages." Some students keep a journal of favorite selections along with their comments about the writing. (See an example in Figure 4.2.)

Listening for New Words

Read-alouds provide excellent opportunities for word awareness and vocabulary development. It is easy and natural to stop and savor interesting and new words while reading to the class. New terms that students will need to know can be introduced informally through read-alouds from informational trade books, newspaper articles, and magazines. Before starting, the students can be asked to listen for new words or for words already on a classroom list they are creating. After reading, leave time for student talk including attention to the new words encountered and their meanings, as well as alternative definitions of words already introduced. Then these words can be added to the ongoing vocabulary list that is displayed during the read-aloud. (See Figure 4.3 for a list generated for *lepidoptera.*)

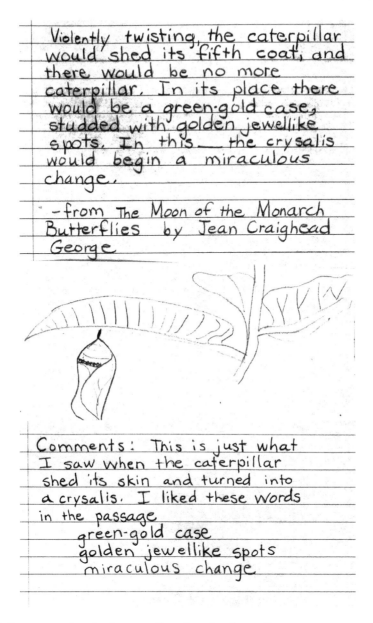

Violently twisting, the caterpillar would shed its fifth coat, and there would be no more caterpillar. In its place there would be a green-gold case, studded with golden jewellike spots. In this ___ the crysalis would begin a miraculous change.

—from The Moon of the Monarch Butterflies by Jean Craighead George

Comments: This is just what I saw when the caterpillar shed its skin and turned into a crysalis. I liked these words in the passage
    green-gold case
    golden jewellike spots
    miraculous change

FIGURE 4.2. Example of selection for class book on favorite passages.

Words to Know about Lepidoptera

camouflage | Colors or patterns that blend into the surroundings so that an animal is hard to see. Also provides protection.

caterpillar | A baby lepidoteran after it comes out of an egg. Synonym: larva.

chrysalis | Case that holds the butterfly or moth. Synonym: pupa.

cocoon | A covering that protects the pupa of an insect. Moths spin cocoons around the pupas.

metamorphosis | The process of changing from egg to adult in lepidopteran life.

migrate | To move a long distance from one place to another.

nectar | A sweet liquid made by flowers that is eaten by butterflies.

osmeteria | A caterpillar's "horns."

predator | An animal that eats other animals.

prey | An animal that is eaten by other animals.

proboscis | A long mouth tube used by lepidoptera for sucking nectar.

prolegs | Leglike stumps that help a caterpillar cling to twigs and leaves.

scales | Tiny, flat shapes that cover lepidoptera wings.

FIGURE 4.3. A classroom vocabulary list.

Films, videotapes, filmstrips, special TV programs, and science technology also offer opportunities for vocabulary development. As in the read-aloud, students can turn an ear toward new words and meanings, adding them to the growing classroom list of unit-specific words. When teachers praise students' attentiveness to new terms, they learn to look for words and develop confidence as learners. Another way to build students' attention to words is to assign different students to listen or look for words that are associated with a specific topic. For example, some students in the second grade studying lepidoptera may be assigned all the words relative to the caterpillar stage, others to the pupa stage, and still others to the adult stage. Everyone will be responsible for discovering additional vocabulary words and information on metamorphosis. After the visual presentation is complete or the computer program has been run, new vocabulary can be discussed and new concepts and meanings explained. In this way awareness of words, deeper understandings, and new definitions will develop.

Teachers Must Be Models

Teachers can constantly model their own interest in words and in the specific terms the students will encounter in discussions and during reading for content. They do this through read-alouds and during a guided reading of texts. The importance of words can be communicated easily by encouraging students to use targeted words orally and in written work and praising them for their efforts. It is also important to model using the words in complete sentences, with appropriate diction and correct grammar. Many teachers also keep a dictionary close by at all times as a reference to use when a definition or pronunciation may be unknown. This also shows students the importance of using a dictionary or glossary when needed.

EXPERIENCES PROVIDE FOUNDATION

Science is one of the easiest subjects for building vocabulary because students have a natural interest in it and words are necessary to communicate what one sees and does. It is especially useful if science lessons are activity oriented, because then teachers have a ready-made laboratory for words as well as for discovery of science concepts. In fact, when incorporating vocabulary into science instruction, the most productive opportunities are based on actual experiences. Hands-on real experiences allow students to see and feel the meaning of words instead of just hearing the definitions.

Students who enter elementary classrooms are still in the concrete-operational stage of development characterized by hands-on thinking. Through the children's experiencing things they can see and touch, the vocabulary becomes more concrete and will therefore be retained and understood better than if a teacher just talks about concepts and expects students to form their own (Woolfolk, 2001).

Most students have excellent strengths in learning modalities other than the auditory. Kinesthetic and visual modes are in operation during hands-on or experience-oriented work, which serve to encourage more efficient use of language and stimulate improved concept development. These experiences help students successfully define vocabulary better than the use of teacher-talk or dictionary definitions. They help students to achieve solid cognitive links between the words they are learning and what the words represent. Hands-on activities allow teachers to provide new vocabulary as a natural and welcome extension of their explorations.

Observing

One of Judy's current jobs is running an elementary school garden. She is responsible for offering a full complement of experiences for the more than 600 students who attend the school. Language is richly embedded in the experiences the students have in this beautiful place, so she encourages and develops it. Students often observe butterflies there as they fly, light on plants, drink nectar, (sometimes) mate, and lay eggs. They are encouraged to talk about what they see, which helps them to expand their vocabularies and use the "scientific" words associated with these observations. "Did you see the butterfly 'perch' on the flower petal as it took its drink?" "The butterfly used its 'proboscis' to drink 'nectar' from the flowers" or "Let's think of as many words as we can to describe how a butterfly flies. Think about what you saw to help you. . . . Yes, 'flutter' is a good one." Back in the second-grade classrooms, an ongoing list of synonyms and modes of flight can be generated and expanded as the units on the butterfly life cycle progress. When teachers keep lists of new terms visible in the classrooms, the children can keep referring to these words and can use the words as they write in their own journals or discuss what they have seen.

Experimenting

Students can improve their language skills as they observe and handle living things or do science experiments. Describing, discussing, and comparing come naturally as they see and experience the meaning of words instead of only hearing the definitions. Teachers need to allow time for reflection and for talking about what was experienced to enable the students to interpret what they have experienced and to verbalize about it accurately, putting vocabulary into context.

Shared Experiences

Savvy teachers build on shared experiences, with the students helping them to use words to precisely define those experiences. An example of such an experience is the "Science Day Surprise" documented in Figure 4.4. A cocoon brought in by one of the students had been saved in a container throughout the winter. What a thrill it was when a child discovered what had happened one day in May! The occurrence just happened to coincide with a special day set aside for an array of science activities and related language arts, which the students had named Science Day. Minutes after witnessing the amazing event, the students gathered on the

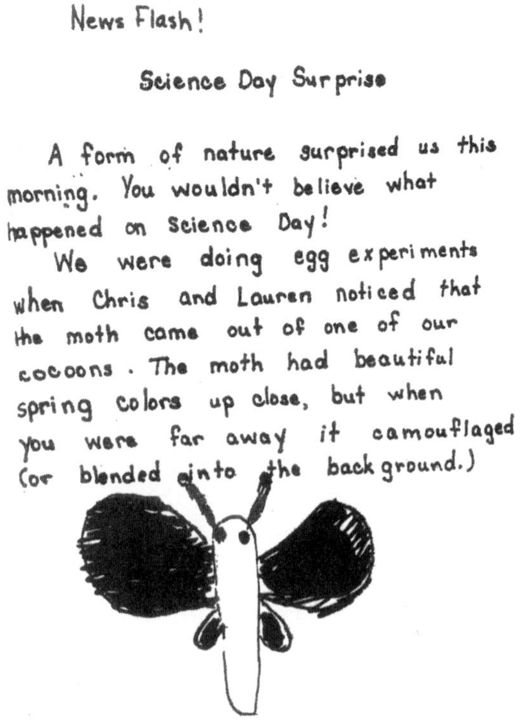

News Flash!

Science Day Surprise

A form of nature surprised us this morning. You wouldn't believe what happened on Science Day!

We were doing egg experiments when Chris and Lauren noticed that the moth came out of one of our cocoons. The moth had beautiful spring colors up close, but when you were far away it camouflaged (or blended into the background.)

FIGURE 4.4. Class-generated story.

floor in the rug area of the room. Together they summarized what was important. Words germane to the story were listed on chart paper. The teacher then helped to frame ideas offered by the students to create the written piece. As you can see in Figure 4.4, vocabulary words from their unit-specific list are included in the story.

Making Meaning from Experiences

Students may use labels without really understanding the meanings behind them. In science we want to build concepts rather than labels. To form an abstraction or concept derived from a particular experience may take time; in fact, students may need several experiences in several grades at different developmental stages in order to fully understand the concepts we require of them. For instance, the idea of magnetism is a complicated one. Early in school, students playfully experiment with magnets, learning how they push and pull or attract and repel. They can experiment to find out what materials are magnetic and which are nonmagnetic. They can discover how magnets help us by going on a magnet hunt at home. After having had a significant amount of experience with magnets and the associated vocabulary, they will understand the concept of magnetism developmentally appropriate for their age. But to understand how magnetic fields function with atoms and electric charges is too abstract for them. Introducing more advanced concepts should come later when the experiences they have had with magnets to that point can help them understand the complexity of the concepts.

Vocabulary Assists Concept Formation

The newly acquired vocabulary helps students form and understand abstract concepts. Appropriately planned experiences geared to the developmental level of the students lay the groundwork for understanding more difficult and more abstract ideas presented in later science instruction. Students will also be developing an awareness of how specific words define these experiences and understandings.

DEVELOPING CONTENT-SPECIFIC UNDERSTANDINGS

Every unit of study has its own vocabulary that helps students see and understand better. Over time students become more attentive to the way vocabulary conveys meaning in science. However, sometimes so many new terms are introduced that students can feel overwhelmed, especially if they don't have particularly strong vocabularies. When this happens, teachers can help students differentiate the most important concept-laden words from interesting but less essential terms in several ways. As a new unit is introduced, teachers can help students check their prior knowledge and familiarity with key terms. When students monitor their own need to know more about these terms, they are often more willing to focus their energy on learning. Instructional activities can also help students elaborate their definitions of the key terms and practice using them until they are learned. Examples are provided in the following sections.

Rate Your Knowledge

The Rate Your Knowledge activity (Blachowicz & Fisher, 2002) permits students to see key terms and assess their own level of familiarity with them at the outset of instruction. The teacher prepares a list of terms (not more than 12 and appropriate to the age and ability level of the group) and places them on a chart like that shown in Figure 4.5. Students individually complete the activity by supplying the definitions of the terms they mark as known. This added step helps students monitor their own honesty in identifying words as ones they know and establishes that being able to explain what a word means is part of knowing it. After this activity, the students, as a class, discuss which words they knew and what they think others mean. The teacher can then guide them to keep the less familiar terms in their vocabulary notebooks or in some accessible place so they can be referred to regularly and located in what the students read or see.

RATE YOUR KNOWLEDGE—SOLAR SYSTEM				
Vocabulary terms	Unknown	I've seen	I know and can use	Definition
Orbit				
Meteor				
Asteroid				
Planet				
Rotation				
Atmosphere				
Revolution				

FIGURE 4.5. Rate Your Knowledge sheet for the solar system.

At the end of the unit, students can return to the Rate Your Knowledge sheet and evaluate the growth of their vocabularies. By the end of the unit, all of the terms should be known by the students, because the list is fairly short and focuses on important aspects of instruction.

Connect Two

Another prereading activity that permits teachers to focus attention on key terms is Connect Two. As in the Rate your Knowledge activity, the teacher selects important terms that he or she wants to be sure everyone learns. The teacher puts the terms on the board or on a transparency and reads the words aloud so that students can hear the words and connect them with their written forms. Then the students are instructed to connect two of the words to create a sentence, and to continue doing so until all words are used. This can be done individually with students writing their own sentences, in partners with both members creating the sentences, or as a group oral activity. The first time the activity is introduced the teacher needs to clarify the purpose for thinking about the terms and the expectation that, by the end of the unit, all the words will be familiar. The teacher also makes it clear that for the initial activity the words don't have to be known, but that students should make up sentences that seem plausible. Great fun can ensue as unfamiliar terms are combined in "possible sentences, " another name for this activity. At the end of the unit students can be assessed according to the sentences they write using this list of key terms.

Content Word Walls

It is important that the students have ready access to the words they will use during a science unit. Some teachers have a special Word Wall for the current unit of study, and others keep a chart of these words in an easily observed spot.

As units progress, words are continually added to the list. Words of the Day can be added as well. The collection of words should also be open-ended so that students can add words they find in their study that they and the teacher agree are important ones. The key to the effectiveness of a Word Wall is that the frequently used and important words are visible to students. When the words on the wall or chart become familiar, teachers can provide added incentives by giving students extra credit when they use these terms in class discussions or in their journals and papers. As the list of words grows, students can also learn to group or classify terms that fit together. These groups of words can then be labeled—a form of the activity called "List–Group–Label." Particularly at the upper levels, some students seem to need encouragement to work with new terms.

Some teachers encourage students to add words that they have encountered, but before doing so a student must demonstrate knowledge of its meaning. Of course, the teacher will also add to the list as the need arises. Lists generated with each unit are then saved and easily accessible for the rest of the year.

Student Word Book

As we learn new words, we need to practice using them frequently in order to make them our own. One way teachers can help students develop their understanding of new terms is to have them keep Word Books or Vocabulary Notebooks. These can be useful across all school content areas, but can naturally be introduced in science. Students then have their own lists of words being mastered, with personal associations, descriptions, examples of where they are found, and illustrations that help them to retain them. Words that students didn't know during the initial Rate Your Knowledge or Connect Two activity would be appropriate. Students may want to add new words to their Word Books as they are encountered during lessons or more expansive independent readings. Illustrations can be made to reinforce meaning, and sentences using the words can be included in the book.

Concept of Definition Maps

An easy way to help students understand what is involved in knowing words is to have them create concept of definition word maps (Schwartz & Raphael, 1985) of key terms. At first the teacher needs to model the creation of a concept map, explaining that there are three components on the map. For each word selected, the students need to think of the attributes of the term, some examples, and the larger category of which it is part. For example, the teacher might begin with the term *compound*. If students don't have a clear idea of the scientific meaning of the term, they can turn to their textbooks or notes and other materials to see how it is defined by experts. Then they insert some descriptive terms or phrases in the boxes—"What is it like?" Some students may be able to give examples of compounds based on their experiments and reading. They also need to think of the category of words in which *compound* is a subset. In this case, they may not know a scientific term, but *combination* or *mixture* might work. See the example in Figure 4.6.

Word Card Collections

Another way to help students practice new words is to develop a set of word cards. Each card is for one new term. Two variations are useful. The first is to have students write a word on one side of a card with the definition, concept map, or other personal connections or elaborations on the term on the back. The other is to have students create an illustration of the word on one side of a card and have the word, definition, and a sentence in which the word is used meaningfully, on the other. We have found (Ogle, 2000) that many students develop more interest in the new words when they can have the fun of guessing what scientific concepts are illustrated on classmates' cards.

Primary students can use index cards, punch one corner of each, and keep them together on a ring. The cards can also be kept in zip-lock bags at their desks

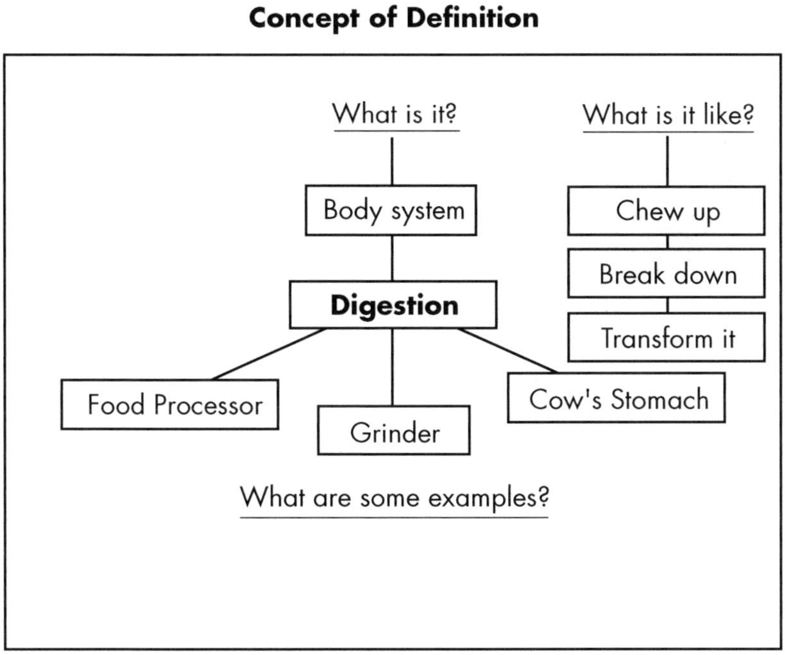

Concept of Definition

FIGURE 4.6. Example of a student-generated concept of definition map.

for easy access during written work. In this way they can always have their words near them and can use the word ring for a variety of activities. These cards can be sorted (some students use different colored cards for separating word categories), used for alphabetizing, for creating poetry and written messages, and for practice when there is downtime in the classroom.

Older students can also keep vocabulary terms on index cards and have them available when there is time for review Some teachers take a few minutes at the end of each class period to let students test each other on words they are learning. Some use the words on the index cards for partner games and review. Having words accessible to the students allows them to develop the expectation that learning new words requires practice—which can be fun!

Illustrating Vocabulary Words

Younger students profit from illustrating some of their words. An illustration can act as a visual clue when they come to read the word or must find it quickly when it is needed to use for written work. This technique is especially good for students who are learning English as a second language (English language learners; ELL) and need as many visual cues as possible to master the overwhelming number of new words they encounter daily.

Chiroptera

echolocation = sounds
bounce off things to
help bats find their
way in the dark

navigate = fly

roost = 1) place
where bats hang
during the day
2) what they do
when they hang

FIGURE 4.7. Example of simple bookmark.

Bookmarks

During fact-finding searches involving note taking, older students can go back through their notes and underline vocabulary words new to them. Then, during follow-up discussions the words can be added to the class list. Some teachers encourage students to use a bookmark as they go along. Students jot down new words on the bookmark, page numbers for later contextual reference, synonyms, or other associations, which can serve as memory aids to help them retain meaning. (See Figure 4.7.)

Bookmarks can also be developed by teachers and given to students when there is a text to be read that might overwhelm some students with the high proportion of very technical terms. The important words with their definitions, as used in the particular text, are put on the bookmarks so students don't have to slow down their reading and thinking to find these words in a glossary or dictionary. In this way the teacher saves students a great deal of time doing a very low level task of searching for definitions and lets them focus on getting the meaning. If students find this form of bookmark useful, teams of students can be designated to prepare vocabulary bookmarks for others before subsequent units of study. Working with the teacher, they can ensure that the most important terms will be included, and the teacher can also learn from the students' selections of terms just how difficult the material will be for them. See Figure 4.8 for an example.

Synonyms

A list of synonyms can be generated to help expand word knowledge. For example, the words *larva* and *caterpillar* have the same definition in discussing and observing the caterpillar stage of the butterfly/moth life cycle. Some teachers keep a continually growing synonym list visible in the classroom throughout the unit.

BIOMES

biomes—Natural areas on Earth including climate, soil, plants, and animals.

ecosystem—There can be thousands of ecosystems in a biome.

energy—All living things in a biome need energy from the sun to live and grow.

energy—Flows through all living things.

food chains—Plants use energy from the sun and carbon dioxide in the air to make food and grow.

Animals must eat plants or other animals to get energy.

Animals that eat other animals that eat plants form a food chain (illustration).

food webs—Chains in a biome that are connected make a food web.

FIGURE 4.8. Example of bookmark to be given to students prior to new unit.

Semantic Maps

Building relationships between words is important in vocabulary development. Semantic maps or word maps provide a way for students to access prior knowledge and organize information visually according to categories. The following example relates what happened when Judy's class was beginning a study of bats.

1. She placed the word "Bats," the key word, on chart paper and turned to the students: "Think of as many words as you can that fit with (are related to) the word "Bats."
2. The students brainstormed words for the list.
3. She then asked the students if some of these words fit together in some way. After some discussion, she used new chart paper to make the semantic map. In each such study, words pertaining to physical characteristics, habitats, myths, and so forth, were grouped together and given category labels. For instance, she might point to the words "wings" and "vampire teeth," and the students might come up with "What They Look Like." Later she would suggest that the label "Physical Characteristics" be used. "Scary" and "dangerous" were put under the heading "Feelings." Judy downplayed anything to do with vampires, sucking, and blood, because only 1% of bats in the world are vampire bats, a fact she would tell the students as they brainstormed. She might place "vampire" words under the label "Myths," planning to discuss them and other misconceptions in more depth later. "Vampire bat" was placed under the label "Kinds of Bats."
4. A class discussion was held about the map. Judy added more information and cleared up misconceptions. She showed the class a rubber Halloween bat

SEMANTIC MAP (BEFORE)

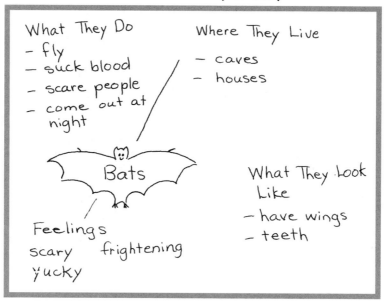

What They Do
- fly
- suck blood
- scare people
- come out at night

Where They Live
- caves
- houses

Bats

What They Look Like
- have wings
- teeth

Feelings
scary   frightening
yucky

SEMANTIC MAP (AFTER)

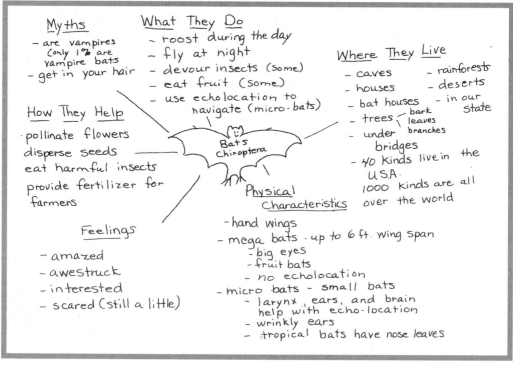

Myths
- are vampires (only 1% are vampire bats)
- get in your hair

What They Do
- roost during the day
- fly at night
- devour insects (some)
- eat fruit (some)
- use echolocation to navigate (micro-bats)

Where They Live
- caves   - rainforests
- houses   - deserts
- bat houses - in our state
- trees bark leaves
- under branches bridges
- 40 kinds live in the U.S.A.
1000 kinds are all over the world

How They Help
- pollinate flowers
disperse seeds
eat harmful insects
provide fertilizer for farmers

Bats
Chiroptera

Feelings
- amazed
- awestruck
- interested
- scared (still a little)

Physical Characteristics
- hand wings
- mega bats - up to 6 ft. wing span
    - big eyes
    - fruit bats
    - no echolocation
- micro-bats - small bats
    - larynx, ears, and brain help with echo-location
    - wrinkly ears
    - tropical bats have nose leaves

FIGURE 4.9. Example of classroom semantic maps. The first semantic map indicates prior knowledge. The second one shows a map with new information added.

and explained, "Bats aren't really like this. They are very helpful, and as we learn more about bats, we'll add 'How Bats Help' to the word map."

5. As the unit progressed, new information was added. The map was soon transferred from chart paper (or the overhead transparency) to the chalkboard so that there would be room for many more words or concepts. See the example in Figure 4.9.

In generating the semantic map, the students first use prior knowledge and personal experiences as a starting point in developing language for the science unit to be undertaken. They pool their knowledge and pertinent vocabulary as they discuss the less familiar words on the list. As their research and learning experiences continue, they are encouraged to review the map to uncover inaccuracies, refine information, and add new ideas and vocabulary. Before something was added, Judy encouraged class discussion about the information. Often, there was indecision as to where it should be placed on the map. For instance, should the word "echolocation" be included under "Things They Do," or should a whole new category be formed? The process of allowing the students to decide, guided by the teacher, encourages them to gain ownership of the map.

The graphic organization offered by a semantic map can be valuable in helping students think, call up prior information, categorize facts, develop concepts, and synthesize information. By leaving it prominently displayed, the teacher can then assign a written project, expository or creative writing, using the map as a resource for ease in accessing vocabulary, correct spelling, and accurate information.

MASTERING THE NEW VOCABULARY

The traditional way of teaching science is the lecture–discussion method, whereby teachers tell the students what they are to learn, and then ask them to answer questions about what they heard. This limited approach provides little opportunity for students to discuss issues, solve problems, or ask their own questions, which ultimately result in developing thinking skills. There is little sense of ownership, and chances to discover and use related vocabulary are reduced. Rather than requiring students to memorize word lists (which is very difficult for many students), but instead stressing language skill development and comprehension by having them practice the necessary vocabulary and language in a real-world setting, is of significant benefit to students (Reutzel & Cooter, 2000).

Teachers who value the power of words take time to allow plenty of classroom talk. Daily classroom discussions are held so that the teacher can assess understandings and concepts and correct the misuse and mispronunciation of words. Students are encouraged to describe an observation or experiment or to repeat information from the text in their own words. Vocabulary is reinforced in a natural way as the students learn from their experiences and readings.

Cooperative Groups

Cooperative learning groups can be effective because they foster language development through interstudent communication. Drawing conclusions from observations and experiments, as well as answering assigned questions or those generated by the group, are appropriate science-related activities for group work. A grasp of unit-specific vocabulary and communication skills are natural outcomes. The classic design of cooperative learning is characterized by structured groupings, clear purpose and instructions, and a balance of group interaction with individual responsibility. It involves assigning a specific task (i.e., chief experimenter, observer, recorder, mathematician) to each student. Tasks should be rotated among the students from lesson to lesson to provide each person opportunities for varied contributions and experiences. Some teachers successfully engage students in smaller cooperative learning groups.

While working in cooperative groups, students should be given ample opportunity to discuss observations, choices, decisions, and results. They must be allowed time for understanding and reflection through discussion, and for repetition of the language heard and spoken. After a lesson is completed, group members can be encouraged to evaluate their own work as well as that of others in the group, though they may want to do so privately.

When students are asked to find the answers to problems they pose for themselves about a topic, they become invested in the work. They master vocabulary as they articulate the problems and their efforts to solve them. This process also encourages students to learn independently. Ideally, teachers should provide a variety of resources to support the activities undertaken: materials for science laboratory investigations; reference materials such as books, newspapers, and magazines; films and computer programs; and outside resource people. The objective of forming cooperative groups in science is to allow students to acquire science information through their own efforts. Communicating with one another by using content-specific vocabulary already introduced and hearing and discovering new words that evolve from the experiences and discussions are natural consequences.

Think–Pair–Share and Think–Pair–Square

Think–Pair–Share and Think–Pair–Square are strategies that can be used to encourage conversation about science-related experiences or information. The first of these methods is to ask students to think about a problem or an open-ended question, making sure they can justify the reasons for the answers generated. Other ideas that work well for science are making predictions about an experiment and discussing it, talking over the charts and graphs, drawing conclusions and developing concepts through discussion.

After the "think time" it's time for the students to share their thinking with a partner. The two might come to a consensus or simply take turns listening to each other and explaining their thinking. Another possibility is to use this time for students to teach each other if necessary. The conclusions or results in Think–Pair–Share are ultimately shared with the rest of the class.

Think–Pair–Square is similar to Think–Pair–Share, but instead of sharing with the whole group, the partners are asked to share with another pair to compare thinking. This stretches out the process a bit more and gives more accountability to each member of the pairs.

There are good reasons for using both of these effective strategies. For one thing, they are easy to use on the spur of the moment. Moreover, because students don't feel the peer pressure involved in responding in front of the whole class, they are more willing to participate. Misunderstandings about the topic are often revealed (and resolved) during these small-group discussions in a nonthreatening way.

Time to think and share deepens the comprehension of concepts so that more information is retained. This is critical in many classrooms, as teachers often present so much information that much of it is lost. Of course, the discussions are only as deep and rich as the extent to which they incorporate specific vocabulary to enhance understanding. Therefore, the students need prior input and access to the vocabulary they will need to use.

CONCLUSION

It is common knowledge that students learn vocabulary best when directly involved in rich experiences to help them construct meaning. Memorization of definitions and dictionary work are not effective means of vocabulary enrichment. In addition, teachers must plan for effective word acquisition by allowing for plenty of classroom talk by discussing experiences and thinking about words, by relating new vocabulary to background information, by helping students see relationships between words, and by helping students build deeper understanding of the words they encounter. All of these strategies can enable students to better reach the goals we set for them in concept development. Other important results include improved reading comprehension and students' ability to incorporate additional complexity in their written work.

CHAPTER 5

EXPLORING THE REAL WORLD WITH INFORMATIONAL TEXTS

When I read a good book, it makes me think of things like: I'm learning so much from this book! When I read it, I could read day and night.

—BRANDEN, grade 4

Science content provides a stimulating context for students' learning, as illustrated in the previous chapters. Students' excitement about topics and units of study leads naturally into reading as a way of developing deeper understandings. Yet without instruction, many students become frustrated because textbooks, magazines, and informational trade books are organized and structured very differently than pieces of fiction and poetry. Because it is important that all students learn to use these kinds of reading materials, even with their first experiences with books it is natural to teach the needed skills in conjunction with science. And because most of the reading we as Americans do is in nonfiction or informational materials, it is important that teachers give students ample experiences in using a variety of such materials. Focused teaching about informational texts is critical; science provides a natural context to develop students' ability to read for information.

In this chapter, we offer an overview of the key features of informational texts that students need to use as they read in science. Both textbooks and trade books are included, as students need to learn to use both kinds of resources well. Then we describe how teachers can build classrooms in which students have access to quality books and magazines and are given regular opportunities to engage in reading to learn science content. We provide many ways in which teachers can help students to use the information they gather from their reading for writing and research.

We devote a separate chapter (Chapter 6) to using fictional texts to introduce students to scientific concepts and experiments. There are many very engaging books that have a foundation in scientific data, yet need teacher amplification to make them most meaningful to students. In the examples provided some of the fictional texts are linked to nonfiction pieces. Other examples show how fiction can be used independently to create more interest in science and help students explore concepts. Some of the interesting projects can whet students' appetites to learn more.

LEARNING TO USE INFORMATIONAL TEXT

> Reading fills our head with interesting questions that can be
> answered by just reading another book.
>
> —ELIOR, grade 2

Science requires that students learn to use a variety of print materials that are different from those generally taught in language arts instruction. The relationship of printed materials to the "activity" of science is also different. When students are engaged in scientific inquiry, books, websites, and articles serve as reference points, as extensions of their thinking, and as sources to resolve unanswered questions. Even when teachers use a textbook series to provide the framework for teaching science, the experiments and demonstrations are the focal points for learning. The words and explanations help students make sense of actual phenomena. With literature, reading and responding form the heart of the experience, but in science the reading of texts is done to confirm and provide a language and context for what students experience, see, and explore. Also in contrast to reading literature, when reading most scientific materials (unless the class is reading through a section of a textbook) students don't need to start on page 1 and read to the end in sequential order. Students can learn to look for the section of the text that contains the specific information they need to answer their questions. They can use a glossary, a table of contents, and/or an index as tools to help their search. In addition, most science texts (textbooks, trade books, magazines, and newspapers) rely heavily on visuals to illustrate the

Every classroom library should have both fiction and nonfiction selections to enhance science units.

content. Most young readers need guided instruction in how to read various forms of diagrams, charts, maps, and pictures. They need to learn to associate the visual displays with the narrative text and combine these different types of information if they are going to comprehend what the authors of the text intend. Too many teachers assume that students know how to read the visual information, yet when students are tested they regularly demonstrate deficiencies in such reading (Illinois Standards Achievement Test, 2000; Moline, 1996).

Some teachers and schools have almost ignored reading as part of their science curriculum under the assumption that science is "hands-on activity," not synthesized ideas. However, this is not good practice. Research studies (Anderson, 1987; Roth, Anderson, & Smith, 1987) have demonstrated that students in these classrooms do not necessarily make accurate interpretations any more than do students who just read about science. A major component of understanding process is prior knowledge. So, even in activity-based science, checking and expanding on students' knowledge is critical. Helping them describe what they experience and put into words what they learn is important, and reading how others describe similar experiences is very helpful to their critical thinking.

Scientists engage in concrete activities and observation, yet they keep careful records of what they observe and share them with others in written form. Scientists also confirm their own observations with the findings of others; they regularly read and compare findings as an essential part of their work. When we teach science, we need to involve students, too, in using literacy as they develop scientific understandings. They can also be taught the formats most appropriate for sharing the results of their studies.

There are several areas in which informational texts in science are different from other materials students read. Teachers should instruct students in their use so that they can succeed with the various materials available. First is understanding the external features and aids provided in the texts—the headings, subheadings, graphics, and highlighted terms. Second, students need to learn to read the different forms of visuals and connect them to the narrative content. Third, they need to learn to read and follow directions for experiments. Fourth, they need to become familiar with the various ways in which texts are organized by science authors. This area is especially difficult because such a variety of text structures are employed. For example, as students read and learn about butterflies, they may find books that compare and contrast various butterflies or contrast butterflies and moths. They will also be likely to find books that use the life cycle to structure the content (e.g., the life of a monarch). Some books are written by selecting descriptive categories and exploring them (habitat, stages of life, body parts, enemies, migration). Yet others focus on the relationship of butterflies to their habitat and how they can be protected (e.g., Karner's blue or monarch). If students learn to look for the organizational patterns used by authors, they will be able to organize their own learning better (using categories for chunking ideas and information) and then write in a more organized way. Major organizational structures used in science include:

➢ Life cycle (biology)

➢ Steps in a process (chemistry)

➢ Problem/solution (biology; astronomy)

➢ Compare/contrast (classification)

➢ Description (biomes—Earth science; astronomy)

Helping students to become familiar with these ways of organizing information and presenting it in engaging ways is well worth instructional time. Teachers can draw attention to writing structures by previewing two books on the same topic that are organized differently. Sharing the table of contents of the two books and asking students what they reveal about how the books are written opens students to thinking about organization. After a few experiences, by looking at the cover of a book, students can be asked to predict, what its table of contents will likely contain. Children enjoy guessing how an author will organize a book once they have their attention drawn to this important feature of books.

BASIC FEATURES OF INFORMATIONAL BOOKS AND ARTICLES

The reading skills needed for reading informational texts can generally be applied to trade books, magazine articles, and textbooks. It is critical that students gain familiarity with the kinds of reading and viewing skills commonly needed for reading science texts through teacher explanation and lots of guided practice. They can then navigate the variety of interesting magazines and trade books now available, as well as make sense of the textbooks that most students find quite challenging. Teachers must help students to identify the special features of informational texts, to preview texts to identify special features and ways of presenting information, and to note the differences among texts they can select.

Using the Table of Contents

Luckily, many good materials are now available for teachers to use in helping children note the key features of informational books. Among them are the "Big Books" in science that are available through some trade publishers. By putting a Big Book on an easel, the teacher can show students the various features and model previewing a book by using the title, the table of contents, the index, and other features. If students are asked to read informational books, they can include an overview of the structure of the book as they describe it to others in their oral reports. A team of primary teachers in Glenview, Illinois, asks students to write monthly informational book reports using a format that can be folded into a little book. The second page of the report form asks students to check off the features that each book contains. In this way the students are reinforced in looking for these elements. If elements are lacking, as is the case in many of the older science books for children, students can use sticky notes and add them. For example, some books still don't have tables of contents and indexes. Students enjoy adding these features to books in their classroom collections.

As students are engaged in an inquiry, the teacher can collect several books related to the study. As questions emerge, they can be written on poster paper or a transparency so they can be retained and answered over time. Kelly Lane, a third-grade teacher, collects important student questions and puts them on tagboard strips on her bulletin board ("What we want to find out"). She then distributes a book on the topic to each student and asks everyone to turn to the table of contents (ToC) in his or her book. She next takes one of the question strips and reads it aloud. She asks students to use their tables of contents and guess in which chapter the answer might be found. Some books clearly don't seem to contain sections on all questions, but the activity leads to an understanding of the value of using the ToC as an initial organizing tool when engaging in research. (When students are familiar with the ToC, she adds lessons on the index and repeats this kind of activity, asking students to use books of their own choice.)

Students can also become sensitive to book parts by writing their own chapter books. Second graders taught by the same team that has students write book reports on informational books, regularly create class books on various topics they study during the year. Their book on animals included contributions from all class members related to their areas of study. The table of contents they developed is shown in Figure 5.1.

Table of Contents

Chapter Title	Pages
History of local animals	1
Animal classification	9
Life cycles	21
Habitats	29
food chain	36
Adaptation	47
getting rid of animals	58
Interrelationships	60

FIGURE 5.1. Student-generated table of contents.

As children progress through the grades, their science study includes using printed resources as part of their work. The books they write become increasingly individual, and with the use of a computer they can contain a wide array of visual and graphic information. The students of a fourth-grade class, as part of their study of plants, divided into teams, each creating a book about its investigation. The group that studied root systems took digital photographs of some root systems and produced a book with chapters on different forms of roots (tap and fibrous), how the plant uses the system for transportation of nutrients, and the importance of roots. These books looked very professional when they were completed and now are part of the classroom library.

By reading, reviewing, editing, and creating books, students discover how to use the table of contents as a major organizing tool in learning. At all levels, teachers need to help students use this resource. In the upper grades it can be helpful to make a transparency or other visual form of a table of contents before students begin reading the material. This is especially valuable when a new textbook is introduced. Looking over the ToC and "thinking aloud" about the organization and content can help students think more deeply about what is going to be included and how it is organized, link the ideas to their own knowledge, and build interest in the topic.

Headings and Subheadings

Informational materials generally provide visual support to readers so they can understand how the material is organized. Skill in using the table of contents can be used to help students look for the titles, headings, and subheadings in book chapters or within textbooks. Again, to focus students' attention on these important features of informational texts, using a Big Book and demonstrating the headings of the text can be most useful. "Think aloud" with students about the headings and what they might mean; predict content based on the headings and subheads. Ask questions and engage students in thinking about the possible content.

As a second step, using a shorter text, perhaps a magazine article that the class will read, put the title and headings of the article on a transparency or on the board and ask students to think about the potential content—how the author has organized the information, what they may expect to learn, and what questions would be good to ask of the text. Each heading might be turned into questions or stimulate questions. For example, using the headings in an article on tornadoes, students might conjecture about the content in the three sections: "Funnel Facts," "Tornado Tips," and "Tiny Tornado." Simply turning a heading into a question wouldn't be very useful, but elaborating on the questions that might be answered in the sections would be. A class might predict that the section on facts would likely tell what tornadoes are, where they are found, when they occur, how long they last, and how strong or harmful they are. The section "Tornado Tips" might explain how to avoid being caught in a tornado, how to know if there might be a tornado, and so on. In this way the headings help to activate the students' prior knowledge and offer a way to predict and form questions to guide their reading.

Following Steps in an Experiment or Process

Many science programs, like those discussed in other chapters, rely heavily on students' conducting experiments and following directions as they try to understand scientific phenomena. The shorter experiments conducted in the primary grades translate into more complex activities that students must be able to handle at the upper level. We have found that many students have trouble reading and following the steps in simple processes and experiments (Blachowicz & Ogle, 2001, p. 222). Some forget to read through the steps first. They need to create a visual image or draw what the experiment looks like as a preliminary step. They also need to think through the equipment or supplies needed and collect them before starting. If diagrams of any part of the experiment are provided, students need to connect them appropriately with the steps in the process and check to see whether they interpret the visual and printed text correctly. As a class focuses on doing experiments or creating artifacts, it is useful to create a list of steps that should be followed. Having students participate in "metacogntively" reflecting on what works best, they can come up with their own steps, which will be more memorable than any produced otherwise. Such a list may look something like this:

➢ Read through all the steps.

➢ Note any special terms that might be confusing.

➢ Look at diagrams and connect them to specific steps.

➢ Visualize the process before starting. Create drawings that can help you to be successful.

➢ Check to see if you have the necessary materials.

➢ Clarify any steps or parts that aren't clear before you begin.

➢ Begin the process, and reread after each step to be sure you have been accurate.

➢ Keep notes of what you do and what happens.

➢ Make a drawing showing the results.

➢ Write down questions that arise as you are working.

Diagrams

At the heart of many science texts are the diagrams and charts that help explain the content. Students steeped in reading fiction may tend to ignore these aspects of the "text" because they are unaccustomed to encountering them within the books they read. Students need to learn to read these graphic forms of information and to relate them to the narrative portion of the material. Again, Big Books can be very helpful as a starting point, with the teacher modeling how to read the visuals. In the upper grades, making transparencies of some frequently appearing forms of diagrams and charts can serve the same purpose. Initially, students benefit from seeing the variety of ways scientific material can he presented visually, and then focusing on one form at a time. First, show students a variety of good diagrams. Include examples of diagrams showing a side view, then a cutaway, and finally a bird's-eye view. It is helpful if the diagrams are of the same object—for example, a flower, animal, or land form. Point out that the caption is very important in explaining the perspective of the diagram. Then emphasize the labels on the parts that help readers understand the various aspects of the object. Once you have introduced the components of a number of diagrams, ask students to locate diagrams in books and articles. Comparing several diagrams can help students note their features and begin to build a framework for evaluating them.

Later, it is helpful to model creating diagrams of objects under study. Teachers like Judy who guide primary students in creating science journals, can build the creation of diagrams into their modeling for journal entries. Diagramming can become a skill students use individually or in groups. Some students will be much abler to use their artistic and representational skills than others will. This is an opportunity for students to work in teams, drawing on these strengths. It can also lead to students creating their own diagrams as they read and work on their projects.

A good example of students creating diagrams comes from a fifth-grade team in Evanston, Illinois. During their study of insects the classroom teacher and the drama teacher combined efforts. They helped the teams studying different insects to create a "body poem" of each insect. For example, to create a firefly one student curled up on the floor while two others sat at her feet creating the "light" of the firefly. Two others, one on each side, became the wings. After creating their figures the students returned to their desks and diagrammed each insect, using a side view and a bird's-eye view.

Charts and Graphs

In considering how much emphasis to place on charts and graphs, it is a good idea to skim the materials you use with your students and make a list of the different charts and graphs they will likely use during the year. Primary texts have few charts or graphs, but upper elementary texts may have many. Again, beginning by modeling different kinds of charts and graphs draws students' attention to these graphic elements. Many charts involve comparisons of elements, and students need to read the titles and captions carefully to understand what is being represented.

As students learn to read these formats, involving them in creating their own charts and graphs makes them much more meaningful to the students. Primary students can chart heights of classmates, preferences in foods, daily temperatures, and many aspects of life close to them. Creating charts of animals, gerbils' eating and moving, and stages of the life of moths or butterflies make natural and highly interesting experiences for groups of students. As students get older, being familiar with visual ways of representing data opens a range of possibilities for recording and reporting on what they learn. The use of the computer can turn the data into high-quality presentations.

SELECTING BOOKS CAREFULLY

Whenever we study something I learn a lot from reading. It feels like I'm right in the book and I think how interesting the book is.

—SAM, grade 2

Today's trade books offer students appealing, up-to-date opportunities for learning in science. They are plentiful, inexpensive in paperback, and widely available for purchase in bookstores, online, and in educational catalogues. Because they are easily integrated into thematic units, teachers seek effective titles. Nonfiction trade books are far more interesting to students than most science textbooks, which can often prove overwhelming to struggling readers. When books on topics that fit into the curriculum at various reading levels are selected, more students have access to informational text. The photos, colorful illustrations, and graphics help with comprehension of abstract ideas and difficult concepts. Trade books are more likely to celebrate diversity and gender equity in their illustrations and graphics than textbooks. They support inquiry, offer opportunities to compare texts and facts, and promote thinking skills when used appropriately. Because of the current popularity of using nonfiction trade books to teach science, even the publishers of elementary science texts have included trade books among the supplemental products that accompany their series.

The following discussion addresses the selection of suitable nonfiction books to teach science concepts and how they can facilitate reading and writing, as well as learning, about science.

When teachers first began to integrate curriculum, they tended to collect any books, nonfiction or fiction, with the subject in their titles. If the texts were not accurate and up-to-date, their use may have contributed to students' acquisition of numerous misconceptions. Concern about the accuracy of content in nonfiction trade books was raised early on when the wide use of trade books instead of science textbooks began. Research on misconceptions indicated that all of the following were responsible for the erroneous ideas acquired by students: children's literature, storytelling, popular children's films, and teachers. Research in science education suggests that such misconceptions are difficult to change or correct (Anderson, 1987; Roth et al., 1987). Misconceptions are unintended but, unfortunately, they are also often undetected in the classroom. Conscientious teachers know that this can happen no matter what the teaching mode: trade books, textbooks, hands-on science, websites, guest speakers. The teacher must constantly be aware of students' learning and monitor for misinformation. Students usually view the content of any book as truth, despite its containing inaccurate information. Therefore, we must choose books carefully to avoid unintended learning outcomes.

Not only are nonfiction science books filled with interesting facts and illustrations, but many valuable informational books of today are written in forms designed to entice students. Books such as the Caldecott Award-winning *Snowflake Bentley*, written by Jacqueline Briggs Martin and exquisitely illustrated by Mary Azarian, is an example of the many successful books written in narrative form. Jane Yolen's *Welcome to the Greenhouse* is a book chockfull of richness in words and illustrations to make the rainforest come alive through poetic prose. Some books are published as cartoon books. A series of four books called *A Cartoon History of the Earth*, by Jacqui Bailey and Matthew Lilly can appeal to readers who need extra motivation. And what child has not been turned on by the Magic School Bus books written by Joanna Cole, and illustrated by Bruce Degen? Dorling Kindersley has put out a series of DK Readers filled with facts to build general knowledge. *Superman's Guide to the Universe* by Jackie Gaff is a level 4 (for Proficient Readers) and includes the Man of Steel taking young readers on a tour of the universe. Sidebars display science fiction related to Superman, along with real facts, in such a way that it is easy to tell the difference between the two on the page.

Criteria for Selecting Books

The National Science Teachers Association (NSTA) and the Children's Book Council (CBC) have worked cooperatively over the years to select a list of books, Outstanding Science Trade Books, published every March in *Science and Children*. Members of a book review panel appointed by NSTA assemble the list by looking at both content and presentation. Here are the criteria they implement in the selection process:

➢ The book has substantial science content.

➢ Information is clear, accurate, and up-to-date.

➢ Theories and facts are clearly distinguished.

➢ Facts are not oversimplified to the point where the information is misleading.

➢ Generalizations are supported by facts, and significant facts are not omitted.

➢ Books are free of gender, ethnic, and socioeconomic bias.

In selecting nonfiction a critical factor to consider is when the books were published, to make certain that the facts are up-to-date and accurate. It is important to select books with current copyright dates, because many can be obsolete in only a few years. Today new information is being churned out in all scientific areas at a record rate. Certain topics, such as astronomy and dinosaurs, two favorites of students, are especially vulnerable. For these and other subjects it is good to cull classroom books from time to time and to encourage the school resource center director to do the same.

The Importance of Accuracy

As mentioned earlier, in selecting nonfiction, one must consider whether the facts are up-to-date and accurate. The standard of accuracy must also include photos and illustrations. A few years ago, when Judy's second graders were studying butterflies and moths, they discovered an inaccurate photo in their reading textbook. The photo showed a Cecropia moth cocoon. There was no reference in the text or in the caption to moths, a different kind of lepidopteran from butterflies. In fact, the class had collected a Cecropia moth cocoon and was waiting for the moth to emerge in the spring, something Judy did yearly with her classes. The students quickly pointed to the mistake, and all agreed, after reading and rereading the book, that the picture should not have been used. Together the class composed the following letter, which they sent to the editor of the textbook:

> Dear Editor,
> There is a mistake in "The Caterpillar's Surprise" in your book. You have some things mixed up. The book said that a butterfly comes out of a cocoon but we think it really comes out of a chrysalis. You put a picture of a cocoon in the book when the story was all about butterflies.
> We would like to know if maybe there are butterflies that come out of cocoons on other continents like Africa or South America. We don't know of any that come out of cocoons in the U.S.A.
> This is from the second graders in Mrs. McKee's classroom at [name of school] in [city and state].
> Sincerely,
> [all students signed the letter]
> P.S. Please write back.

A month later they received a letter from the then-current editor of the series, thanking them for the information. She stated that the students were correct in their comment that butterfly caterpillars do not spin cocoons but instead come out of a structure called a chrysalis. She said that she was not knowledgeable enough on the subject herself and referred the students to an expert in the field who had been extremely helpful to her in answering their question. She ended her letter by saying that it is "because of discriminating young readers like [you] that we are able to produce better reading textbooks for students."

The students were ecstatic. Copies of both letters were sent home to parents, along with copies of the original piece from the book. The children decided it would be fun to read the story to their parents, asking them to decide what information in the piece was incorrect. Then they could proudly show their parents the mistake in the text to let it be known that they had learned to be "critical" readers. Notes from the parents indicated how impressed they were with the discovery, the follow-up correspondence, and the thinking and learning involved in this discovery.

Text Organization and Layout

There are further considerations in selecting nonfiction trade books for the classroom: Is the text laid out in an easy-to-read form? Will it match the ability level and learning style of the students who will use the book? (Fortunately, many books are leveled, although we veteran teachers know that because there are a variety of ability levels in any given classroom, the levels should be used only as a general guideline.) Is the text large enough and easy enough for a struggling reader? Is there too much busyness on the page for some students to cope with? It often happens that some books will work for one type of student but not for others.

The use of graphic information is also critical in selecting books. Some books designed for the youngest readers have confusing visual information. For example, a beginning book on growing and using rice included a two-page spread showing a large machine harvesting rice. An insert photo at the bottom center of the picture showed birds eating what was left in the fields. As we looked at the pictures with children, some worried that the machine was going to run over the birds. They didn't understand that the small photo, with a dark frame around the edges, was an insert.

Inserted pictures layered on larger ones create problems when children don't know how to interpret them. Another example of this problem came to our attention when children were reading a book about different plants. Each page had a large picture of a plant and an insert showing the bulb or root system. However, on one page the bulb was the large picture and the plant was shown in the insert. Relating the large pictures to the inserts was challenging for the first graders who were attempting this. The shifting relationship between the two pictures was needlessly confusing. Although pictures are very good supports to help children develop scientific understandings, we need to analyze them carefully before giving them to children to use. If they contain important content, then it is necessary to teach students how to read the pictures and connect the different presentations.

Science concepts are shown visually in many books. Demonstrating steps or changes is often done with photographs. A text that teachers were using in their unit on where foods come from explained the making of breakfast products. A series of illustrations on where orange juice comes from had pictures going horizontally across two pages, as well as from top to bottom on the page. The students were naturally confused, because they had learned to read one page at a time, not read across pages. Being aware of the visual layout of pictures and shifts from the expectations we develop is important, too. Again, doing a "picture walk" before handing books over to children will help them use the books effectively.

At the intermediate level many interesting science trade books are full, and sometimes too full, of engaging pictures and photographs. The Magic School Bus series written by Joanna Cole and illustrated by Bruce Degen deserves special notice. These books offer great ways to teach many complex science concepts and phenomena. However, teachers need to show students the three levels of text: the story line in the running text, the dialogue among the class members carried by the cartoon text bubbles, and the elaboration on scientific information in the marginal notebook pages and displays.

Another area in which teachers can help students with visual and graphic information is to help them locate and use the captions that often accompany the displays. Many students overlook captions unless directed by their teachers to consider the information contained within them. Moreover, some captions are hard to identify as such. Therefore, in considering trade books it is also important to look for the way visuals are labeled and the clarity and informative nature of the captions.

Positive Images

When selecting books, be sure they communicate positive images of science and scientists. Avoid those with titles that refer to anything having to do with science as "weird" or "icky"; for instance, the title of *The Icky Bug Alphabet Book* presents insects in a less than positive way. Many parents and teachers communicate negativity about science because of their own experiences or because they view science as messy and some of the experiments disgusting. Unfortunately, girls often pick up existing cultural cues and decide to avoid getting involved with science experiments or the natural world because science is more for guys than girls. Books that show girls and women engaged in science are important to include in your classroom collection. For example, Sophie Webb (2000), a biologist, has written an engaging account in *My Season with Penguins: An Antarctic Journal*. This book provides a very positive example of a scientist in action and models how scientists keep journals to record their observations and their thinking while in the field. In addition, negative stereotypes about "mad scientists" abound. Make sure that none of these stereotypes are reinforced in the classroom literature you select for your students to enjoy.

There are books, such as the Extreme Readers series, that feature high-interest topics using dramatic photography and illustrations to captivate students. *Predator Attack!* by Katharine Kenah presents animals from all over the world in a thrilling manner, complete with facts and maps. This title may be a bit strong, but it need not be called "negative," because on each page several short, clear sentences about hunting and capturing prey will spark interest in reading more. Although it describes adaptations for the successful capture of prey, such as teeth, claws, paws, and jaws, it is ultimately appealing, as it gives students a sense of mastery through acquiring a realistic understanding of the life of predators in the natural world that they may have considered frightening before.

ORGANIZING THE CLASSROOM SCIENCE LIBRARY

A classroom library should be brimming with informational books and magazines. Nonfiction resources can be organized for easy access as references or for choosing during periods of independent reading. Although there are many genres other than science to consider in organizing a classroom library, the different types of nonfiction reading discussed here pertain to science teaching and learning.

An easy way to organize science-related materials is to put them in labeled tubs that relate to a specific area of study. Tubs of books are then always available in the science center. Some are arranged by topic and include books written by the children. Others contain series books that are related in other ways. For example, tubs may contain a series of nonfiction resources, including Dorling Kindersley's Eyewitness Books, titles published by Usborne, Scholastic's First Discovery Books, Joanna Cole's Magic School Bus books, and magazines like *Ranger Rick*. Other tubs could include:

➢ Separate tubs for each of the following animal families:
  ➢ Fish
  ➢ Amphibians
  ➢ Insects
  ➢ Mammals
  ➢ Reptiles
  ➢ Invertebrates
➢ Tubs for special-interest areas:
  ➢ Astronomy
  ➢ Dinosaurs
  ➢ Science experiments
  ➢ Other topics, as they come up during the year

During specific science units, additional tubs are used for particular units, such as:
  ➢ Bats
  ➢ Butterflies and moths
  ➢ Light and color
  ➢ Life cycles

➤ Air and water
➤ Sound
➤ Arctic plants and animals
➤ Australian plants and animals
➤ Rainforests

Color-code the books so that guided reading levels are represented in each tub. Scholastic lexile units for determining reading levels for books are available, and many of the series identify books by levels, especially at the beginning for primary levels. (See the Rigby and Newbridge leveling.) Some publishers also have their books available in Spanish so English language learners can participate fully in the classroom explorations of science. These leveled science books can then be used for guided reading instruction, with the teacher developing students' reading abilities while they enjoy the science content. Many of the skills needed for reading informational texts can be taught and practiced in this reading time. In addition, with books coded by difficulty, students can select their own books for independent reading and reinforce their reading skills and especially, their vocabulary acquisition.

Teachers who lack books for their classrooms might consider the following ideas:

1. Scholastic and Trumpet book clubs offer bonus books.

2. Book companies have sales of remaindered books, some of which may be appropriate for your class.

3. Inexpensive books are often on the sales counters in bookstores. For example, we found the Handy Science Answer Books on sale at our local bookstore, and for a small amount of money, we bought three of the books—one on science, one on insects, and one on space.

4. Ask families to contribute books as part of their children's birthdays and special events. The gifts can then be recognized on bookmarks inserted at the front of the books, and the children can continue to note those contributions as the books are used year by year.

Jim Tingey's method for organizing the books in his classroom makes it easy for students to use them and check them out. Each book is color-coded according to genre and placed on bookshelves with the Library Service Center nearby. The Service Center is a file box used to keep track of books that are checked out. A library book pocket and index card are placed in each book. When students check out books, they put their names on the cards and put them in the Library Service Center file box. When a book is returned, the student finds the correct card and puts a dot after his or her name to indicate if the book was read cover to cover. From time to time during class time Jim encourages the students to report on their at-home reading, critiquing the books read and telling whether they would recommend them to others. Jim reports that he seldom has problems with his book checkout system because of the strong attitude of responsibility he develops with his students through frequent class meetings to resolve problems of all kinds, including issues that surface regarding the checkout and return system.

TEACHER AND KIDS' READ-ALOUD TIME

It is important that teachers read aloud from nonfiction materials daily so that students can enjoy the ways in which authors express understandings about the world around us. Reading from informational books, magazines, web-downloaded articles, and articles from newspapers demonstrates to students that science is all around us in the literate world. When you decide on a piece to read orally, be sure to rehearse before reading it to the children. The intonation and fluency with which material is read contributes a great deal to the pleasure of hearing someone read orally. It is also valuable to encourage and support students in reading orally from special science materials they find. They, too, need to practice the texts they are going to read before reading them while other students listen. In any case, whether the teacher or a student is reading, the children should be guided to listen for:

➢ New information

➢ Information that confirms what they are learning

➢ Information that contrasts with that from another source

➢ New vocabulary

➢ Interesting ways in which experiences and ideas are expressed

➢ Special interesting facts or details

➢ How scientists have uncovered new information or engaged in exploration—the personal stories of doing science

BEGINNING OF BASIC RESEARCH

How to begin a unit is discussed in Chapter 3. Here we discuss fact-finding and the use of nonfiction books. Before beginning a unit, collect as many well-chosen books as possible from the school library or public library. Then introduce a selection of the most intriguing books to the students, talking about their attributes and generating interest in the selections. Spread them out on a counter, on a shelf, or below the chalkboard so the "researchers" can easily see the ones that appeal to them.

Although the following strategies are well used in the first and second grades, we have found, when working with teachers in higher grades, that they are quite interested in trying them with their students. In many schools the required skills are not taught earlier, so when the time comes in the intermediate grades for nonfiction reading, writing, and research, students flounder. They need to go back to the beginning and build from there.

Amazing Fact Sheets

First, the vast amount of interesting information students encounter as they read independently for information must be dealt with, so assisting students in recording these facts on "Amazing Fact Sheets" begins their process of making notes (see Figure 5.2). Students learn how to write down the fascinating information they uncover in books in their own words and use these sheets in a variety of ways.

Judy kept a box of the fact sheets on top of a bookcase so that students could take one anytime they found a fact they wanted to record and share later. The fact

An amazing fact about _____

is _____

_____

found by _____

in the book _____   by _____

An intriguing fact about _____

is _____

_____

found by _____

in the book _____   by _____

A fascinating fact about _____

is _____

_____

found by _____

in the book _____   by _____

FIGURE 5.2. Amazing Fact Sheet.

was written in the student's own words along with his or her own name, but as students became more proficient, the title and the author of the book in which the fact was found were included. During "sharing time," Judy gave students time to read their special facts. Thus, by the end of second grade these children were already making research "note cards"—something traditionally reserved for much older students. They were also learning to cite references and to share the excitement of knowledge with each other.

Here are some tips to make fact-finding work for all students:

➤ Read some factual information aloud from a book to the whole group. Let several students select some facts and practice telling the information in their own words. This is one of the most difficult components of fact-finding. Be sure to give students much practice with selecting and summarizing ideas.

➤ Model how to fill out a fact sheet on an overhead projector or chalkboard.

➤ When they are first searching for facts, let students work with partners.

➤ Allow young students or struggling readers to read and use the captions under the pictures.

Whenever we look at coffee table books, those beautiful large volumes containing outstanding photos for our perusal, do we read the text? Rarely do we take the time to do so. Most of us inspect the pictures and read the captions. It is amazing how much we can learn just from this legitimate way of gathering information. We can encourage readers to do that to glean information from a book. Then, if they want to learn more, they can go back into the text.

Here are things to do with the fact sheets:

➤ Students always enjoy seeing their work displayed, so teachers often use the Amazing Fact Sheets on bulletin boards along with posters and pictures of the subjects at hand.

➤ Teachers of younger students can reach into a container, pull out a fact sheet, and ask the student who wrote it to read it to the class.

➤ Group the fact sheets together, along with illustrations, to make informational books for the class to read.

Using the Facts in Paragraphs

Sorting skills should be taught in kindergarten and first grade. Students practice sorting things according to their attributes, buttons and assorted objects first. Sorting words into groups such as animals, plants, number words, and so forth, is next. These background experiences help when students must organize their research in later grades, starting with organizing for paragraphs.

Before asking students to write their own paragraphs, some teachers spend time reading paragraphs to their students that have an obvious topic sentence and asking them to tell the class what the paragraph was about. Then a discussion defining what a "topic sentence" is can take place. Students will need to practice reading paragraphs and underlining topic sentences. At first these sentences are simple, but they can offer information concerning a subject being studied at the time.

Students need to group facts from their fact-finding assignments into categories that make sense. When doing this for the first time, the teacher will have to work with the group to come up with categories to be used. While discussing what the students already know, the teacher can use an overhead projector, chart paper, pocket charts, or computer program to generate categories with the students. Examples of categories for a study of whales include habitat, physical characteristics, life cycles, endangered status, and location in the wild. From these groupings the students may chose one subject to cover in a summary paragraph containing a main idea, with specific pieces of information to provide elaboration. Later they can write whole reports in this manner.

Judy Sawdey, a veteran teacher who has taught second through fourth grades, has made helping students learn to write one of her major goals through the years. Among other pursuits, she has successfully refined the process of turning research into paragraphs. Here are the steps she takes to help her students:

➤ First, she models sorting information by using a topic that the students all know something about. The students brainstorm many facts about that subject on chart paper. *Example*: Cats.

➤ She then writes the facts the students have generated on cards. Using a pocket chart, she places the facts in the pockets in random order.

➤ The students are asked to begin to think of ways the facts fit together. *Example*: What they look like; what they eat; and so on.

➤ These facts are written on sentence strips and placed in the pockets on the chart. Then students place the facts beneath the related strip. They will always find that some facts fit in more than one place. It is then a matter of judgment as to where that fact should be placed.

➤ She introduces the concept of *topic sentence* for them and asks them to think of topic sentences for facts that have been researched, displayed, and sorted in the pocket charts.

➤ The class members then compose a paragraph together from the organized information, using the topic sentence they have created.

Judy is cautious about writing paragraphs in a formulaic way. She doesn't want to squelch creativity but gives guidelines to help students get started.

Reporting in a Variety of Ways

When it is time for students to write their own reports, they will be prepared to think of how to structure their information. Do they want to write a description of an animal by simply addressing different attributes (categories in description), or do they want to deal with a problem the animal has in competing with human encroachment on its territory (problem–solution)?

Because there are many different structures used by authors of elementary science materials, students can explore a wide variety of interesting formats. Some teachers have students write new content using a predictable pattern from a favorite book. For example, the framework used by M. W. Brown (1947) in her *Important Book* has each page begin with "The important thing about . . . is that it has/is . . . But, the most important thing about . . . Is. . . . " This structure is repeated as each new item is described. Carol Skalindar, a third-grade teacher, used this framework as students wrote about insects they were studying. The results included the following:

➢ The important thing about a bee is that it stings. It is true a bee has two pair of wings and collects honey, but the important thing about a bee is that it stings!

➢ The important thing about a ladybug is that it has sticky pads on its feet. It is true that it does not bite, it has a round shell and it spits out yellow spit, but the most important thing about a ladybug is that it has sticky pads on its feet (see Figure 5.3)

These books help students attend to simple structures, which then serve as bridges to the more abstract organizational frameworks writers use. With some teacher guidance, students can have great fun writing group books, building from the structure of a favorite children's book to create their own informational texts.

Class Big Book

Amazing Fact Sheets can be used to make a "Big Book." After the students have sorted their own individual facts into appropriate categories, the teacher has them lay their facts on large sheets of construction paper labeled with the categories. Then a cooperative group of students is assigned to each of the categories. They are asked to create a page, or pages, of information for a class Big Book. They may enhance the pages with illustrations or cut-

FIGURE 5.3. Student page for *The Important Book about Insects*.

outs from magazines. During the process, information sorting is further refined. Gaps in facts are sleuthed out with more research. For instance, a team of students preparing a page on the location of whales in the wild might have to find information on where orcas (killer whales) are found. Then they must decide how best to convey that information along with the research on where other whales live. The students in one group decided that they needed to create symbols of specific whales and place them on a world map.

Class Question-and-Answer Book

Another way to use the facts is in a class question-and-answer book. Each student is responsible for one page. One side has a question, the other side often has the illustrated answer. For example, the following pages were found in the question-and-answer book on arctic animals.

> Side 1: What arctic animal can take the cold better than any other animal?
> Side 2: Arctic foxes don't really get cold until the temperature is minus 70 degrees below zero (F). That's when they start to shiver.
> From: *Arctic Babies* by Kathy Darling
> Side 1: Were there always polar bears in the far north?
> Side 2: Scientists think polar bears evolved from the brown bear where Siberia and Alaska met 25 to 100 thousand years ago. It took a long time for them to become adapted so well to their life in the ice and snow of the frozen north.
> From: *Great Ice Bear* by Dorothy Hinshaw Patent (p. 11)

ABC Books

Many teachers have used the popular alphabet book format to involve students in synthesizing what they are learning. First, teachers present alphabet books written by several authors to compare styles. Jerry Pallotta (1986) has made this structure very popular with his wide range of science topics. Adults and children alike enjoy *The Butterfly Alphabet* by Sandved (1996), with its photographs of letters of the alphabet found in butterfly wings and poetry for each page that captures the wonder of these creatures. The book begins, "On wings aloft across the skies—an alphabet of butterflies."

Soon the students are ready to make their own book. Each student can be assigned a letter. *X*, *Y*, and *Z* always are problematic, so it's good to refer to the published ABC books to see how their authors resolved the issue.

Hands-On Additions to Reports

The students in Judy's class are always enthusiastic about Report Day. That's when the third graders present oral reports based on their completed written reports. In presenting one of the facts, the students are to include some sort of hands-on way to help students know more than they would by merely hearing the fact. For instance, in reporting about koalas in Australia, one student brought in a 23-foot rope to show the class the length of a koala intestine. Koalas need long intestines to digest the tough eucalyptus leaves they eat. Another student had the class do a scale drawing of a 50-foot whale shark on the playground asphalt. Each classmate was responsible for a square of the grid the student had created so that the whale could be reproduced. Another member of the class handed out 10-foot pieces of string and had the other students put them on the playground in a straight line to show how long an adult blue whale is (100 feet). To show what a million was for a report on star clusters, a student brought in two reams of paper (1,000 pieces), each page having 1,000 dots, to equal one million.

Instruction Book for Science Experiments

Students can try some easy experiments selected from a book on science experiments. Then they can write about and illustrate the experiments on single sheets of paper. These can be gathered and duplicated to make a class book for everyone to take home and use there.

Nonfiction Book Reviews

> Reading is good for your brain. You should look for good passages and good words the author chooses. You should think what you are learning. You should also think how you would recommend the book to others.
>
> —LOURDES, grade 3

A collection of nonfiction book reviews can be developed. Students can tell what they liked or did not like about a book and some of the interesting facts they learned. There should be room for illustrations on each page.

Children enjoy deciding whether or not to recommend a book.

Using the Facts in Story Problems

Have the students use their facts to write story problems for other students to solve. For instance:

➤ A full-grown male polar bear usually weighs about 1,000 pounds. Females usually weigh about 700 pounds. How much more does the male weigh than the female?

➤ Do you think all of the 22 kids in class weigh as much as two silverback mountain gorillas? Hint: A mountain gorilla weighs 600 pounds.

With the gorilla problem the students need to figure out a way to answer it. In one class, the students decided they needed to weigh each child and then combine all the weights, using calculators, to see if the total weight was as much as that of two adult male gorillas. In this case, the teacher opted out of being included in the combined class poundage. Without her, the class weighed about 1,200 pounds, or as much as the two gorillas.

Story problems can be written by the students, put on story problem worksheets, and distributed for the class to solve.

CREATIVE WRITING

Students often use their facts when writing pieces of fiction, just as real authors do. In fact, it is a worthy endeavor to encourage students to find and make note of (even if only a mental note) factual information within pieces of fiction as they read. A creative writing assignment written to include facts learned during a unit will have greater complexity and richness.

The Goose
by David, age 7

I am a goose.
When I'm migrating south, I'm flying high, high up,
winging over land and sea.
When I'm leading sometimes I'm frightened.
Some of the members of the flock
might get injured and fall into foaming waters.
When we land to rest and eat,
our enemy, man, with his fearsome
loud stick might lift it and hurt us.
We might not fly fast enough
to flee from ice covering our food.
We travel day and night in our formation
exhausted and determined.
Once we are in our pleasant winter feeding
grounds and our trip is done, we can
can be grateful to rest in peace.

David had learned much from his research on the migration of geese. But his writing also indicates that he has been exposed to passages of well-chosen words. In his classroom, his teacher takes the time to read aloud, asking the students to listen for examples of "words that help us make pictures in our minds about what is happening." He has students select well-written passages and illustrate them in their own way. He also spends time during writer's workshop in class to help students form vivid passages, both individually and with the group. There are lessons on adjectives, with synonyms listed, along with examples of their use in sentences. Words to express feelings are also color-coded on another chart. Therefore, the results of student writing projects in this classroom often demonstrate the willingness of students to explore writing with strong descriptions and feelings. Furthermore, students feel comfortable in taking risks by using words in new and different ways. When students read their pieces to the class during Author's Chair time in the class, other students compliment them on, among other things, word choices, passages that "helped us know what was happening," passages that "helped us identify the feelings of the characters," and the facts they put in their writing to make it more interesting.

A second-grade class was studying the migration of monarch butterflies. Their teacher read aloud about this amazing phenomenon, and students read from multiple copies of nonfiction trade books. They were given maps of the various migratory routes of monarchs. They also observed monarchs in the school garden and looked at monarch butterfly wings under a microscope. All was in place for the culminating written piece of fiction assigned to the class. A checklist was given to the students with the necessary components for their story. One of the items on the list was, "My monarch came across at least one challenge at each stop or city." The way this was worded seemed to indicate to some of the young writers that the butterflies would be making stops in cities along the way. However, monarchs actually stop to "nectar" in the same large open areas each year to fill up and gain weight for their strenuous journey. After waiting for thousands and thousands of butterflies to come every fall, local residents marvel at this event. The stop cannot be done in a city, especially because the monarchs fly in large groups.

The adventure stories that were written by the second graders were well done. They had a sense of story and included problems that the butterflies had to solve as they made their way to their overwintering grounds in the forested mountains of central Mexico. But many of the stories involved stops in major cities on the way, rather than in the fields, meadows, and open areas that the butterflies usually use. Thus, the writers of these stories will have reinforced misinformation and will miss one of the important reasons for preserving natural habitat for these magnificent creatures. Their teacher can clear up the misunderstanding with discussions and maps, showing where the butterflies congregate each year, so all is not lost.

Following is a well-written example that includes many facts the class had learned.

The Travels of Monarch Flutter
by Emma

Monarch Flutter filled up on flower nectar in Canada. Then she flew with her friends over Lake Huron and stopped to eat in a beautiful park. 1000 other butterflies were flying with her. She fluttered by lots of people who were there to watch her. A boy tried to catch her but she flapped her wings as hard as she could to get away.

She flew over Indianapolis. A bat tried to catch her but the bat was too slow and she got away. When she was flying over Arkansas a tornado was there. The edge of it blew her and another time some of the butterflies got hit by cars on the highways.

Monarch Flutter flew on the wind all the way to Texas. She stopped to eat more nectar in a beautiful field of flowers. A farmer and his wife were there to say hello. A hungry shrew tried to eat her when she was sleeping. The shrew was too noisy so Monarch Flutter woke up and flew away. Some other butterflies did not get away.

Then she flew on to her winter home in Mexico. But 75 of her friends were lost or killed in the trip. She snuggled up with many of her friends from Canada and they had a nice winter together.

When generating inventive ways to use facts, don't forget that rhymes, poems, raps (see page 54 in Chapter 3), and plays can provide opportunities for the infusion of information. You can use the beautiful books of poetry by Paul Fleischman, *I Am Phoenix: Poems for Two Voices* (1985).

Cereal Boxes and Candy Bar Wrappers

Sam, in Susan Dennison's fourth grade, used the facts he had gathered about Saturn during the class Astronomy Unit to create a cereal box of Frosted Saturns made by the Solar Cereals Co. The pieces of cereal pictured on the box had a Saturn-like shape. An alien is shown on the outside of the box, bragging that the cereal inside has "a taste that's out of this world!" There is a sign on the box inviting the reader to "find all five facts about Saturn on this box!" One had to look carefully, but there they were!

1. Saturn is nearly 10 times farther than Earth from the Sun.
2. It is the sixth planet from the Sun.
3. It has seven major rings.
4. It was formed billions of years ago.
5. It has very little gravity.

Sam mixed other pertinent facts into his list of "Nutrition Facts" on the side of the cereal box, including temperature, −300 degrees F; size, 74,900 miles in diameter; distance from the sun, 889 million miles; and moons, 33. A Tip Top Recipe using Frosted Saturns with another cereal made by the Solar Cereals Co. was featured on another side of the box:

> *Frost Mix*
> 1 cup of Solar Cereal's Frosted Saturns
> 1 cup of Solar Cereal's Titan Trixies
> ½ cup Karo syrup
> Mix together and put in the freezer for 1 hour.
>   Take out, cut, and enjoy!

It is much easier for students to do such an assignment if the expectations are clearly laid out. Many teachers, like Susan, use product descriptors. The description for the cereal box listed all the things the cereal box had to include: a name, a slogan and picture, nutrition facts, ingredients (or planet composition), a company name, and a logo for that company. Additional ideas were also included, such as box tops, coupons, recipes, and other creative ways to show the information that was gathered during time designated for research. There was a clear expectation that the project would be neat, colorful, detailed, creative, and would use accurate facts.

Other classes have used the same directions, but instead of making cereal boxes, the students created candy bar wrappers.

Cartoons

Some students show a gift for making cartoons. Others need a unique way to stretch their thinking and their repertoires for reporting information they have gathered. Judy remembers Michelle, who was a very bright first and second grader when she taught her for 2 consecutive years. She had unusual interests for a child of her age. Because her father was a physicist at a major university, she overheard conversations other children might not be exposed to. Believing that students should have times when they pursue their own interests, when Michelle asked her if she could study "atoms," Judy agreed to help her, smiling to herself and thinking, "What next with this child?" Judy secured some appropriate books, and off Michelle went, quite motivated on her own to read them.

Later Michelle came to Judy wondering what she should do now that she knew about "atoms." Judy

FIGURE 5.4. Student-created science cartoon.

gave her several suggestions, but one of them was to make a cartoon to show a bit of what she had learned. After laboring over her project for an hour or so, she presented Judy with the cartoon shown in Figure 5.4.

RODENT CLUB: A STUDENT-SELECTED MINI-UNIT

Another example of using students' interest to enhance learning comes from one of Judy's classes. She has learned that reluctant students can often be enticed to participate in productive learning if their interests are recognized. To accommodate one of her struggling readers who just happened to have a passion for rodents, as well as one for science, Judy guided a small group of students to embark on a series of inquiry experiences to learn as much as possible about the class gerbil, Speedy. The group members chose to call themselves the Rodent Club and decided to meet at noon recess time. The struggling reader was selected to be the Rodent Club president. The following are the steps the group took during its meetings, according to one of the students who wrote about the activities after each meeting:

> ➤ First Meeting: We made a KWL [what we already know, what we want to find out, what we have learned] to get us started.
>
> ➤ Second Meeting: We read in partners and talked about facts about rodents with each other. Then we put some of the most important things on our KWL chart.
>
> ➤ Third Meeting: We thought about questions we still had that needed to be answered and on how we could find the answers by conducting experiments. We designed an experiment to answer this: What does Speedy, the classroom gerbil, like to eat? We thought of problems we might have and how we could solve them. We decided what we would need for our experiment and who would be responsible for getting them to school. We made a list.
>
> ➤ Fourth Meeting: We conducted our experiment. Later the Rodent Club President, one of his assistants and I wrote up a report to give to the Rodent Club members.
>
> ➤ Fifth Meeting: We analyzed our data and then we thought of other questions for research.

READING DIRECTIONS

Throughout students' experience in school, learning should be connected to real-world experiences. Discrete information and concepts need to be integrated into meaningful contexts so that application and transfer can occur.

In a beginning unit called Matter: Solids, Liquids, and Gases, students learn a number of isolated concepts. Kitchen chemistry can be used to help develop concepts. Students learn that matter can change into different states. They learn about dissolving when they make salt and sugar solutions. They learn how heat changes matter when sugar melts into a puddle and when water turns into steam, using pans on a hot plate. They learn that when a liquid and a solid mix together, they may form a gas, as when vinegar and baking soda are mixed.

As Judy's own children were growing up, they often made Crazy Cake, a delicious chocolate cake that always drew compliments to the young family cooks. Judy decided that making this cake with students would realize a goal of connecting science to meaningful life experiences. She found the book *The Magic School Bus Gets Baked in a Cake* by Linda Beech (1995), which supports some of the science that happens in the cake recipe and adds many more ways in which science is at work in the kitchen. In addition, the recipe was always sent home and is reported to have become a favorite with the families of many former students, just as it was with Judy's own family. The recipe is given in Figure 5.5.

To read this recipe is intrinsically motivating for students. The activity itself dramatically strengthens concepts taught during the unit and reinforces science vocabulary they will need in the future. Each time they make the cake, a review will take place.

CONCLUSION

Informational texts are very appealing to young students. They introduce children to the world around them and expand their horizons in many ways. However, as this chapter has indicated, informational texts pose many reading demands that are different from those encountered in reading fiction. Students need good instruction in how to read resources with a variety of structures, layouts, and types of materials. Teachers can begin by modeling the reading of articles and informational books and then guiding students' use of instructional-level materials. Recording important facts and sharing the outcomes of information searches enhance the learning of the whole class. Inquiry is most successful when students possess the tools to read and critically reflect on information.

Make this cake with a parent or an older brother or sister. Here's what you need:

8-inch cake pan	cocoa
sifter	baking soda
measuring cups	salt
measuring spoons	cooking oil
fork	vanilla extract
flour	vinegar
sugar	water

1. Sift the following *solids* into the cake pan:
   1½ cups of flour
   1 cup sugar crystals
   3 heaping tablespoons cocoa
   1 teaspoon baking soda
   ½ teaspoon salt crystals
2. Mix or sift the *solids* well and then spread everything out evenly in the cake pan with clean hands. Feel the solids between your fingers.
3. Poke 5 holes about 4 centimeters in diameter in the mixture. Place one in each corner and one right in the middle.
4. Next carefully put the following *liquids* into the holes:
5. Put 6 tablespoons of cooking oil into 3 of the holes in the corner.
   (Put 2 tablespoons in each hole.)
6. In another corner hole put 1 tablespoon of vanilla.
7. In the last hole in the middle put 1 tablespoon of vinegar.
   Watch what happens. Do you see *gas* forming? The vinegar is mixing with the baking soda.
8. Pour 1 cup of water over everything.
9. Mix it well with the fork.
   Watch for more signs of *gases* forming.
   Check to see if the *solids* are dissolving by taking a small amount between your fingers and rubbing them together. Can you feel small pieces of *solids*?
10. Put the cake in the oven and let it bake at 350 degrees Fahrenheit for 30 or 35 minutes. It is done when a toothpick poked in the middle of the cake comes out clean. While the cake is baking, talk about how heat changes things and what the heat is doing to the cake in the oven.
11. Cool the cake. Look at the top to see the holes where the *gases* came out. Frost it if you wish.
12. Eat it, but before you do inspect it carefully. Look for:
    Signs of *gases* that formed during baking
    Signs of the salt and sugar crystals that were once there
    Signs of the *liquids*
13. Leave a small piece of your cake out uncovered for a day or two. Don't let anyone eat it! What happens to the cake?

Note: The gases that form in this cake are carbon dioxide (from the mixture of vinegar with the baking soda) and steam.

FIGURE 5.5. Recipe for Crazy Cake.

CHAPTER 6

THE SCIENCE–FICTION CONNECTION

Teachers have long used fiction as well as nonfiction selections when teaching science units because children, science, and literature naturally go together. In fact, as the print and photo processes continue to make books ever more appealing, they are even more valuable as part of the science curriculum. Science educators and reading experts share their expertise on linking literature with science experiences. Books can be used as a springboard to hands-on, minds-on learning, or they can act as reinforcement of desired science concepts. Science experiences can also enhance a piece of literature, enabling a richer understanding of the text.

In this chapter we present a rationale and criteria for the selection of appropriate fiction. We include background information and science activities as examples of how one can use fiction, nonfiction, and science in classrooms. We start by emphasizing the need for care in choosing the books to use when connecting them to science learning.

SELECTING THE RIGHT PIECE OF FICTION

Although there are thousands of books, there are far fewer options when discriminating choices are made. We must choose only the best of the lot for teaching and supporting science concepts.

D. A. Mayer (1995) has developed a series of 10 questions for evaluating fiction trade books for a science class, but, as you can see, they can be used for nonfiction as well:

1. Is the science concept recognizable?
2. Is the story factual?
3. Is fact discernible from fiction?
4. Does the book contain misrepresentations?
5. Are the illustrations accurate?
6. Are characters portrayed with gender equity?
7. Are animals portrayed naturally?
8. Is the passage of time referenced adequately?
9. Does the story promote a positive attitude toward science and technology?
10. Will children read or listen to this book?

Books written for younger students often anthropomorphize animals, causing them to believe that animals can feel and communicate like humans. Illustrations can also be misleading as a result of inaccurate representations. The fact that a book is fiction can, in itself, complicate matters if the fictional components somehow muddle the science concepts presented. In her research, Mayer (1995) concluded that young students learned erroneous concepts about whales by reading a children's book in which a whale writes letters to a young child containing factual information about the species. Although it was a charming book containing accurate information, students came away thinking that the whale in the book was a person, along with other misconceptions.

In their research, Rice, Dudley, and Williams (2001) found that children may start out with correct concepts, but these can change if material presented in books is inaccurate. These researchers found that students believe that what they read is truth. The findings of these authors do not mean that they think trade books should not be used to teach science, however. In fact, they encourage teachers to use trade books as one strategy to help students to become interested in and to learn science.

It seems obvious to most experienced teachers that misconceptions can occur no matter what they are teaching with; trade books, textbooks, hands-on science. In their daily lives, students spontaneously construct naive theories and misconceptions. The teacher has a huge responsibility to be constantly aware of what students are actually learning and to monitor for misinformation. To undo misconceptions, teachers have to challenge pupils' thinking and give them new experiences and perspectives from which to view the evidence.

We must emphasize that trade books, whether fiction or nonfiction choices, are not substitutes for real hands-on science teaching, although they can certainly lend themselves to science experiences. However, trade books can be a stimulus for students to engage in some hands-on investigations of their own.

ENHANCING SCIENCE WITH MATH CONNECTIONS

The National Standards emphasize process and scientific inquiry through activity-oriented lessons. A basic construct in designing such inquiries is to use "fair tests" (controlled experiments) when students are planning experiments. A useful way to explain this kind of experimenting to students is to suggest that a fair test is like two children running a race. They both want the race to be a fair one. They want to start and finish in the same place, and they need to begin at the same time. There will have to be two paths, and the paths have to be equal. If one is muddy or bumpy and the other one is on asphalt, then it won't be a fair test. Later they can take on a more formal consideration of controlling experimental variables.

Students need to learn how to think, ask questions, design experiments, use instruments to extend their senses and make measurements, collect data, ask more questions, synthesize information, and share information. All of these experiences not only help students to learn science, but will also assist them in becoming knowledgeable about everyday events. In fact, by providing such experiences, teachers will be helping them to become everyday scientists who can think and function in the real world.

FICTION AND SCIENCE ACTIVITIES

Sometimes a simple activity accompanying a book experience can make a significant difference in student understanding. When reading the award-winning book *Working Cotton* by Sherley Anne Williams, a book that respectfully and honestly captures a long, hot, arduous day in the life of a close and loving family of migrant cotton pickers in the 1940s, students can better understand what the people experienced if they are simply allowed to examine a boll of cotton. By feeling the tough, almost thorn-like parts of the boll and weighing it (which is almost impossible using the typical equipment found in an elementary classroom because it is so light) one can better understand how difficult it was for these people, who had to pluck thousands of cotton bolls every day, to have enough, even with the whole family contributing, to afford the most meager subsistence living.

It is impossible to leave the subject of suitable fiction books that lend themselves well to classroom science without mentioning Megan McDonald's *Insects Are My Life*. This delightful book presents girls who are passionate about subjects many would find peculiar. The story's delightful humor and the lively and entomologically correct illustrations add charm and flare. It is just so much fun!

The rest of this chapter is devoted to a careful selection of trade books, both fiction and nonfiction, with accompanying activities designed to help students better understand and extend their knowledge of the science content in the books. These books and activities can be used in related science units or can stand on their own.

Several of the activities include fair tests, others have mathematical components allowing for the use of measuring tools, an important part of science, and others include opportunities for students to design and experiment. In order for teachers to answer questions and help generate new ones, they must be informed themselves. Naturally, classroom teachers often have to learn right along with the students, but it is good to start out with enough knowledge to be comfortable with the material. Therefore, a small amount of background information is included.

AFRICAN ANIMALS

NATIONAL SCIENCE EDUCATION CONTENT STANDARD C (LIFE SCIENCE)

As a result of activities, all students should develop an understanding of:

➢ The characteristics of organisms

➢ Life cycles of organisms

➢ Organisms and environments

Elephants

Fiction

Grindley, Sally, and Butler, John, *Little Elephant Thunderfoot*, Peachtree, Atlanta, GA, 1996.—Poachers alter the life of a baby elephant. Grades K–2.

Nonfiction

Kulling, Monica, *Elephants: Life in the Wild*, Step into Reading, Random House, New York, 2000.—Describes life of elephants in the wild. Grades K–2.

Lewin, Ted, and Lewin, Betsy, *Elephant Quest*, HarperCollins, New York, 2000.—Researchers report on African Savannah ecosystem while studying elephants. Grades 2–6.

Background Information

Because these largest living land mammals have intrigued people all over the world, much important research has been done on elephants in the wild. The African savannah elephant that once roamed the entire African continent in abundant populations is now reduced to living in much smaller groups scattered in smaller areas south of the Sahara Desert. An African adult male (bull elephant) can weigh as much as 14,000–16,000 pounds (6,300–7,300 kilograms) and grow to 13 feet (4 meters) tall at the shoulder.

It was recently discovered through DNA testing that a second species of African elephant exists under cover of the thick African forests. The African forest elephant was formerly thought to be a subspecies of the savannah elephant. It is smaller, standing only 8 feet (nearly 2.5 meters). Its ears are rounded and its tusks are straight and thin with a pinkish tinge, which makes this species prized by poachers. Its long jaw gives its face a long, narrow look.

Asian elephants average 5,000 pounds (2,300 kilograms) and 9–10 feet (3 meters) tall. Their ears are much smaller than those of the African savannah elephant. Females do not have tusks, as female African elephants do, nor do many males.

Elephants have developed the adaptive behavior of flapping their ears to cool themselves because they don't sweat to cool down. The ears of the African savannah elephant are roughly about 42 inches wide by 53 inches long (dimensions taken from the elephant in the lobby of the Field Museum of Natural History in Chicago). They are three times the size of Asian elephants' ears, most likely because they live in hotter places.

Wild elephants have strong family ties. The females and young are quite social. Males are generally solitary but communicate with their family groupings over distances of many miles using low-frequency sounds well below the range of human hearing.

Activities

LIFE-SIZED ELEPHANT EAR

Materials:

> Large pieces of gray or brown construction or butcher paper
> Tape

Question: How big is an African savannah elephant's ear?

Referring to pictures of elephants, create a life-sized African savannah elephant ear 42 inches (1.1 meters) wide by 53 inches (1.4 meters) long by taping together pieces of paper to fit. If possible, laminate the ear and display it. Ask the students to guess what it is. Then ask them to estimate the size. Allow them to measure the ear themselves.

Note: The shape of an African savannah elephant's ear closely resembles the shape of the African continent.

COMPARING HEIGHT AND WEIGHT OF AFRICAN MAMMALS WITH THOSE OF STUDENTS

Question: How much bigger is an African elephant than me?

Have the students research the height and weight of an elephant species and compare these measurements to their own height and weight. "How much more does an elephant weigh than you do?" "How much taller is an elephant than you?" "How many students would it take to weigh as much as an elephant?" "How can you find answers to these problems?" Other animals can be compared in the same way.

ANIMALS OF THE ARCTIC AND FAR NORTH

NATIONAL SCIENCE EDUCATION CONTENT STANDARD A (SCIENCE AS INQUIRY) AND CONTENT STANDARD C (LIFE SCIENCE)

As a result of activities, all students should develop an understanding of:

➢ The characteristics of organisms

➢ Structure and function in living systems

➢ Life cycles of organisms

➢ Organisms and environments

NATIONAL SCIENCE CENTER EDUCATION CONTENT STANDARD B (PHYSICAL SCIENCE)

As a result of activities, all students should develop an understanding of:

➢ Properties and changes of properties in matter

➢ Transfer of energy

Polar Bears

Fiction

Grindley, Sally, *Polar Star*, Peachtree, Atlanta, GA, 1997.—To learn how a polar bear mother protects her offspring until they can live independently, we follow a mother polar bear and her two cubs from their birth to a dangerous encounter with a hungry male bear. Grades K–3.

Nonfiction

Patent, Dorothy Hinshaw, *Great Ice Bear: The Polar Bear and the Eskimo*, Morrow Junior Books, New York, 1999.—Gives information about polar bears that inhabit the arctic regions of Russia, Norway, Canada, the United States, Denmark, and Greenland. Good teacher reference. Grades 3 and up.

Background Information

Polar bears, the most recent bears to appear on earth, are extremely well adapted to life in the frozen north. They are marine mammals, spending much of their life on the ice or swimming in the water in search of the abundant prey there. Adult males are 5 feet (1.5 meters) (to shoulder) with a standing height of 8–11 feet (2.5–3.4 meters). The average male weighs 880–990 pounds (400–450 kilograms); females, 650–770 pounds (295–350 kilograms).

Their short, thick underfur is densely packed. The longer, coarser outer hair is hollow, allowing for trapped air to help insulate the bear's body from cold arctic temperatures. The hollow, transparent hairs also trap the warmth of the sun and carry it to the bear's black skin, where the heat is easily absorbed. Polar bears also have as much as 4½ inches (11.5 centimeters) of blubber for insulation in arctic temperatures that can fall below –50 degrees Fahrenheit (–46 degrees Celsius or colder). Because polar bears have adaptations so well designed for insulation and heat absorption, they experience almost no heat loss.

Not only does their fur help keep the animals warm, it also helps them to maintain buoyancy in the water because of the trapped air within and between the hollow hairs. The blubber is also helpful.

Fresh water freezes at 32 degrees Fahrenheit (0 degrees Celsius) and ocean water has a lower freezing point. Average temperatures are 28 degrees Fahrenheit (2.2 degrees Celsius).

Activity: Black versus White in Transfer of Heat and Light Energy

Materials:

> White and black pieces of construction paper
> Two aluminum cans, same size
> Black and white paint

Question: How does the polar bear's black skin help keep it warm?

To experience how black absorbs heat, lay pieces of white and black paper in the sun. Black paper should absorb the warmth enough to allow a person to feel the difference quickly. Discuss how one can feel the hot sun through dark clothes more easily than through white clothes, which reflect the sun's rays.

Another way to check this out is to paint two cans, one with white paint and the other with black paint. Fill them with equal amounts of water. Place a thermometer in each and put them in the sun. Check the temperatures after an hour.

Note: This is a fair test, so the cans, where they are placed, the thermometers, and the amount and temperature of the water in both cans should all be the same. The only thing that will be different is the color of the cans.

Because blubber is also an insulator for polar bears, see the Blubber Glove experiment in the following section on whales.

Whales

Fiction

George, Jean Craighead, *Water Sky*, HarperCollins, New York, 1987.—A young boy who is eager to learn about his Ologak ancestry learns the importance of whaling to the Eskimo culture. Grades 4 and up.

Nonfiction

Petty, Kate, *I Didn't Know That Whales Can Sing*, Copper Beech Books, Brookfield, CT, 1998.—Amazing facts about cetaceans, including physical characteristics, adaptions to their environments, hunting, migration, and reproduction. Grades 2–6.

Background Information

Paleontologists have learned that the ancestors of whales were once four-legged, furry mammals with hooves and sharp teeth, living on land near rivers and large bodies of water. Slowly, over millions of years, these animals developed adaptations to a sea environment. Now they have blowholes, which are actually nostrils on top of their heads; tiny holes where ears used to be; and flippers instead of front legs. Species of cetaceans (whales, dolphins, and porpoises) that spend time in cold polar waters, or live their whole lives in that environment, have developed the important adaptation of blubber for insulation.

Whaling has been integral to native cultures of the far north for more than 1,000 years because the bowhead whale, the species hunted, had many uses, and no whale parts were wasted. Everyone in the community was involved in the whaling process from beginning to end. The whole community helped to haul in the whale, butcher it, cook it, and distribute it. Elaborate celebrations were held surrounding a successful whale hunt each year.

During the mid-1970s the International Whaling Committee (IWC) decided that Eskimos were harvesting too many bowhead whales, the species of whale featured in *Water Sky*. Although the scientists did not have a good estimate of the bowhead population, which turned out to be larger than they thought, they still called for a complete moratorium on hunting this species. Compromises were reached, and today native whalers can continue their cultural traditions with annual controlled hunts overseen by the Alaska Eskimo Whaling Commission (AEWC).

Bowhead whales grow to 60 feet (18.5 meters), weigh 1 ton (907 kilograms) at birth, and can weigh more than 60 tons (54,431 kilograms) as adults. They spend their entire lives in northern waters, insulated by blubber more than 2 feet (61 centimeters) thick.

Activities

BLUBBER GLOVE

Materials:

> Four quart-sized zip-lock bags
> Strong tape
> Ice
> Can of vegetable shortening

Plastic tub
Thermometers

Question: How does the whale's blubber help keep it warm in cold waters?

To make a blubber glove, use two quart-sized zip-lock bags. Turn one inside out and cover it on all sides with a thick (at least ½ inch) layer of shortening. To do this, it works best if your hand is inside the glove and if you leave the part of the bag near the closure free of the shortening.

Next, cover the "blubber" with the second zip-lock bag. You should then be able to zip the bags shut, closing off the shortening. It is wise to use some strong tape over the zip-lock part to make sure it stays closed off. There will now be an opening for a hand to be placed that will be protected from the greasy shortening. Then make a second glove that contains no blubber.

Fill a plastic tub with cold water and lots of ice. Check the temperature of the ice with a thermometer. If the water has enough ice, the thermometer will read 32 degrees Fahrenheit (0 degrees Celsius). Explain that the freezing temperature of salt water is lower depending on how salty it is.

Ask one student to hold a hand encased in the blubberless glove in the ice water for as long as possible. Discuss how difficult it is for warm-blooded animals like seals, whales, and penguins to survive in cold waters, especially at the poles.

Then ask the student to put the other hand (not the one that was in the cold water) into the "blubber glove" that has a thermometer inside and hold it in the icy water. It will be fairly warm inside the glove, and the student will be able to feel the warmth immediately. Discuss how the "blubber" protects the hand from the cold and is an adaptation that most marine animals living in polar regions have developed.

Check the temperature of the thermometer in the blubber glove with the child's hand inside to see how well the insulation works. *Hint*: Someone should keep a hand inside the blubber glove (with a separate thermometer from the one used in the blubberless glove) when it is not being used in the experiment so that body warmth keeps the inside warm (just as a warm-blooded animal would be warm inside its blubber). Otherwise, it takes too long for a thermometer to warm up to the temperature the hand is giving off inside the blubber glove when it's being immersed. (See Figure 6.1.)

Note: This is a fair test, so the only thing that is different in the two experiences (immersion into ice water with and

FIGURE 6.1. Blubber glove.

without the blubber) will be the absence of blubber in one of the gloves. This is a good activity when studying any of a number of marine animals, such as polar bears, who live in polar regions.

DO WHALES HAVE EARS?

Background Information. Whales have no outside ear flaps as we do, only holes, one on each side of their head, which do not seem to help them hear. Sound is picked up by the lower jawbone and travels to the eardrum, where it is passed to the whale's brain for interpretation. The whale's skull also transmits the sound waves.

Whales communicate with each other by making a variety of sounds. Scientists really aren't sure how they make the sounds, but many suspect that the sounds originate in air sacs near their nasal passages and are sent out through a fatty area of their foreheads, called the melon. Whales pick up the sounds through their jaws, as described earlier. (See Figure 6.2.)

Scientists think that most toothed whales, such as dolphins and porpoises, use echolocation. A sound travels through water until it strikes something and bounces back as an echo. The echo is picked up by the whale, which interprets the sound as coming back from a fish, rock, boat, or other object. Whale researchers continue to study this incredible phenomenon. Humpback whales and bowhead whales are baleen whales, the kind of whales that do not use echolocation.

Sound is a form of energy that is produced when an object vibrates or moves. It travels in waves, called longitudinal waves, through molecules of matter—solids, liquids, and gases—at differing speeds. The faster it travels, the louder it sounds.

Sound is sent out from the whale's forehead

It travels through the whale's jawbone

FIGURE 6.2. Whale communication.

Sound travels fastest in solids, slower in liquids, and even slower in gases. Molecules vibrate faster in warm air and water as compared with cold air and water. Salinity and depth also affect how sound travels in water.

We hear when sound travels through gas (air) molecules. Whales hear through liquid (water) molecules.

Materials:

Old dinner forks for all

Question: How can I hear like a whale?

Ask students to strike an old dinner fork against a table, then place the handle of the fork next to an ear. What is heard? (A ringing, or sound vibrations, should be heard.) Now ask them to predict what will happen if the fork is struck again and the handle is placed between the front teeth and bitten. Then have the students try it. What is heard or felt? (The sound is a much more profound sensation as it travels through bone to the eardrum.) Try it by biting with the molars. (See Figure 6.3.)

Note: A tuning fork can be used, but it doesn't work as well. To use one, strike the fork on the heel of a shoe or on a rubber mallet, then press the handle firmly into the chin, making sure that the vibrations continue. (The vibrations will be felt and heard in the lower jaw.)

ASTRONOMY

NATIONAL SCIENCE EDUCATION CONTENT STANDARD D (EARTH AND SPACE SCIENCE)

As a result of activities, all students should develop an understanding of:

➢ Earth in the solar system

NATIONAL SCIENCE EDUCATION CONTENT STANDARD G (HISTORY AND NATURE OF SCIENCE)

As a result of activities, all students should develop an understanding of:

➢ History of science

by Jenny

FIGURE 6.3. Student illustration of child using a fork to "hear" like a whale.

Fiction

Asch, Frank, *The Sun Is My Favorite Star*, Harcourt, New York, 2000.—Celebrates a child's love of the Sun and its wonder. Grades K–2.

Nonfiction

Tomecek, Steve, *Sun*, National Geographic Society, Washington, DC, 2001.—Describes the physics of the Sun. Concepts are presented in an easy-to-understand manner enhanced by colorful illustrations. It includes historical thought on the relationship of the Earth to the Sun. Grades K–2.

Activities

What's a Million?

Duplicate 1,000 pages (2 reams of paper) with 1,000 dots (periods) on each page. Use 20 lines of 50 periods on each page. Put the reams of paper in a plastic tub and make a cover for it with the title "What's a Million?" Add "Look inside and see one million dots." Use this to help the students develop the concept of one million.

Beach Ball Sun

Materials:

Beach ball
Small dried pea

Question: How big is the Sun as compared with the Earth?

Inflate a beach ball. Tell the students that if the ball were the Sun, one million Earths would fit inside it (volume). Show a dried pea (small one), and say that this is somewhat like the size of Earth as compared with the size of the Sun. Explain that if a string of these peas/Earths were strung through the center in a straight line, it would take a hundred peas to do it (diameter).

CENTER OF MASS/CENTER OF GRAVITY/BALANCING

NATIONAL SCIENCE EDUCATION CONTENT STANDARD A (SCIENCE AS INQUIRY) AND CONTENT STANDARD B (PHYSICAL SCIENCE)

As a result of activities, all students should develop an understanding of:

➢ Motions and forces

Fiction

McCully, Emily Arnold, *Mirette on the High Wire*, Putnam Publishing Group, New York, 1992.—Mirette learns tightrope walking from a man who has given it up because of fear. Grades K–3.

Nonfiction

Gerstein, Mordicai, *The Man Who Walked between the Towers*, Roaring Brook, Brookfield, CT, 2003.—A lyrical telling of Philippe Petit's 1974 tightrope walk between the World Trade Center towers. Grades 2–6.

Background Information

Vocabulary: The center of mass is the point at which the entire mass or weight of a body can be considered to be concentrated. The center of gravity is the point in the body around which the mass or weight is evenly distributed, or balanced, and through which the force of gravity acts. These concepts are especially evident in high-wire acts that demonstrate for us a combination of hard work, courage, and a little bit of magic, with physics "thrown into the balance as well!" according to the piece in *Newton's Apple*, a public television family science show.

To understand high-wire acts, we can think of the wire as an axis and the performer's center of mass as having the potential to rotate around the axis. The center of mass must be directly above the wire or gravity will cause the performer to begin to rotate around the wire. Eventually, if the performer cannot recover, gravity will continue to cause a fall.

A high-wire artist often carries a long balancing pole, shifting it from side to side, not up and down, to assist in maintaining his or her balance. Poles range in size and weight, depending on the physical size and personal preference of the performers. They may be as long as 39 feet (12 meters) and weigh up to 31 pounds (14 kilograms). High-wire artists often use a drooping balance pole with a weight on each end, to change the center of gravity. The longer and heavier the pole, the easier it is to keep a sense of balance. The lower the center of gravity is, the easier it is for the performer as well. In fact, if the center of gravity is below the wire, the performer needs very little sense of balance.

Philippe Petit, a daring young Frenchman, succeeded in walking across the 130-foot (39.6-meter) gap between the twin towers of the World Trade Center on a tightrope on August 7, 1974. The feat was watched in amazement first by a few, then by hundreds of thousands of bystanders. Although his act was illegal, he became such a folk hero that all formal charges were dropped.

Note: Squirrels use their tails like a high-wire artist uses a pole to maintain balance.

Activity: Balancing Act

Materials:

> Paper clips
> Pin
> Masking tape
> Battery

Question: How do tightrope walkers keep their balance?

Have the students bend two equal-sized paper clips and tape them (front and back) to a pin. Balance the pin on the bump of a battery by hanging a paper clip on each arm. *Hint*: If it tilts, bend the higher arm outward. Have the students work to make the pin stand as straight as they can by manipulating the paper clips. This will prove to be a fine example of inquiry. (See Figure 6.4.)

This activity comes from TOPS Learning Systems at the TOPS website (www.topscience.org).

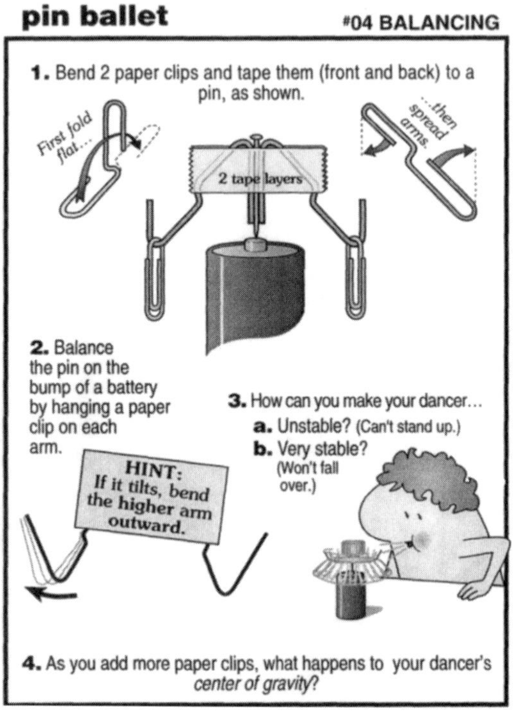

pin ballet   #04 BALANCING

1. Bend 2 paper clips and tape them (front and back) to a pin, as shown.

First fold flat...   *...then spread arms.*

2 tape layers

2. Balance the pin on the bump of a battery by hanging a paper clip on each arm.

3. How can you make your dancer...
  a. Unstable? (Can't stand up.)
  b. Very stable? (Won't fall over.)

HINT: If it tilts, bend the higher arm outward.

4. As you add more paper clips, what happens to your dancer's center of gravity?

FIGURE 6.4. This experiment helps students understand how tightrope walkers use poles (and dancers use their arms) to help keep their balance. Copyright 2003 by TOPS Learning Systems. Reprinted by permission.

Eggs

NATIONAL SCIENCE EDUCATION CONTENT STANDARD C (LIFE SCIENCE)

As a result of activities, all students should develop an understanding of:

> ➤ Life cycles of organisms
> ➤ Structure and function in living systems

Fiction

Bunting, Eve, *Secret Place*, Clarion Books, New York, 1996.—A young boy discovers a patch of wilderness in the city where birds find a place to nest. Grades K–3.

Nonfiction

Burton, Robert, *Egg*, Dorling Kindersley, New York, 1994.—Eye-catching photographs chronicling eggs and hatching are presented along with a wealth of information. Grades K–4.

Jenkins, Martin, *The Emperor's Egg*, Candlewick, Cambridge, MA, 1999.—A look at the fatherly duties of the male emperor penguin. Grades K–4.

Background Information

A bird's egg is one of the strongest shapes in nature. Shaped like a dome, eggshells can support a significant amount of weight because the weight doesn't press down on any single point; instead, it travels down along the curved side to the widest part of the dome, the base. No single point of the dome supports the whole weight. This structure helps protect the growing chick inside. It is an amazing fact that the staff at the Ontario Science Center in Toronto have demonstrated that a single egg can support a 200-pound (90-kilogram) person! Because of their strength, domes are often designed by architects for big buildings that can't have pillar supports, such as hockey rinks and arenas.

The babies of chickens, ducks, and penguins use a small point on the tip of the bill, called the egg tooth, to break through the eggshell. Prior to hatching, penguin chicks call to their parents from inside the eggs.

Eggs come in many different shapes and colors, depending on the environment in which the species lives. Some are very pointy at one end; these eggs are laid by birds who make their nests on cliffs and ledges. The pointy eggs roll in very tight circles, so they don't fall off. Some eggs have markings and colors for camouflage.

Chicken eggshell quality is affected by the type of feed the hen gets, so not all eggshells are equally strong.

Activities

Question: How strong is an egg?

CAN'T CRUSH AN EGG

Materials:

Plastic bags
Raw eggs

Allow each student to try to crush an egg (over a bowl or wrapped in a plastic zip-lock bag, just in case) by squeezing it with both hands. Be sure there are no rings on fingers. The egg should not break, because the force is spread over a fairly large area of the shell. Normally, when an egg is broken, it is cracked against something hard so that the force of the tap is concentrated on a small area of the eggshell.

EGGSHELL POWER

Materials:

Several raw eggs
Small scissors (manicure scissors work well)
Masking tape
Many hardcover books, like encyclopedias, that are all the same size

Gently break open the small end of one of the raw eggs by tapping it on a table or counter. Peel away some of the eggshell to make a hole large enough to pour out the raw egg inside. Then put a piece of masking tape around the middle of the empty eggshell. This will keep the eggshell from cracking when you cut it. Now, using a small scissors carefully cut the eggshell in half through the masking tape, so that you have a half-dome with an even bottom. Repeat until you have four equal-sized halves.

Put the eggshell halves on a table, open end down, in a rectangle, which will provide a base for the stack of books you will lay on them, one by one. Ask the students to estimate how many books the eggshells will hold before they break. Lay the books slowly on the shells until there is a stack of them. Be sure to listen for cracks! Keep adding books until the shells give way. Ask the students to estimate how much the pile of books weighs. Then weigh the books to learn how close they were to the right answer.

An inquiry approach would be to try this using different types of eggs from the grocery store: cage-free eggs, brown eggs, eggs from a chicken factory.

EPIDEMICS

NATIONAL SCIENCE EDUCATION CONTENT STANDARD C (LIFE SCIENCE)

As a result of activities, all students should develop an understanding of:

➢ Life cycles of organisms

NATIONAL SCIENCE EDUCATION CONTENT STANDARD F (SCIENCE IN PERSONAL AND SOCIAL PERSPECTIVES)

As a result of activities, all students should develop an understanding of:

➢ Personal health

➢ Natural hazards

➢ Science and technology in society

Fiction

Anderson, Laurie Halse, *Fever 1793*, Aladdin Paperbacks, New York, 2000.—In 1793 Philadelphia, a 16-year-old girl learns about perseverance and self-reliance when she is forced to cope with being separated from her sick mother amid the horrors of a yellow fever epidemic. Grades 5–6.

Nonfiction

Kalman, Bobbie, *The Life Cycle of a Mosquito*, Crabtree, New York, 2004.—High-interest, comprehensive nonfiction resource. Grades 4 and up.

Ward, Brian, *Epidemic*, Eyewitness Books, Dorling Kindersley, New York, 2000.—Discusses what an epidemic is, how it evolves, various causes and carriers, and efforts to prevent epidemics. Grades 4 and up.

Background Information

Yellow fever is spread by mosquitoes just as malaria and various forms of encephalitis, such as West Nile virus, are spread. Yellow fever struck Philadelphia in 1793, and in 3 months it killed close to 5,000 people, nearly 10% of the population. Because medicine in those days was crude, people didn't know how the disease was spread nor how to treat it.

Mosquitoes become infected with West Nile virus when they feed on infected birds. These infected mosquitoes then can transmit West Nile virus to humans and to other birds and animals through a mosquito bite. However, even in areas where mosquitoes do carry the virus, very few mosquitoes (usually fewer than 1 in 500) are infected.

West Nile virus is occurring in many parts of the country, and most human cases occur in late summer and fall. Mosquitoes bite more frequently at dawn, dusk, and early evening. They can lay their eggs in the smallest bodies of water, even in a puddle formed inside an old tire, a tin can, or a flowerpot. These hidden places can make insect control very difficult. (See Figure 6.5.)

Activities

Question: How can we help people avoid West Nile virus?

Mosquito Abatement Day

A class Mosquito Abatement Day can be organized, with a search for

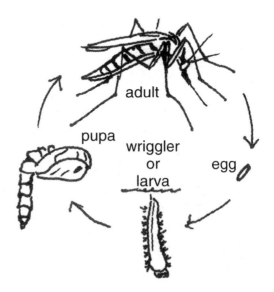

FIGURE 6.5. Mosquito life cycle.

breeding areas on the school grounds, in the neighborhood, or in the students' own backyards. They may find larvae or "wrigglers" or even a puddle with egg rafts laid by female mosquitoes.

Safety precaution: When looking for breeding areas, a repellent containing DEET should be worn. The directions on the bottle should be read carefully.

Reducing the Risk of West Nile Virus

Students should be informed about avoiding mosquito bites by using repellent and wearing long pants and long sleeves during times of high risk. The clothing should be sprayed with repellent. They can also reduce risk for their families by making sure that the screens in their homes have no holes. Dead birds should be reported to authorities, who will then check them for the disease.

Safety precaution: Do not touch dead birds. Though West Nile virus is not spread by touching dead birds, students should not touch any dead wild animals.

GEOLOGY

NATIONAL SCIENCE EDUCATION CONTENT STANDARD D (EARTH AND SPACE SCIENCE)

As a result of activities, all students should develop an understanding of:

➢ Structure of the Earth system

➢ Earth's history

Fiction

Kehret, Peg, *Earthquake Terror*, Puffin Books, New York, 1996.—When an earthquake hits the isolated island in northern California where his family has been camping, a 12-year-old boy must somehow keep himself, his partially paralyzed younger sister, and their dog alive until help arrives. Grades 4 and up.

Skurzynski, Gloria, and Ferguson, Alane, *Over the Edge*, Mysteries in Our National Parks Series, National Geographic Society, Washington DC, 2002.—While she studies condors in the Grand Canyon, a scientist's life is threatened, and a strange teenage boy may be involved. Grades 4 and up.

Nonfiction

Vieira, Linda, *Grand Canyon*, Walker, New York, 1997.—Visitors to the park learn the history and geology of the area, which are depicted with visual drama. Grades 3–6.

York, Penelope, *Earth*, Eye Wonder series, Dorling Kindersley, London, 2004.—Offers clear informational text along with powerful photographs of our geological world. Grades 3–6.

Background Information

Earth's crust is made up of huge pieces, called tectonic plates, that have been moving slowly for millions of years. As they drift and shift, they cause dramatic effects. When plates slip past each other, they can cause tremors or earthquakes on the Earth's surface. During earthquakes, faults move or break rock under the surface, which often doesn't show at the surface. Volcanoes and mountains form along a fault, a place where two plates run along side by side. Magma—molten rock from inside the Earth moving within Earth's crust—often follows the path of least resistance, such as through fractures between layers, to form igneous rocks at the surface or between layers of rocks.

The Grand Canyon is 277 miles (446 kilometers) long, and in places it is a mile (1.6 kilometers) deep. There was once a tall chain of mountains in the Grand Canyon area that have since been eroded away. A layer of basalt proves that there was also some volcanic activity in the long-ago past. Early on, uplift from inside the Earth elevated the land. The Grand Canyon itself was formed by ice and wind, but the strongest factor in its formation was water erosion in the form of flash floods. The erosion has uncovered layers of rock that were formed millions of years ago.

Activity: Sedimentary Rock Sandwich

Materials:

> Breads: white, pumpernickel, wheat with sunflower seeds or nuts (find out whether any students are allergic to nuts, and check for them in the ingredients)
> Apple jelly
> Apple butter
> Small paper cups
> Plastic knives
> Paper plates
> Baster filled with red jelly
> Pictures of sedimentary rock that forms the Grand Canyon

Questions: How do some rocks form? What happens when tectonic plates move? What are magma intrusions?

Make sure that everyone has washed his or her hands. Divide the group into pairs to make the following sandwich:

The bottom layer is white bread. Explain that it represents *white sandstone*, composed of broken pieces of rock that formed long ago when the Earth was young and cooling off. Water broke the rock into small pieces as it splashed back and forth over the rock for millions of years to finally form sand. Sand is often made of tiny pieces of quartz. Other layers of sediment settled over the sand and water (which is very heavy) also weighed down on it, so that, over time and with this pressure, the sand became solid white sandstone.

Spread apple butter over the sandstone. This is *claystone*, which forms when brownish, reddish clay spreads out over the sand that later became sandstone, and with time and pressure from the layers of sediment and water on top of it, it, too, turned into rock.

Pumpernickel bread, added next, is *shale*. Mud spreads out in layers over the other two layers and, over time and with pressure, it also hardens into rock.

Yellow apple jelly is layered on next. It represents the *limestone* that formed in oceans millions of years ago. Many kinds of limestone formed from the shells of animals that lived in those oceans. Other kinds formed from the chemical that made the shells, calcium carbonate. Time and pressure changed the shells and chemical into limestone.

Wheat bread with nuts or sunflower seeds goes on last. This is *conglomerate* rock or small rocks cemented into sand or clay over time and with pressure.

Note: Explain that this is not the geological story of the layers in the Grand Canyon, all of which are depicted and labeled on the inside front and back covers of the book *Grand Canyon*. Perhaps the students can research these layers later.

Discuss and show pictures of layers of rock that have been bent or broken. (Some excellent pictures are found in *Grand Canyon*. Many of the rock layers are not horizontal because of the movement of Earth's crust. Have the students bend the sandwich to form hills and valleys. Have them tear the sandwich into two pieces and demonstrate the different ways faults can move (apart, pushing together laterally, one moving up and the other down, one over the other).

Demonstrate how layers sometimes move so that they slide deep down into the crust to become metamorphic rock over time and with heat and pressure. If hot enough, the rock may melt into magma and recool as igneous rock. Use a baster filled with red jelly to show intrusions of magma between layers or volcanic activity above the surface.

Last of all, everyone can eat the sandwich if he or she wishes.

RAINBOWS

NATIONAL SCIENCE EDUCATION CONTENT STANDARD B (PHYSICAL SCIENCE)

As a result of activities, all students should develop an understanding of:

➢ Light, heat, electricity, and magnetism

Fiction

Freeman, Don, *A Rainbow of My Own*, Puffin Books, New York, 1966.—A child gets a rainbow surprise caused by light refraction. *Note*: This is a delightful book, but a discussion on discerning fact and fantasy is important. This is always an important concept to develop with young children. Grades K–2.

Nonfiction

Krupp, Edwin C., *The Rainbow and You*, HarperCollins, New York, 2000.—Explains how rainbows are formed by the colors in sunlight shining and bending through raindrops and gives many other fascinating facts. Grades 2–4.

Background Information

Rainbows involve a complicated process of reflection and refraction within a raindrop. A rainbow displays itself as a portion of a full circle. We don't see a full circle because the Earth gets in the way. The lower the Sun is to the horizon, the more of the circle we see; right at sunset, we would see a full semicircle of the rainbow with the top of the arch 42 degrees above the horizon. When the Sun is higher in the sky, the arch of the rainbow above the horizon is smaller. Occasionally, a rainbow can be viewed in its entirety from an airplane.

Activity: Rainbow Physics

Materials:

> Small circle templates for students to share
> White construction paper
> Markers or crayons

Question: What is the shape of a rainbow?

Have the students use a circle template to outline a single circle as a starting point for coloring a rainbow. The acronym ROY G BIV gets its name from the seven colors of the rainbow (red, orange yellow, green, blue, indigo (purple), and violet (reddish-purple). This name will help students put the colors in order, remembering that violet is the shortest band of light in the spectrum and red is the longest. Next, the students will use another piece of paper and cut a horizon to cover the rainbow circle so it is viewed as we usually see it. Trees, mountains, and other landscape details can be added. (See Figure 6.6).

The rainbow as a
full circle.

A horizon covers
the circle.

FIGURE 6.6. Rainbow physics.

Suggestion: These make charming Mother's Day cards along with a special note.

RAINFORESTS

NATIONAL SCIENCE EDUCATION CONTENT STANDARD C (LIFE SCIENCE)

As a result of activities, all students should develop an understanding of:

➤ Structure and function in living systems

NATIONAL SCIENCE EDUCATION CONTENT STANDARD D (EARTH AND SPACE SCIENCE)

As a result of activities, all students should develop an understanding of:

➤ Structure of the Earth system

Poetic Prose

Yolen, Jane, *Welcome to the Green House*, G.P. Putnam's Sons, New York, 1993.—Beautifully illustrated poetic description of a tropical rainforest. Grades 2–6.

See other examples of fiction and nonfiction trade books in the "Children's Literature" section at the end of the book.

Background Information

Although tropical rainforests once covered more than 14% of Earth's land area, they now amount to less than 6%. Rainforests are defined in several ways. They are located in a belt between the Tropic of Cancer and the Tropic of Capricorn. They are distinguished by distinctive layered vegetation, and they are home to more than half of the world's plant and animal species. Some experts claim the figure is more like 80%.

Rainforests receive an annual rainfall of 80–400 inches (2–10.3 meters). Nights are cool, causing high humidity and early morning mists. These mists evaporate with the rising sun, and by late morning an upward convection current causes water-laden air to rise and form clouds. The higher the clouds go, the colder the air is. When water vapor rises, the cold air causes the vapor to form droplets. When the droplets get big enough and heavy enough, they fall as rain. Often in a rainforest, every day by late afternoon there are thunderstorms.

Activity: Rainforest Terrarium

Question: How is a terrarium like a real rainforest?

Do this with your students. Collect some small rainforest plants (houseplants such as pothos or African violets purchased at the supermarket). Put a layer of

FIGURE 6.7. Creating a classroom rainforest terrarium is easy.

gravel in the bottom of a terrarium or a gallon jar with a lid. Add several inches of potting soil. Plant the smallest plant first by poking a hole in the soil with your finger. Put the roots of the plant into the hole, and fill the hole around the roots with soil. Water just enough to make sure the roots are watered and the soil is damp. Put the lid on the terrarium or jar. There should be some small holes in the top, but they should not be big enough to let much moisture escape. Keep the container in a warm place out of direct sunlight. (See Figure 6.7.)

As time goes on, the water will continue to recycle inside the jar, just as water does in the rainforests of the world. Students can observe the condensation on the top of the container gather and coalesce until it slides down the sides, making "rain-tracks." Sometimes the droplets just disappear as water vapor, only to return again as condensation. Explain that this is what happens in rainforests of the world.

The moist environment inside the terrarium will keep the plants healthy. The terrarium may need to be watered from time to time, and the plants inside may need trimming.

WATER CYCLE

NATIONAL SCIENCE EDUCATION CONTENT STANDARD B (PHYSICAL SCIENCE)

As a result of activities, all students should develop an understanding of:

➤ Properties and changes of properties in matter

NATIONAL SCIENCE EDUCATION CONTENT STANDARD D (EARTH AND SPACE SCIENCE)

As a result of activities, all students should develop an understanding of:

➤ Structure of the Earth system
➤ Earth's history

Poetry

Locker, Thomas, *Cloud Dance*, Harcourt Brace, New York, 2000.—Superb illustrations and lovely poems describe clouds. Grades 2–6.

Locker, Thomas, *Water Dance*, Harcourt Brace, New York, 1997.—Once again, Thomas Locker provides lyrical poems and glorious paintings to describe the various states of water. Grades 2–6.

Martin, Bill, and Archambault, John, *Listen to the Rain*, Holt, New York, 1988.—Wonderful poetry for choral reading. Grades K–4.

Nonfiction

Hooper, Meredith, and Coady, Chris, *The Drop in My Drink: The Story of Water on Our Planet*, Viking, New York, 1998.—Examines the amazing story of water, how it is always changing, and the essential role it has played and will continue to play in life on Earth. Grades 2–6.

Background Information

There is the same amount of water on Earth as there has always been. It just keeps getting recycled (see Figure 6.8).

Activity: Hydrological Water Cycle Bottle

Questions: How does the water cycle work inside a hydrological bottle? How is it like Earth's water cycle?

Pour about a cup of water into a 2-liter soft drink container. Close it and place the bottle horizontally on the seat of a chair or on a table. Clip a lamp onto the back of the chair, or on something else, so that the light will shine directly on the center of the container of water. Tell the students that the lamp is like the Sun shining on the Earth's water. An evaporation/condensation process should begin quickly, and within an hour the students will be able to see tiny droplets form. Have a magnifier handy for viewing. These droplets will coalesce, getting bigger and bigger until they slide down the sides of the bottle as "raindrops." Keep this set up for a few days, but turn off the light at night. Also try the bottle in a window with sunlight shining on it. (See Figure 6.9.)

CONCLUSION

We hope you will discover some science lessons among your students' favorite pieces of literature. As you can see from the numerous ideas presented in this chapter, there are many ways teachers can use trade books, fiction alone or combined with nonfiction, effectively to teach science and many ways that science experiences can be used to enhance a work of fiction. We also hope the suggestions will inspire you to incorporate some fiction into your science teaching, and some science into your fiction.

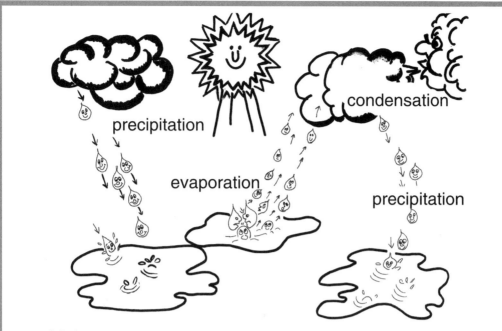

1. Rain falls from the clouds.
2. The sun warms the water in the ground, in puddles, in streams, in lakes, and in other bodies of water.
3. Water molecules begin to move and bump into one another. They bump each other right out into the air, forming water vapor.
4. Water vapor rises to form more clouds.
5. When the clouds contact cold air, the water vapor begins to condense to form new raindrops.
6. When they become heavy enough, the raindrops fall, continuing the ongoing water cycle.

FIGURE 6.8. The illustration and text help explain the water cycle in a simple way.

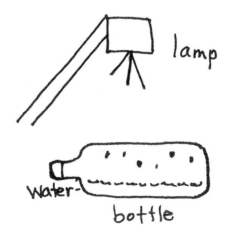

FIGURE 6.9. Hydrological water cycle bottle.

CHAPTER 7

WRITING TO LEARN IN SCIENCE

Just as science provides a natural context for students to develop their reading skills and strategies, it also provides a natural context and real purposes for students to develop their writing abilities. As soon as primary students can record their own heights or eye and hair colors or make observations of animal behaviors, they should make records of their findings and write conclusions about what they observe. As students extend their inquiries and use books and articles to locate answers to their questions, they should write notes on the information they find. At all grade levels, as students engage in making notes, recording, summarizing, and describing events, they are using writing as a tool for recording their explorations, observations, and thinking. When they consolidate their learning by writing news articles or reports, they extend their writing to more formal formats. Many examples of how writing is an essential part of students' learning have been included in earlier chapters.

In this chapter we focus specifically on how teachers develop writing abilities in their students as they involve them in learning science. We use an example from Judy's second-grade classroom to illustrate how valuable writing can be for the science program and how important modeling and scaffolding are in helping students use writing as they experiment and develop concepts. She and other teachers who integrate science with literacy create classrooms in which students are regularly involved in a variety of types of writing. The examples we include are illustrative of how easily science serves as a real context for writing and exploring various forms and conventions. Our experience also makes clear how important writing can be to help students keep track of their own learning and develop skill in evaluating what they have learned.

Students need to understand how important writing is to science. A good way to start is to develop a class list of the ways in which scientists use writing. Reading books to your students that include examples of how important writing is in science can also reinforce the value of developing their own writing. We have found S. Webb's *My Season with Penguins: An Antarctic Journal* (2000), Jim Arnosky's *Bug Hunter Nature Notebook* (1997), and, for older students, W. Hampton's *Meltdown: A Race Against Nuclear Disaster at Three Mile Island, A Reporter's Story* (2001), to be the kind of books that help students understand how important writing is to science. They are great models of ways to keep notes about observations.

Introducing students to websites where scientists collect and share data is also useful. For example, students at all grade levels are interested in the "frog problem" that was first discovered by middle-level students in Minnesota. Now there is a website where all children can participate by adding their sightings of malformed frogs, and collecting, reporting, and submitting these data to the scientists working on the project (frogweb.nbii.gov/index.html). The U.S. Geological Survey also maintains the North American Reporting Center for Amphibian Malformities (NARCAM), to which students can also report data on the Internet (frogweb.nbii.gov/narcam).

Science news is happening all over the globe, and students can become aware of and develop interests in important issues through various news magazines. There are good magazines available for all grade levels. Having subscriptions to a few of these, at the appropriate reading level for students, can build their awareness of another kind of writing about science. Reading some of the articles to the students and discussing the features together can stimulate their interest in science news. Some of the articles can serve as models for the students' own writing. By comparing the various formats of the articles, students can learn about ways to present their own research to others.

It is also valuable for teachers to bring in science articles from local newspapers and read them to the class. This helps students understand that science is an ongoing, important part of society. Every week, there are articles on newsworthy subjects, ranging from human health, to pollution, to astronomical exploration to read to students. Putting an article you select to read on a transparency and pointing out the features of the article and how it is organized will help students begin to think of ways of composing their own information when it is time to write.

Scientists report their findings both informally to their colleagues and to the public and more formally in scholarly reports and papers. Students can take a step toward this kind of sharing of information by communicating with other students via the Internet in news-making topics. All of these kinds of writing can easily be included in an engaging science/literacy classroom.

Another important part of recording and sharing information in science is drawing and creating diagrams. Scientists write and make illustrations as an integral part of their work; as students participate in the science curriculum, they need to do the same. In the primary grades children can learn the difference between scientific diagrams and creative drawing. They also learn the power of drawing as a means of representing ideas. The teachers with whom we work have helped students learn to combine words with illustrations. The relationship between these two forms of representation is especially strong in scientific writing.

The use of diagrams provides an additional way for students to express ideas they are developing. It is often difficult for them to put into precise words what they think. Diagrams can build a bridge. An important benefit is that when they share their representations, students learn to appreciate different interpretations. Diagrams give students a different way of expressing what they know and permit them to compare their interpretations with each other. It is also true that children often learn better when they can visualize a concept, make careful observations, and record what they see with detailed illustrations.

CLASSROOMS WHERE CHILDREN WRITE

Classrooms where children use writing to learn are generally classrooms where students are involved in many different types of writing. Writing workshop is an important linchpin in many writing programs because it puts children at the center of writing as they explore ideas and choose what they want to write about, create drafts, make revisions, confer about their pieces, and take some to final copy or publication. Shared writing has also become a popular instructional strategy for teachers to model and collaborate with children in composing texts. As they write with students, teachers can teach the conventions and forms of written language the children are ready to experience.

Dictated language experience articles and stories are also valuable. Many teachers and reading specialists who work with struggling readers find that serving as scribes for students frees them to express their thoughts in more elaborated language than they would use if asked to write themselves. These personal compositions are more motivating as sources of reading and are easier to decode because the stories are written by the children. In the intermediate grades word processing becomes a useful resource, freeing students to create more elaborated pieces of writing and to create "professional looking" pieces.

When teachers value children's writing, science provides a particularly motivating content. We have worked with many teachers who use their science units to help students learn to

➢ Record observations

➢ Reflect on what they are learning

➢ Make notes of information as they collect it from print materials, videos, and the Internet

➢ Compose reports

➢ Engage in self-reflection

In the following sections we share some examples from these classrooms that illustrate how, even in kindergarten and first grade, teachers can involve students in meaningful writing and build strong writing skills.

GETTING STARTED IN THE PRIMARY GRADES

A few years ago we collaborated in analyzing how Judy was able to develop children's abilities to communicate at a very sophisticated level, both orally and in writing. What follows is a brief description of how she develops children's writing and understanding of science in an integrated program. Judy, like many good primary teachers, has children writing independently every day—responding to what they read, creating their own stories, writing letters, and keeping personal journals. In addition, she uses a rich language experience program in which teacher and students together create stories and articles. She uses these group experiences to model conventions and extend students' thinking.

A central part of her scaffolded writing is the creation of a daily news article. This is done as a group experience; the class reviews the events of the day and then summarizes what is important. The students dictate to her, and she records their ideas. As together they create the text, she often rereads the emerging text so students can contribute their ideas and make revisions, deepening the students' ownership of the writing. She uses these times to guide students in using correct forms, punctuation, and capitals and in expressing ideas in complete sentences.

By the end of the day this news article is reread and is often copied for the children to take home and read with their parents. Students and parents become accustomed to this missive, and it often becomes a shared reading at home. The newsletter provides parents with an ongoing idea of what is happening in the classroom and helps them talk more extensively with their children about school.

Composing these newsletters and other more extensive texts is one of the most important foundations for writing. Judy believes it is critical that all students develop a sense of ownership in the group writing. She lets the children know that she considers each student's contribution essential to the whole group. She gives the children time to prepare ideas for the articles: "I want you all to think of a sentence that would fit this article. When you think you are ready, let me know." If a child's idea has already been contributed, she explains that they too can claim and share part of the article or story. The goal is for all children to feel that they have made a contribution and that they own the text. It takes some time in the fall before the class can function as a unit in creating meaning. Yet the value in developing this process cannot be overlooked. The group writing ensures that all students think of themselves as composers and serves to model and nurture student thinking and writing.

MODELING AND DEVELOPING WRITING IN SCIENCE

Science journals are a basic tool Judy uses to help children learn to think through writing. In units that are based on active inquiry, as well as those that are more text-based, children learn to record their ideas with careful teacher modeling and scaffolded experiences. We use a unit on light to explain her approach. Children begin the unit with hands-on experiences. It is designed to help students develop an understanding of the properties of light—that it interacts with materials (transparent, translucent, and opaque), that when it goes through some substances, it bends, creating various illusions, and that it refracts into a spectrum.

At the beginning of the unit, key terms and important vocabulary that children can use to reference in their own writing and oral language are written on the board and form a "Science Word Wall." Because these words remain accessible to the children over an extended period of time, the children gain confidence in using the language and are able to think more precisely about what they see and do.

Linking the unit to children's prior knowledge is also a key. Judy knows that the children have studied the sun, moon, and planets in kindergarten and first grade. As she discusses with them some of the things they have already learned about light, she leads them in constructing a chart of what they already know. This gives the students a sense of confidence and ownership and provides a foundation for new learning.

With this foundation, Judy guides the children in developing their understanding that light and objects interact in different ways. She demonstrates with the overhead projector how this occurs and writes the key terms on the board. With the help of the children, she constructs definitions for these concepts, which are also written on the board. A lace handkerchief on the projector is determined to be translucent by the children because some light passes through it. In contrast, a plastic lid does not allow light to pass through it onto the screen and is therefore called opaque. A glass of water on the projector permits all the light to pass through, and so the students label it as transparent.

On the basis of these experiences, the children together write their definitions. Light goes through transparent things. Some light goes through translucent things. No light goes through opaque things. These definitions are written and posted so that all the children can see and use them in the independent journal writing that follows.

After this introductory activity, the children do a series of sorting and classifying activities in teams of three and record their findings in their journals. For their first experiment they work with the overhead projector and sort materials into transparent, translucent, and opaque categories. Each child makes a list in his or her own journal for each category. When they do this, Judy insists that they also write the concept that is being exemplified. Therefore, the list of translucent objects includes the explanation that translucent objects let some light pass through them. (See Figure 7.1 for an example of one child's journal entry.) Subsequent experiments are done in teams or individually, and each is recorded in the journals.

The unit continues as children learn about refraction of light. After each experiment, they illustrate examples of refraction in their journals and explain what happens. In contrast to their initial entries, these entries reveal that the children are showing more of their thinking on paper. Sentences appear and higher-level thinking is evident. Christy's entry on refraction is a good example of this development (see Figure 7.2). She indicates the concept being studied at the top of her page and then explains four activities she undertook at the science table. It is obvious that she has learned a great deal about refraction and can explain it in her own way.

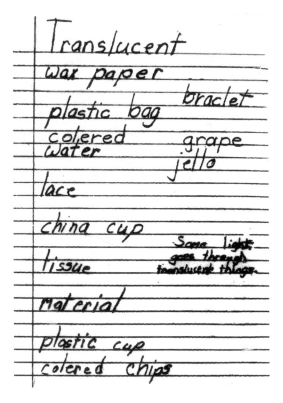

FIGURE 7.1. Example from a student's science journal with simple explanation.

One of Judy's goals is for the children to make the link between the concepts they are learning in science and everyday experiences. Again, she uses the journal to encourage each child to construct ideas and reflect on their hands-on experiences as they make connections. To help in this transition between science in school and home, she sets up a classroom fishbowl containing four fish. Then the children perform independent observations to see what concepts they can apply to their understanding of what they see in the fishbowl. The children write their observations in their journals. This year, some noted that they saw reflections on the shiny fish in the water. Some also noted refractions—from the right perspective, they could see double the number of fish. (See Figure 7.3 for an example of a child's observations.)

In addition, Judy brings in photographs and copies of artworks, such as Mattisse's *Goldfish*, and encourages the children to read and look through art books. She periodically shares pieces of art with the children and discusses what they observe in the paintings and photos. The children note shadows, sunsets,

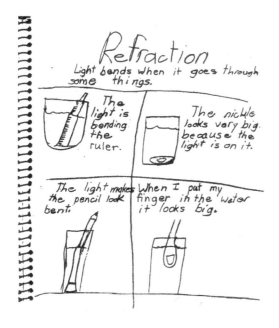

FIGURE 7.2. Journal entries describing what happens during science explanations of light refraction.

reflections, and refractions. Some of them save these experiences by writing in their journals.

The culmination of the Light Unit is Rainbow Day. The children wear rainbow-colored clothes, and the whole day is planned around rainbows. When the students arrive in the morning, they find prisms on their desks. They proceed to learn about the spectrum through exploration. They journal, draw, and compose stories and poetry. Central to the reading/writing on this day is Don Freeman's *A Rainbow of My Own*. In this story a boy wants to have his own rainbow and explores what he could do with it. After they read this imaginative story, Judy encourages the children to think about what they might do with their own rainbows. As a group they can construct a collage poem.

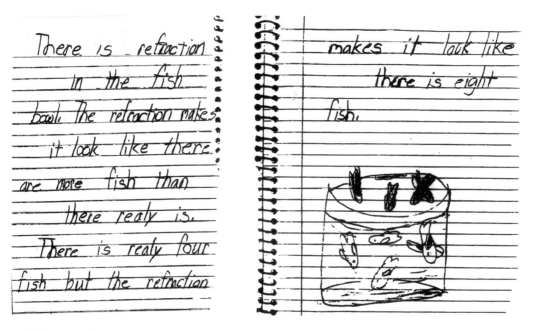

FIGURE 7.3. Journal entry describing observations of light in a fishbowl.

My Very Own Rainbow
Rainbows make me feel:
happy
surprised
excited
Rainbows look:
pretty
awesome
spectacular
I wish I could:
climb on one
slide down one
play on one all day
use one as a water slide
go to the end and find a pot of gold
Would you please be my rainbow?

Finally each child writes his or her own rainbow story. Thus ends a rich, integrated unit. The end is only a beginning, however, for during the rest of the year the children continue to note light and color and periodically bring in examples and discuss their observations informally.

During this unit, which comes early in the year, the children build on their group experiences with daily messages and learn to record what they are learning in science. Initially, science activities are modeled in large group experiences, and the children's task is to continue the exploration, with partners or individually, and describe the outcomes of what they do in their journals. Later their writing is more extensive—students describe and record the science experiments and the conclusions they draw from them on their own. According to their teacher, this marks an important milestone in the use of journaling; it requires internalization of the process and a much higher level of thinking. Students must know the concepts before they can write about them. Judy watches for this change and supports students as they make the transition in their own work.

THE DEVELOPMENT OF JOURNAL WRITING AND LEARNING

As we reviewed the journals created by different students, it was clear that over the year they developed considerable skill in writing and thinking on paper. Their paths were quite individual in this process. Yet some key elements were apparent in all journals.

First, all students were able to think and communicate more fully because the journals contained a combination of drawings and illustrations with writing. From the beginning of the journaling process, Judy encourages students to illustrate their writing. This is an especially important component for the children who are less secure with writing. Through elaboration in their drawings, children can display or demonstrate their knowledge and understanding of a particular activity or concept. Some relied on the visual forms very successfully.

Judy also encourages this use of visuals by periodically photocopying diagrams, illustrations, and elaborations on concepts being studied so students can read, cut out, and paste them into their journals. Children like to embellish their journals by incorporating these materials. It gives the journals an interesting, sophisticated flavor and demonstrates that knowledge is built from a variety of sources. These diagrams, photographs, and bits of information also help the children focus on important concepts they might have difficulty expressing in their own words. (See Figure 7.4.)

FIGURE 7.4. Examples of pages from two science journals. Skeleton drawings in Figures 7.4 and 7.5 are from Figure 2 of Thewissen et al., 1994, *Science*, Vol. 263, pp. 210–212. Copyright 1994 by AAAS. Reprinted by permission.

Second, the focus on Amazing Facts (see Chapter 5) is motivating and exciting. It keeps the amount of writing manageable and provides a concrete purpose for writing, because the children know they can share these writings with their classmates. As the children become more comfortable writing in their journals, Judy suggests that they keep a record of Amazing Facts they find in their independent reading. In this way she encourages students to integrate their independent reading and writing. When they record the information, it is saved for them so they can share it later with the class. Often, children also like to read silently from each other's journals during independent reading time.

Judy has found the Amazing Facts to be a jumping off point for many students, whose inquisitiveness prompts them to write more extended pieces in their journals. By the end of the year, full-blown articles emerge and are shared. The goal is for students, throughout the year, to continue to read and select interesting information about curriculum topics. An example from Les's journal illustrates his increasing skill in writing to consolidate and reflect on new learning. (See Figure 7.5.)

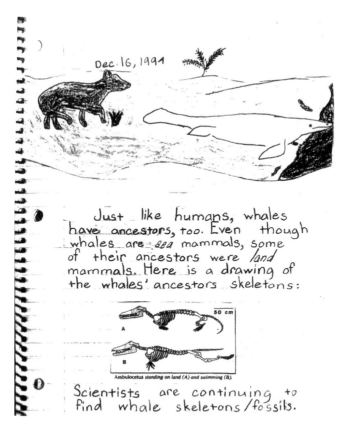

FIGURE 7.5. A record of new information in a science journal.

Third, Judy models the uses of writing and reading throughout all her units. She scaffolds each new kind of writing experience for the children and then monitors their ability to use it in their journals. She is constantly engaged with the students, reading and responding to their ideas and illustrations. The *purposes* for the journal are clear to all the students. Their ideas are important and central to the class's learning. The journals become a wonderfully personal text for a continuing dialogue about science and literacy.

Judy has found science journals to be a powerful tool in developing children's thinking and independence in learning. Journals also provide a rich data set for ongoing assessment in determining students' progress in language learning as well as in meeting science objectives. They offer concrete evidence, to the children, parents, and teacher, of the ongoing instructional program and of each child's own learning. Rather than comparing children with each other, the journals permit an evaluation of an individual child's own growth over time. This makes the journal a wonderful archive that children are proud of and may keep for years.

THIRD-GRADE STUDENTS DEVELOP SKILLS IN RECORDING SCIENCE

Carol, a third-grade teacher from another school district, also uses science as the foundation for literacy. She has found many of the same advantages mentioned earlier in linking science with writing and reading. Her class includes many English language learners, and she is careful to model and provide carefully scaffolded experiences for the children. She finds that by using science, she can also provide reading materials at a variety of levels and that children can interact easily and learn with each other despite their language differences. She, too, has students keep science journals and is careful to model writing on the overhead so that those who need support can copy her correct spelling and forms.

Carol begins an Insect Unit with a KWL activity in which students share orally what they already know about insects. She records their contributions on a transparency on the overhead projector. (She will later ask students to copy this information on paper strips and put them on the large KWL chart on the wall. See Figure 7.6.) After many students have shared, she asks the children to record these ideas in their personal journals and to add anything else they know about the subject. The initial discussion focuses the students and stimulates more ideas. Carol gives the children time to keep writing and circulates to help any who get stuck. (See Figure 7.7 for an example of one student's work.) When they are finished, she asks them what they most want to learn about insects. She records their questions on a large piece of chart paper and keeps adding questions during the unit.

FIGURE 7.6. Classroom KWL chart.

Vocabulary terms are important in this unit, so Carol highlights key terms early in the unit to help students develop their understanding of these words. She gives each child a list of the words (*abdomen, thorax, cuticle, larva, pupa, nymph, camouflage, compound eyes, paraphrase*) on a worksheet that includes space for a sentence using each term, the child's definition, and the glossary definition (see Figure 7.8). While they are reading in the variety of books in the classroom, students keep adding to their vocabulary worksheets.

One of the most engaging aspects of the unit is that students are given mealworms to study. Each keeps a journal of his or her observations. Because of the variation in language skills of her students, Carol often initially models her own journal entries and then posts some of the important words the students will be using where they can easily be seen. Children make their periodic observations of the mealworms with partners and then record what they see in their own journals. With their excitement over the worms and the opportunity to work with a partner, the children talk animatedly about what they see and then write freely. Even children with little English write and draw in their journals. (See Figure 7.9 for examples of children's work.) Writing and drawing go hand in hand. Carol also helps the children extend their inquiry by having them write questions they want to answer. Figure 7.10 shows one child's questions from her journal with some preliminary answers. Note the precise drawing this child is able to do as a result of the careful attention being paid to the animal.

As the unit continues, Carol helps students begin to categorize the information they know about insects, and they group related ideas on the KWL chart. She wants them to know that scientists differentiate animals by their body parts, stages, habitats, protective devices, eating habits, and other characteristics. At this point students select insects for their individual study. Carol helps them begin to compare and contrast different insects. One day the students are asked to find out which body parts particular insects use for detecting sound vibrations. Carol makes a matrix on the board and lists as heads for the rows "most insects, mosquitoes, crickets, and lubber grasshoppers." Across the tops of the columns she puts

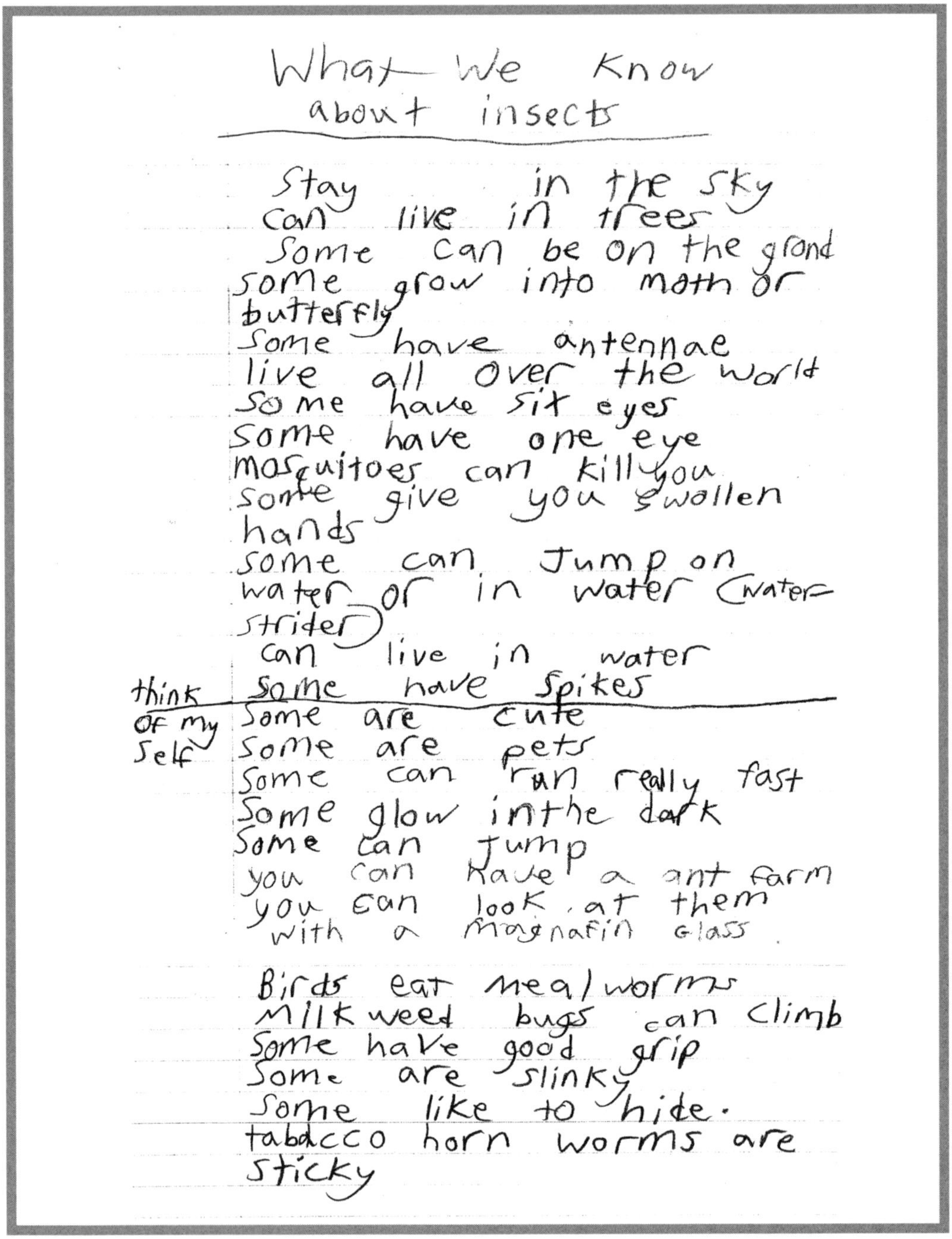

What We Know
about insects

Stay   in the sky
can live in trees
Some can be on the grond
some grow into moth or
butterfly
Some have antennae
live all over the world
So me have six eyes
Some have one eye
mosquitoes can kill you
some give you swollen
hands
some can Jump on
water or in water (water
strider)
can live in water
think Some have spikes
of my Some are cute
self Some are pets
Some can run really fast
Some glow in the dark
Some can Jump
you can have a ant farm
you can look at them
with a magnafin glass

Birds eat mealworms
Milkweed bugs can climb
Some have good grip
Some are slinky
Some like to hide.
tabacco horn worms are
sticky

FIGURE 7.7. A student's list on insects.

Vocabulary Work in Progress

Word	Source/ page # Sentence	My definition	Glossary Definition
larva	p. 7	in bettween egg and pupa.	The young of some types of insect. they look vary much like the adults except that they have no wings. they become adults without forming a pupa like a larva dose.
pupa		pupa charges larva into adult.	
nymph		Stage- between pupa and aduld	

FIGURE 7.8. Vocabulary worksheet.

"Body Part" and "Sounds." Drawing from their research, the children write what they have learned. One student wrote, "Most insects have hairs on their bodies that can pick up vibrations. Mosquitoes use their antennae to pick up the vibrations made by the wing beats of female mosquitoes." This level of note making and summarizing is quite sophisticated, and the children feel confident as they share their findings with the rest of the class.

Much of the students' research at this point is done with the books and magazines Carol has collected for them to use. These resources are at various reading levels; some are very basic so that the least able readers can still read and research. The children use a chart to develop the key questions they want to ask about their insects and to record information gathered from various sources. An example of a student's chart is shown in Figure 7.11.

Each child culminates his or her research in a written report. The students create drafts using the word processing feature of their class computers and, with feedback from the teacher, edit and make their final copies with covers and illustrations. These reports are then read orally and shared with other classes.

Tobacco horn worm

Today we measured the tobacco horn worms. Yesterday it was about a $\frac{1}{4}$. Today it was about $\frac{1}{2}$ inch. Their eyes are so tiny. Their eyes are black. Their poop is called frass. Their segments are like tie-dy. The tobacco horn worm their stages are like mealworms. One of mine did a stand up.

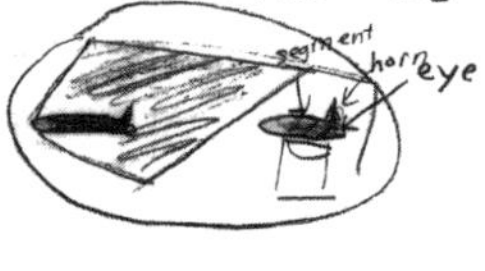

Chapter 4   Nov 7, 2002
(Tabacco horn worm)

I am studing tabacco horn worms today. My partner is Jenna E. We noticed there are white lines and black marks on the side. The one that has a bubble on the horn, is named Bubble. The one that has a sharp horn, is named Horny. The last one is Flashy because he is most active. Somthing is wrong with Bubble. I thought bubble was just a bubble, but it popped and black stuff is over flowing on his uper part of his back. They are about 2 cm and 20 mm.

FIGURE 7.9. Examples of student journals done with a partner.

144

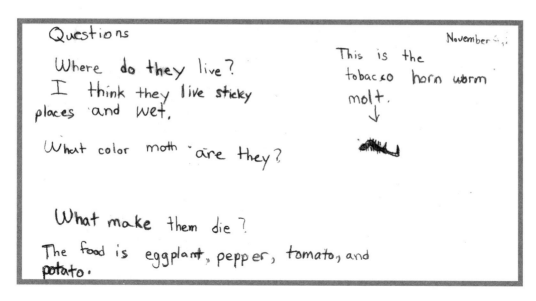

Questions   November 4, ...

Where do they live?
I think they live sticky
places and wet.

What color moth are they?

What make them die?
The food is eggplant, pepper, tomato, and
potato.

This is the
tobacco horn worm
molt.
↓

FIGURE 7.10. Page from a child's science journal with questions and possible answers.

Inquiry Chart   Source: Insekt lives (book)   Name: Sammy

Guiding Questions			
What the bodies look like	A katydid looks like a grasshopper. A katydid also uses little holes by its knees to hear. diffrent insects eat diffrent things. so they need diffrent	Mouthparts, for example: a mosquito has its mouth like a needle to sucks blood, a grasshopper has its mouth like a pair of sissors to chew plants, and a butterfly has its mouth like a straw to sip Nectar	
dangers	insects enymies are birds, bats, and frogs. they have lots of wase to keep safe from enymies. one of the ways is camouflage.	A rain-forest mantid may scare a enymie away by doing a startiled display.	
stages	They all start from eggs. Some look like ther parents when born, but some insects don't look like ther parents at all.	Some insects example of insects that look like ther parents when born are: milkweed bugs and baby roaches.	

FIGURE 7.11. A student's research chart.

SELF-SELECTED RESEARCH

Marj Steiner believes strongly in allowing time for students to pursue their own interests through research. She waits until she is sure her class has acquired independent work skills and a good sense of responsibility for themselves and for class books and materials.

Over a period of a few days, Marj has the students first brainstorm things they've always wanted to study. They write their ideas on a worksheet designed for this purpose and then think about them for 2 or 3 days. After this incubation time, the students rethink their selections and add or delete some ideas. Finally, they choose one topic to explore. It should be noted that, although the subjects are not limited exclusively to science-related topics, they often are related to science. Next, Marj asks the students what they will need to do in order to learn about their subjects. This discussion leads to each child's developing a list of resources to do the research. A typical list might look like this:

Websites
Books
Magazines
Supplies for experiments
Talk to my grandfather

Marj is fortunate to have a cadre of carefully selected parents who believe in what she is doing. They willingly devote time to this class endeavor by taking several of the students' lists and spending a day or two accumulating some of the resources necessary to complete the project. They work with these students throughout the study. The students, too, gather things they will need. Everything accumulated for each student is placed in a large file.

First, the students are encouraged to read and gather information from print materials or websites. The parents are there every day for over an hour to supervise, ask questions, help in accessing websites, and assist the students in narrowing their topics and formulating specific questions for inquiry. Always the students are to feel as though they are in charge, but Marj and the assistants are the guides in the process. Sometimes, if the text is too difficult for a student to read independently, an adult will read the passage out loud to the individual child. After each informational piece is read, the parent supervisors present help the students record answers to the following: What did I read? (title and author, or website), What is interesting to me? and What have I learned? These "notes" are helpful later as the students move into the project stage.

In some cases the parents assist students in conducting experiments in order to gather information. After 2 or 3 days, the students usually have a handle on their subjects, so they can move into a project to share what they have learned. This stage requires the use of their reading and writing skills. They are allowed to present anything to the class, but it must include writing. Again, parents are there to help their assigned students accumulate the supplies, conduct experiments, and do whatever the students need to make the projects their own. In the process, the students become intrigued with each other's projects and there is much discussion between them about the activities.

On Sharing Day the students eagerly share what they have learned. Because of their enthusiasm and the quality of the results, one can easily tell that these students profit from researching and developing something related to a topic of their own choosing. Marj stresses that the emphasis is on the process, not on the product, but what these students have accomplished is superior. In the past, projects have included a study of lasers with a (safe and understandable) demonstration of how they work; an Impressionist painting done by a student, with a piece written to describe how the Impressionists used light within their paintings; and chocolate treats for the whole class made by a student who studied the origins and production of chocolate.

Teachers can learn from Marj Steiner's experience. Even without the help of several parents, students can form study groups to read about and discuss together topics of their own choosing and common interest. A variety of resources and texts can be used. This approach can invigorate inquiry as students satisfy their curiosity about a topic of their choice. It is also a way to develop an inclusive community.

Proud students display their written research reports.

DEVELOPING RESEARCH REPORTS

The team of fourth- and fifth-grade teachers at Pleasant Ridge School in Glenview has, over a 10-year period, developed an individual project process focused on a theme the team has selected. Students follow a step-by-step guide for doing projects, which begins by having them brainstorm topics of interest that relate to the theme of the group. When they decide on their topics, students list what they already know about the particular topics and the questions they want to answer through their research. Then the students organize their knowledge on a semantic web that has at least four or five subtopics. This gives students a guide as they determine the areas of their further research questions. They are to determine one broad question and 5–10 additional questions that can help to answer the broad question. The more narrow questions become the subtopics of their reports.

In searching for information on their topics, students need to use pertinent sources. The instructions specify that students must use four or more types of resources, including books, encyclopedias, newspapers, magazines, e-mail, Internet, computer software, videos, and CD-ROMs. In their research the students must include articles on current events and show the importance of their topic in the "real world." One way they do this is by conducting an interview with an authority on the topic. They also keep bibliographic information and notes on their research efforts.

When the research process is completed, students use their questions to develop an outline and write their reports. See the first part of the outline Lauren developed for her report on chimpanzees and the first page of her report (Figure 7.12). Students may also create a media presentation using PowerPoint. According to the guidelines, it must have an attractive display that shows the current events and real-world application.

With a clear process outline, students learn to engage in another form of inquiry by conducting research on topics of interest to them. They brainstorm and organize what they know, ask questions that then guide their research, use a range of resources, evaluate what they learn, and organize their findings into a coherent report.

CONCLUSION

Science provides a natural context for students to develop as writers. They learn to observe carefully and take precise notes of what they see. Their observations and journal entries underscore the importance of recording data and drawing conclusions from these observations. Through observing, many students develop new questions and use books and other resources to find more information. This leads them to taking notes and then sharing their findings with others in their class.

Even primary students can make note cards (Amazing Fact Sheets) and begin bibliographic entries. The use of drawing and diagramming to augment writing also develops early when children can see how scientists use drawing as part of their record keeping. Teacher modeling is also an incredibly important part of helping young children develop skills in writing and recording. More formal report writing can be taught when children are highly engaged in science.

Chimpanzee Outline

I. Introduction
    A. *Main Topic: Chimpanzees*
    B. *Suptopics*
       1. Description
       2. Body structure
       3. Physical Characteristics
       4. Habitat
       5. Diet and tools
       6. Chimp Babies
       7. Social Structure
       8. Behavior in an Community

Awesome Outline
Very well-organized

II. Description
    A. *Family*
       1. Family called primates
          a) Smart
          b) Large brains and have hands for grasping
          c) Use fingers to pick up and hold objects
       2. Primates include monkeys, apes and humans
    B. *Apes*
       1. Larger apes are known as great apes
       2. They include:
          a) Gorillas
          b) Orangutans
          c) Chimpanzees
    C. *Apes and Monkeys*
       1. Apes differ from monkeys in several ways
       2. Apes don't have tails and they are bigger than monkeys
       3. Apes also have larger brains than monkeys and are considered more intelligent
    D. *Apes and Humans*
       1. Many scientists believe that apes and human beings had a common ancestor long, long ago
       2. Apes have many similarities with people

(continued)

FIGURE 7.12. A student's outline for her final report.

Excellent flow of ideas!   Lauren

Chimpanzees are apes that live in Central Africa. They are called primates and are like humans in many ways. Using their intelligence, chimps make many tools to survive in the wild, and the staple of their diet is plants. Chimpanzees are very caring and loving to their babies and live in social groups.

Chimpanzees ~~live~~ *are* in a family called Primates. Primates have large brains and are smart. They have hands for grasping and use fingers to pick up and hold objects. Primates include monkey^s, apes and humans. A chimpanzee is considered an ape. Larger apes are known as great apes. They include gorillas, orangutans and chimpanzees. Apes differ from monkeys in several ways. Apes don't have tails and they are bigger than monkeys. Apes also have larger brains than monkeys and are considered more intelligent. Many scientists believe that apes and human beings had a common ancestor long, long ago. Apes have many similarities with people. Apes can stand upright and have large brains and bodies. Also, their muscles and blood types are similar to ours. Lastly, apes often behave the same way ~~we do~~ *humans do*.

Chimpanzees are about the same size as a ten year old child, four feet standing upright. Most adult males weigh from 99 to 176 pounds. Female chimpanzees are shorter and lighter than a male and weigh about 66 pounds. Chimpanzees in captivity are thinner than those in the wild. The chimpanzee body was made to swing and climb. With their long arms, chimps can easily reach from branch to branch. Using their flexible hands and feet they can grab and hook onto branches. Chimpanzees can travel across thin branches without breaking them.

FIGURE 7.12. *(continued).*

CHAPTER 8

EFFECTIVE USES
OF TECHNOLOGY

S kills required to function in the 21st century distinctly differ from those that were needed in earlier years. This is largely due to the effects of technology in our culture, which has changed learning and communication dramatically. How informtion is accessed, organized, processed, and distributed has been altered. There are now many motivating tools to teach, reinforce, and apply what is learned in lessons. Although other technologies such as audiotapes, films, videocassettes, and DVDs are useful, for our purposes much of the discussion will focus on the use of computers in the classroom.

The National Science Teachers Association (NSTA) composed a position paper in 1999 on the use of computers in science education. It is the Association's position that computers should have a major role in the teaching and learning of science.

> Computers have become an essential classroom tool for the acquisition, analysis, presentation, and communication of data in ways which allow students to become more active participants in research and learning. In the classroom, the computer offers the teacher more flexibility in presentation, better management of instructional techniques, and easier record keeping. It offers students a very important resource for learning the concepts and processes of science through simulations, graphics, sound, data manipulation, and model building.

The paper goes on to make a strong statement that computers should enhance, but not replace essential hands-on experiential learning. Computers should be used essentially as helpful tools to achieve educational goals. (The full document can be accessed at www.nsta.org/positionstatement&psid=4.)

The International Society for Technology in Education (ISTE) has been integral in the creation and dissemination of technology standards for the entire education community: preservice teachers, teachers in the field, and students at all levels. ISTE Student Standards provide a framework for linking technology-based activities to curricular areas, as well as broader guidelines for planning, whereby students can achieve success in learning, communication, and life skills. (See website www.iste.org.) *eSchool News,* an online journal, is helpful in disseminating information on current events and trends. Data, resources, and services that schools can use are included, along with information on available grants, networking possibilities, and general information to improve the application of technology.

HELPFUL TIPS FOR SUCCESS

The complexity of computers can be overwhelming in itself to a teacher, and to implement them appropriately requires planning. Here are some suggestions to help make classroom computer use easier for everyone.

> ➢ Phase in the use of a computer in your classroom. Develop expectations and skills slowly and systematically.

> ➢ Select high-quality software and appropriate websites that offer accurate information.

> ➢ Plan lessons with content and objectives in mind. Then decide whether the use of a certain computer-based activity meets the desired goals of the lesson. Next, decide at what point during the lesson the use of a computer can be advantageous.

> ➢ Make certain that students are clear about the goals of the lesson, what they should gain, understand, and be able to do as a result of the lesson.

> ➢ Students who are less proficient with computers can be partnered with those who are more skilled.

> ➢ Keep the computer turned on, and the program you intend to use already loaded or installed. This helps students focus on the learning task rather than on the mechanics of the computer. It also frees the teacher from having to be constantly available for assistance.

SOFTWARE

To make effective use of the computer it is necessary to obtain high-quality software, an ever-increasing challenge as more and more products are marketed. It will be even more difficult in the future when many more options for virtual science software, featuring interactive problem solving and creative thinking, will be developed. It is important to stay current on these new developments and improvements. Fortunately, numerous websites review software programs to help teachers to be discriminating when making selections for classroom use. Software is regularly reviewed in journals such as *Learning and Leading with Technology*, published by the ISTE, and in those of the NSTA. On the web, Children's Software Review provides reviews of thousands of software programs online and has an excellent track record for recommending worthy choices. (See its website www.childrenssoftware.com.)

Before selecting software, you must be clear about what you want it to do and how you might use it. Determine the educational objective you hope to satisfy. Here are some things to consider in the selection process:

➢ Will it help students attain valid educational goals?

➢ Will it enhance hands-on experiential science learning?

➢ Will the students be able to use it independently?

➢ Is the reading level commensurate with the students' abilities?

➢ Can it be modified to meet varying ability levels of students?

➢ Is the content accurate?

➢ Is it interactive, and does it provide immediate feedback of results?

➢ Can students decipher the graphics easily?

➢ Can the teacher track student progress?

Students must be given clear guidelines and instruction before new software can be implemented. They must be able to read and write at the level necessary to carry out the work involved. New decision-making skills must be honed as well. As they become more competent with computers and more independent in making decisions, students must decide whether using a computer is actually necessary for an assignment. For instance, does one really need to use a computer when consulting an ordinary dictionary would be faster? And what is the most expeditious means of finding information when doing research? Students need to decide whether or not to use an interactive encyclopedia or a web search to access information quickly and accurately.

Teachers are helping students learn to make dynamic class presentations and expecting them to be done more and more independently as they progress through their schooling. Therefore, the use of presentation software is important. Electronic presentations, with pictures and sounds accompanying text, offer a captivating way for students to communicate what they have learned.

LITERACY AND TECHNOLOGY

Being literate now includes being able to use technology to locate data, to evaluate it, and to collect, process, and report results, according to the National Educational Technology Standards Project (Thomas & Bitter, 2000). Students must be able to use a computer for word processing, for graphics, and to portray images. They should also be able to use the Internet to access information. Not only does this mean that teachers will have to develop and stretch their own computer skills, but also that they will need to devote a significant amount of class time to the use of technology.

Using computers for classroom science instruction and for related text inquiry and writing can naturally build authentic purposes into lessons because of students' intrinsic interest in computers. This heightens students' motivation to learn to use them in diverse ways for language learning while they learn more about science.

Specific reading and writing skills must be taught and learned before students can interact with computer text productively. Should the material presented be read slowly or skimmed? Should the piece be divided into parts or first read as a whole? Students must read critically to ascertain whether the information they access is accurate. They need to know when to search for alternative sites, or to seek other resources, in order to compare the information in question. These and other skills should be taught and guided carefully so that students can get full value from accessing material on a computer.

There are definite benefits to using computer technology for literacy instruction while acquiring scientific information. Researchers have found that the use of computers motivates students to spend increased amounts of time practicing important literacy skills (Daiute, 1983). In addition, with the continuing advances in science, using websites helps teachers and students stay current. Reading becomes very purposeful. Students love the interactive nature of sites and the visuals available to help build understanding. These, too, give teachers immediate reason for teaching the use of visual and verbal integration for learning. There is, however, a clear need to evaluate the sites critically and cross-check the sources of information.

Using the World Wide Web to gather information has created the necessity for new literacy abilities, such as search and navigation strategies. Students must also learn to use their time wisely because of the glut of information available. When working on the Web they need to learn to sift through information, skim and scan data quickly, think critically to assess its reliability and accuracy, and select relevant information, all within a reasonable time period. They must learn to verify and reference information just as they must do with a book.

After a search and gathering of information, it is important to discuss what was learned, clear up misconceptions, and synthesize and extend new information. The ability to evaluate the accuracy of information is critical, and it will take some time for students to become proficient at it. Unfortunately, much of what is found on the Web is inaccurate unless thoroughly reliable websites are used. Therefore, teachers must constantly monitor the information to check for accuracy.

Although many websites are transient, there are those that have been available for some time and can be trusted. Each of the following websites has lesson plans as well as kid-friendly areas to navigate. Some suggest other websites with click-on availability to access them.

Ask Jeeves Kids: www.ajkids.com
Blue Web'n: www.kn.pacbell.com/wired/bluewebn
Discovery School: www.school.discovery.com
Eduhound: www.eduhound.com
Encyclopedia Britannica: www.britannica.com
Jet Propulsion Laboratory: www.jpl.nasa.gov
Kathy Schrock Guide for Educators: discoveryschool.com/schrockguide
NASA: kids.msfc.nasa.gov
Scholastic, Inc.: www.scholastic.com

Blue Web'n is a huge site with an online library of hundreds of outstanding Internet sites. They are easily located by subject, grade level, and format. *Format* is the term the web designer uses to refer to the following: "tools, references, lessons, hotlists, resources, tutorials, activities, and projects." Teachers can create their own unique lessons using the links available through Blue Web'n. Important science links, such as the Jason Project, are also available.

Discovery School is another excellent site, offering countless possibilities to help classroom teachers. Kathy Schrock's Guide for Educators, a link found there, presents a helpful list of websites for creating lessons and for enhancing professional growth. There are many sites listed there for use by students.

USING TECHNOLOGY TO LEARN TO WRITE

Today teachers are successfully merging the traditional teaching of writing with developing technologies to help students read, write, and think critically. Classroom technology is not an end in itself, but a different means by which to accomplish goals and objectives. In fact, computers have become important tools in learning to write.

Word processing is now widely used as an aid in teaching writing. There are several advantages to using a word processor. Because motivation seems to be heightened when students use computers to write, better writing results, especially for those who have difficulties (Bangert-Downs, 1993). An advantage for the teacher is that text is readily visible for a quick appraisal of the writing assignment. This is helpful for all students, but especially valuable when the teacher needs to monitor the writing of less adept writers. The visibility factor is also helpful during collaboration with peers, leading to easy discussion about the writing. (Dickinson, 1986; Zorfass, Corley, & Remey, 1994).

Revising written pieces is much easier when students no longer have to recopy whole papers. It is effortless to move words, phrases, sentences, or whole passages or to delete portions during revisions. Spell check programs help students monitor spelling and typing errors. Some programs check grammar and will also alert students if certain words are being overused. Researchers have found that when students were compared using word processing revision versus handwritten revision, they were more highly motivated to revise when using the computer. For this reason, they spent more time on their revisions (Kamil, Intrator, & Kim, 2000).

Publishing is an important last step in student writing. Desktop publishing systems combine word processing with layout and graphic design features, allowing students to arrange print and graphics on a page. Posters, banners, signs, forms, brochures, and class newsletters can be designed with the use of desktop publishing. Students can put the finishing touches on their work by selecting or creating illustrations for their writing.

Motivation to complete quality products is high when young writers know that their work will be published. Teachers find that there is less resistance to working to improve their writing if the students know that many people will read their work.

When students are able to share what they've learned and written, science concepts and information are reinforced. The computer provides opportunities for cooperative learning in partners or small groups. Together the students can filter and discuss the accuracy of information gathered from all over the globe. They can try to find the most current information available.

Electronic mail is a frequently used feature on the Internet. Writing e-mail communication is an important skill. Not only do students need the skills of traditional letter writing, they also need to know the mechanics of e-mail, how to use an address book and write a correct address, how to write a subject heading, and how to send e-mail.

E-mail works well to foster students' writing. Establishing links with people in other classes close by, or in far away places, can heighten motivation to communicate and read and write for authentic purposes.

A third/fourth grade teacher started an e-mail exchange with a school in Australia. The students enjoyed sharing information about where they lived, the climate of their region, the native plants and animals, and the Aborigines, the indigenous people who were Australia's first inhabitants. Sometimes the class composed an e-mail together during writer's workshop, with the teacher using a computer to project the message on a large-screen monitor. They shared information about themselves and asked pertinent questions of their e-pals. At other times each child was to compose an independent message to be sent on. The result was a give-and-take composite of information about two separate communities very far away from each other. The information was examined for similarities and differences, resulting in the two groups' agreeing that they had more in common than differences.

Another project at the same school involved a class of third graders who e-mailed a class in Costa Rica. Because of the language barrier, teachers at both ends had to translate the exchanges, so they decided to keep things simple. The U.S. students were interested in learning whether students in the Costa Rican classroom had seen any of our summer resident birds migrating through Costa Rica to and from the United States to their winter homes in the tropics. The students drew pictures of birds that were known to fly through Costa Rica, scanned them, and sent them on with extra information describing each bird's distinctive features, maps where the bird is found here, and facts about the bird's habitat. The students then reported on whether the bird had been sighted. Although only one bird was (possibly) seen in Costa Rica (a Baltimore oriole) the Costa Rican students sent back pictures of some of their native birds.

Science connections that can be made through e-mail are:

1. Networking among students.
   - Sharing information about location, climate, and environment.
   - Sharing information about native plants and animals.
   - Class surveys
     - Things we do in school.
     - Things we do at home.
   - Descriptions of class science activities and new information learned.
   - Descriptions of field trips and new information learned.
2. Networking with scientists.
3. Charts, graphs, and drawings.

CLASSROOMS THAT WORK

The National Science Teachers Position Statement on the Use of Computers in Science Education makes a strong assertion that there are certain basic requirements for all classrooms:

> Every science classroom must have a minimum of one dedicated microcomputer or laptop computer, modem and dedicated phone line, one large screen display (or LCD for overhead projector), and one printer. In addition, each classroom must have appropriate computer based laboratory sensing devices and a science software library. In addition, a well equipped science classroom should have sufficient computers available for simultaneous use by groups of three or four students and the school should have a facility where students can individually use computers for producing reports, analyzing data, practicing skills, etc.

In many schools sets of wireless laptop computers are available for classroom use. This kind of 1-to-1 computing, in which every student has a computing device, is increasing because of its evolving educational value, the usefulness of new software products, and increasing affordability.

Handheld devices (HDs) are also being used with more regularity, often for scientific activities. Though they have been available to scientists for some time, they are being better refined for classroom use, with assorted software to motivate and enhance learning. Probeware, designed to be used with HDs, allows students to engage in active collecting and analyzing data. The prices of HDs have been lowered, and the software is becoming increasingly user-friendly, with many of the attributes teachers are seeking. These and other emerging advances will enable students to learn computer basics from first grade. However, many elementary classrooms have yet to have one functioning computer.

It is a pleasure to view classrooms that are up to par. Not only does Jim Tingey's technology-enriched fourth-grade classroom have several computers for word processing and connecting to the Internet, presentation software, a scanner, and a printer, but he also has access to a class set of digital cameras. His expertise and the ideal equipment available allow students many opportunities to make efficient use of computers in meaningful ways to support his district science curriculum. Whenever one visits his room, something that coordinates with a unit of study is usually visible on several computer screens in the class computer station. Because Jim has mastered the use of a variety of programs that work well with his projects and assignments, he is eager to share the excellent products completed by his class.

Students are comfortable using the computer because Jim is willing to give them extra help whenever he can. During the day they are either assigned to partner or independent projects or may use the computer as a choice when other work is completed.

Jim is competent in using the computer for differentiation, with a variety of materials and websites available for students functioning at various levels of technological skill, who have diverse learning needs and differing reading abilities. He gives a struggling student the important job of accessing a weather site for daily local weather information. The student takes great pride in this responsibility. With this assignment, Jim is working with his student to advance his computer skills as well as his reading and writing.

There are a wide variety of choice CD-ROMs available in class for students to view, explore, and use for taking notes and information gathering. Jim also posts multiple websites that have been critiqued prior to their use to ensure that there are a variety of references to investigate. Jim has added science-related nonfiction book selections that have web links and CD-ROMs that accompany them.

Digital cameras are also available for student use. Students can take photos of field trips, guest speakers, and science projects and experiments, which will be assembled into slide shows using the classroom computers. These can be transmitted to other classrooms or sent to home computers.

Jim and his class create newsletters that are sent home electronically each week. Each newsletter has two or three links to assist parents in helping their children with homework or to access student-generated projects and slide shows.

Extraterrestrial Life

Susan Dennison's thoughtfully developed use of classroom computers is enhancing her fourth-grade lessons and her students' performance. Throughout the year, Susan uses computers for the application of skills gleaned from mini-lessons during writer's workshop.

For example, during a yearly Astronomy Unit, Susan encourages the students to read about the possibility of life on other planets, an intriguing subject for most students. As they learn about the various methods scientists are using to detect such life, by consulting nonfiction books, CD-ROMs, and websites (such as the NASA website: kids.msfc.nasa.gov), they are encouraged to take notes on index cards. There are a variety of resources for the students, because students need to learn that there is not one resource that will give all the answers. This also allows the students to compare facts and check for accuracy. They are expected to record sources of information on the index cards as well. For example, a card might read: Book: *Is Anybody Out There?* by Heather Couper and Nigel Henbest, p. 25 along with the information. These cards are color-coded according to the following categories:

> Astrobiologists' Findings (astrobiologists are biologists who believe there is life in outer space and are studying places on Earth that have unusual life forms, such as deserts, the deep ocean, and Antarctic ice)

> Exobiology (the study of life found outside our Earth by exobiologists)

> History of Space Travel

> History of Search for Extraterrestrial Life

> Methods of Searching for Extraterrestrial Life Today

> The Search for Life in our Solar System

> The Search for Life on Mars

> Newly Discovered Planets

After the students gather and share information, they are asked to complete a paragraph on one of the subtopics. Susan goes over a rubric containing many of the skills that have been the focus in prior writers' workshop lessons.

Another assignment is a science fiction piece using a combination of the subjects listed earlier. Writers' workshop mini-lessons are devoted to science fiction. Before starting this exercise, Susan explains that good science fiction includes much factual information as well as possibilities that have not yet occurred, but may in the future. Because the students have read excerpts of science fiction from work such as *Out of This World: Ethan Flask and Professor Von Offel Take Off on Space Science* by Kathy Burkett and *Freddy and the Men from Mars* by Walter R. Brooks, they have experienced the science fiction genre. They have also seen movies like *E.T. The Extra-Terrestrial* and *Star Wars*, which help build enthusiasm for writing their own pieces.

One of the students wrote the following communiqué, a News Flash designed for television transmission:

> News Flash! NASA has discovered an alien town on Mars! The aliens have developed such technology that it has been undetectable by any object before this. That is why NASA's Hubble Telescope couldn't see it. With heat sensors, Mars rovers, Opportunity and Spirit, were able to detect the town and send back computerized pictures! It is remarkable. No one on Earth has ever seen such advanced technology! NASA's scientists are astonished at the discovery!

It is obvious that this student had been following the news when the Mars Rovers, *Opportunity* and *Spirit*, were transmitting information from Mars in 2004. Susan had wisely capitalized on the excitement surrounding the Mars project and used it as an opportunity to enliven the study of extraterrestrials.

One way that teachers can help students compose a classroom piece in a new genre is to begin developing one together with the whole class or small groups by generating ideas and jointly making decisions about which ideas will work. To do this takes a great deal of skill in eliciting ideas and in the use of questioning to help guide students' thinking and creativity. The piece can be written with the teacher using word processing and projecting it on a screen so that all can view it easily. Students continue to offer ideas and make suggestions for sentences and vocabulary choices. Next, they carefully evaluate the work together to make revisions. They can then take turns using the computer to correctly place punctuation. After the group piece is initiated, some students may choose to finish it independently, and others may want to generate their own ideas and start from scratch.

Whales

During the class study of marine biology, Susan Dennison's students enjoy using CD-ROMs, the Internet, and other sources to research several species of whales. A list of whale species is generated, and pertinent categories for research are listed. Color-coded index cards to coordinate with these categories are used in fact-finding. The students can then retrieve information to use in written work. They write five-paragraph essays using the note cards.

The culminating activity for the unit is the creation of large scale drawings of several species of whales. The students compare information on the sizes of the whales derived from their research, decide which information to use for each species (information sometimes differs), and make their scale drawings, progressing from smaller to larger ones until they reach a reasonable size. The whale drawings are then painted in realistic colors and hung along the hall outside the classroom.

Prairie

It would be advantageous if every school had a class set of digital cameras. Teachers at one school have created effective presentations using their flourishing school prairie garden. Students use the school set of digital cameras to record a variety of species. Using several resources, including the Internet, they research facts about the plants' characteristics, growing conditions, bloom times, and other interesting facts. Here are a few of the resulting projects:

➤ Each student adopts a prairie plant in the spring. Students take pictures of other students standing by their plants in the spring and again in the fall, when the plants will have reached full growth; some plants are eventually several feet taller than the students.

➤ Students identify prairie plants, snap pictures of them, and research the Native American and pioneer uses of the plants. These projects can be made into a slide show or virtual museum on the school website.

➤ Students take pictures of flowering plants in the prairie. They then recreate the plant in the classroom using a host of materials, making certain that they have included important plant parts that have been studied in class: pistil, stamen, leaves, and so forth. The recreations are recorded, and the two pictures are transferred into written reports. Some are placed on class websites.

Other projects inspired by the school prairie garden include posting pictures of the plants students have sketched, along with original student poetry. Research on the history and location of prairies, animal inhabitants, endangered status, and restoration projects is also posted as the students learn more about this lovely outdoor resource.

DIFFERENTIATING MADE EASIER

Teachers who strive to help all students grow as much as possible during the school year begin where students are and build learning experiences on their needs and interests. Computers are helpful in achieving this goal, because students can work at their own levels, independently or in groups, with the aid of the Internet, CD-ROMs, and a variety of programs. When computers were first introduced in schools, it was common for advanced students to use them as a means of accelerating their learning. Today computers provide many opportunities to make the most of the talents of all learners by offering a variety of options, ensuring that students for whom English is a second language, students who are struggling, those with different levels of background experience, and students needing a greater challenge are able to maximize their learning experiences.

Electronic programs with built-in educational scaffolds have been developed for students with cognitive, physical, or visual disabilities who otherwise would not be fully active class participants. The Center for Applied Special Technology (CAST) is a not-for-profit research and development organization working to create educational opportunities for all students, targeting especially those with disabilities. It is creating technology that will make learning more flexible and accessible.

CAST provides a list of excellent recommended products for educators, including *CAST eReader*, which adds spoken voice, visual highlighting, and document or page navigation to any electronic text, including the Internet, word processing files, and scanned or typed-in text. Another is *KidBook Maker*, allowing teachers and parents to create electronic books by importing or scanning in text and graphics, among other capabilities. *KidBook Player* gives children access to these electronic books and provides them with educational supports such as synthetic voices, including English and Spanish, highlighting of text, bookmark capability, and automatic or user-controlled reading. *WiggleWork* software contains a literacy series for students in kindergarten through second grade. It allows students to read, write, speak, and record themselves reading. The students can create and print books using the software. Audiocassettes and lesson plans are included.

Programs are also available that speak the words that students type in (text to speech) for students with impaired vision and very young students. These programs are also helpful for students who need to hear what they've written to discern errors like a missing -*ed* or -*ing*, grammatical mistakes, and missing words. Hearing the words helps them focus on the meaning they are trying to convey and on the flow of the writing. *Write: Out Loud* is one such program.

The use of a computer for English language learners has distinct advantages over more traditional approaches. Programs with audio components that accompany the visuals can be valuable tools in assisting these students. In many programs a built-in ability to make decisions to repeat questions, exercises, and sequences, based on the students' own progress gives them a feeling of control over their learning.

CREATING EDUCATIONAL MATERIALS

Ideas abound on websites for whole units and individual lessons. Teachers are accessing these regularly to create teaching materials that will enliven their classroom programs. In this chapter we have described unique computer programs that can be purchased to enhance and increase learning. Computers also make it significantly easier to design materials to guide and assess student learning.

Creating product descriptors for students using a spreadsheet that presents specific expectations for student work will help both the student and the teacher.

By listing necessary components of the final project or product to be evaluated, product descriptors can effectively coordinate with assessment rubrics and provide a common language for discussion with students during and after the completion of the project. Product descriptors may also itemize the point value that will be assigned to each component for the final score or grade. In awarding points, much thought has to be given to which features of the final product will get the most weight. Having an attractive, beautifully designed product is an advantage, but the appearance should not outweigh accuracy of information and evidence of depth and understanding.

Teachers make informal judgments about student work every day, based on what is expected of the students. Creating rubrics is a great help in assessing student work. Examples of how teachers are using rubrics with their electronic research reports are provided in Chapter 9.

VIDEOTAPES, DVDs, AND AUDIO TECHNOLOGIES

Because it is common knowledge that children are spending too much time passively watching television, if videos or DVDs (digital video discs) are used in the classroom, they must offer clear educational benefits and accurate content. They should engage the students, answer their questions, and stimulate new ones.

There is a current trend toward using more DVDs with far superior video capability, instead of CD-ROMs. Video projectors in the classroom are not used as often as might be expected, probably because of the effort and time required for teachers to record from television and the expense involved in purchasing videotapes (Tiene & Luft, 2002).

When using informational films or DVDs, optimal results can be achieved if students generate questions about what they want to learn before they view a film. Setting purposes can give focus as students look for answers during a viewing. It is a good idea for students to view a video or DVD once without writing anything down, so they don't miss important information. After the initial viewing, there can be a discussion and new questions can be developed. Students can take notes during a repeat viewing. It is helpful to build in some accountability for learning when using these resources.

Jim Tingey has a Library Service in his classroom. It is his classroom system to allow students to check out videos, as well as books, from his vast collection of many years. Every book and video Jim owns can be checked out. Each item has a library identification tag that is color-coded according to genre. It also has a pocket with a card. When an item is checked out, the student signs the card and puts it in a file box designated for that purpose. When the item is returned, the card is put back in the box. Jim also has a file for reviews written by the students. He has never had a problem with this system, because the students have developed a strong sense of responsibility for their classroom, how it functions, and all the materials in it.

Audio versions of books have advantages because they can be played over and over if needed. In addition, sound effects are often included, different voices may be used for different characters, or the author may be the one who has recorded the book. These features are helpful for students with visual impairments at a Listening Center. Audio books can also be helpful for students who need to hear the text as they see words in a book. There are many types of books that can enrich science units, informational books, and selections of related fiction.

CONCLUSION

More and more, science literacy will include the use of computers and other high-tech devices to enhance learning. Students will need to be able to access information from a multitude of sophisticated resources, construct multimedia reports, and disseminate them. To learn and communicate in these ways students will continue to require traditional skills: to read with understanding, to communicate in writing, and to think with clarity. They will also need a specialized, high level of literacy, and they will need to think with flexibility to discern, evaluate, and make decisions concerning data on a particular topic.

We must remember that learning science means that students must engage in activity-oriented, hands-on science as their first mode of instruction whenever possible. Technology should not take the place of real classroom science. But it is helpful in exploring concepts and models not readily accessible in a lab or classroom, such as those that require expensive or unavailable materials or equipment, hazardous materials or procedures, levels of skills students aren't ready for, or more time than is realistic in the classroom. It is important to know when and where to best utilize technology and that it is not necessarily the most appropriate learning tool for every student every time. However, teachers need to make sure that all students have fair access to the available computers.

CHAPTER 9

ASSESSMENT

One of the biggest issues affecting all teachers today is how to assess student learning in ways that are authentic and provide data for multiple purposes. Most important is the use of assessment to guide instruction. Teachers need to know what skills students bring to learning science: skills in engaging in scientific inquiry, skills in collecting and reporting data, skills in reading and writing informational materials and reports. They also need to know what knowledge and scientific concepts students possess so they can plan appropriately and meet the needs of their particular classes.

One of the most difficult aspects of science teaching is confronting and altering the many misconceptions of students about scientific phenomena (Roth et al., 1987). Topics in science vary considerably, so it is important that teachers assess the specific prior knowledge and attitudes of students before beginning each area of study. Teachers must also assess the specific learning tools students possess, inasmuch as the needs vary with the different types of inquiry and learning (from hands-on activities to text-based research). Then, during instructional activities within units of study, teachers need to watch and listen as students are engaged in the activities so they can adjust their focus and time to ensure that students are successful in learning. This ongoing formative assessment is perhaps the most valuable to teachers so they can ensure that time is spent well in the classroom. Finally, teachers and students need to assess their accomplishments at the conclusion of units of study or projects and learn from their experiences.

Assessment must become part of students' approach to their own learning. Some research in science classrooms has indicated that students learn better when they take an active part in their own assessment (White & Frederiksen, 1998). In the field of literacy there has been an ongoing line of research on students' meta-cognitive involvement in their own learning and its impact on their learning. Janet Coffee (2003) explains, "To become a self-directed, lifelong learner, an aim set forth in the National Science Education Standards [National Research Council, 1996], the ability to self-assess becomes essential" (p. 78).

It is also important that assessments are used that can be understood by parents, administrators, and the public. Classroom instructional-based assessments often form the basis of communication with parents about the curriculum and their own children's development. When parents are apprised of what is being studied, and are even invited periodically to participate in the forms of inquiry used, they can become valuable allies in raising the level of engagement of their children. For example, parents are often involved in aspects of science and can share their experiences in the classroom. One family got so involved in studying the problem of the mutation of frogs when their daughter's class was engaged in this inquiry, that they began using their Saturdays to visit a local bog and record what they found. Their journal became part of the class culminating report. Schools that have students keep portfolios of their work have found that sharing them during parent–student–teacher conferences creates a stimulating context for discussing and assessing what the students have achieved. The evidence is concrete and real. This kind of assessment is generally more meaningful to parents than the sampling of knowledge on standardized multiple-choice tests.

Assessments of this performance type combine evidence of learning in both science and literacy. Student journals, research notes, records of what they have read, and the culminating projects or reports provide evidence of literacy in action. When teachers have focused on the skills of writing and careful reading of informational texts, the work in science can be valid evidence of students' learning. Primary teachers who use science units for guided reading activities also have records of students' growth in reading informational books.

The good news is that by combining literacy and science objectives, the assessment process can be much clearer. Students' written pieces can provide a clear indication of science learning. Ongoing records of what students read and the notes they take provide data that indicate the process of building knowledge. In this chapter we provide several examples of how students' ongoing work can be used to assess their learning. The focus is on what can be done in the classroom to enhance teachers' abilities to understand what supports students need to be effective learners, what evidences of their learning can be collected during units of instruction, and how teachers and students can assess the achievement of their learning objectives at the ends of units. We ground these suggestions in the research and some current projects that have integrated literacy and science learning.

NATIONAL SCIENCE TEACHERS ASSOCIATION GUIDELINES FOR ASSESSMENT

The NSTA guidelines for assessment (2001) provide a thorough overview of the various purposes for and types of assessments and relates those to the different audiences for assessment, such as classroom teachers, policymakers, and governmental bodies.

For teachers, the assessments can be helpful in planning teaching, guiding learning, calculating grades, and making comparisons. Various types of assessments are suggested, ranging from paper-and-pencil tests to performance testing, interviews, and portfolios that teachers use in their ongoing instructional routines.

NSTA also links assessments to the major standards students should achieve. For our purposes it seems useful to focus on the Inquiry Standard, as it provides a good example of how valuable writing and reading are in the most basic of scientific activities. According to the basic standard, students need to be engaged in science as inquiry. That means they are able to:

➢ Understand the inquiry process.

➢ Ask questions, to plan and conduct investigations.

➢ Observe and measure.

➢ Use data to explain phenomena.

➢ Check explanations against knowledge.

➢ Communicate the results of their investigations and explanations in spoken, drawn, and written forms.

ASSESSING STUDENTS' ENGAGEMENT IN INQUIRY

Teachers involve students in inquiry both when they are engaged in observing natural phenomena and behaviors of insects and animals (*activity-based learning*) and when they do explorations, using books and other resource materials, in extended units of study (*reference-based learning*). In many cases a combination of both kinds of learning are part of a unit of study. Therefore, the kinds of assessments that can be collected will vary somewhat, depending on the experiences the students have had. Figure 9.1 lays out some of the parts of the inquiry process on which teachers should be collecting data to ensure that students are able to proceed in a "scientific" way in their inquiries. Add the types of activities you use in your classroom to this list so you will have a record to remind you of the kinds of evidence you can collect from your students, both within a unit and across time, to see the improvement in students' skills throughout the year.

STUDENT SELF-ASSESSMENT

Student self-assessment is also critical to inquiry. Therefore, every opportunity to include students in reflecting on their processes of learning and their findings is important. An easy way to include such participation is to have students keep responses to questions like the following in their learning logs, either daily or periodically:

Inquiry processes	Activity based	Reference based	Teacher modeling and criteria
Ask questions.	• KWL chart • Class discussions • Observation of small-group work • Question board • Exit slips	• KWL chart • I-Chart • Guided reading • Group exchanges • Exit slips	• Ask pertinent and essential questions. • Use "fat," not "skinny" questions. • Chunk similar questions together.
Observe/collect data.	• Journal • Diary • Class charts of events	• Amazing Fact Sheets • Notes/note cards • Journals • Diagrams and graphic organizers • Photocopied information and Internet pieces	• Use a chart that fits data needs. • Record accurately—date, time, and data. • Double-check for accuracy. • Ensure neatness and legibility.
Draw conclusions.	• Journals • KWL chart • Discussion with students • Interviews • Reports • Letters home • News articles	• KWL chart • Reports • Letters home • News articles	• Use pertinent evidence. • Rule out alternatives with evidence. • Check against what seems plausible. • Check against authorities if necessary.
Check conclusions against other authorities.	• Verification of conclusions with list of authoritative sources and text-based information • Creation of a bibliography • Interviews of students	• I-Charts • Multiple sources used in research • Observation of students • Student self-assessment	• Confirm with more than one source. • Use current publications. • Consult authority in the field.
Communicate results in spoken, drawn, and written form.	• Oral report—individual or group • Written report or research project • News article • Diagram or drawing • Presentation with PowerPoint or other technology	• Oral report—individual or group • Written report or research project • News article • Diagram or drawing • Presentation with PowerPoint or other technology	• Summarize information clearly. • Provide specifics from research. • Use good illustrations or diagrams that clarify. • Be well organized. • Use precise vocabulary. • Edit work for accuracy and neatness.

FIGURE 9.1. Assessment matrix.

"What did I learn today?"
"What questions do I now have?"
"What bothers me that doesn't make sense?"
"What seems most intriguing?"
"How can I use this information outside class?"

From kindergarten on, children can be engaged in reflecting on their own learning. Debbie Gurvitz's kindergartners and first graders learn to engage in reflection through her guidance and regular provision of reflective activities. She begins each year using reflection sheets like that shown in Figure 9.2. The teacher helps the students reflect on what they have done during the week and writes a dictated language experience story from what the students contribute. Then, at the bottom of the news story, each child writes what he or she liked, both within the classroom

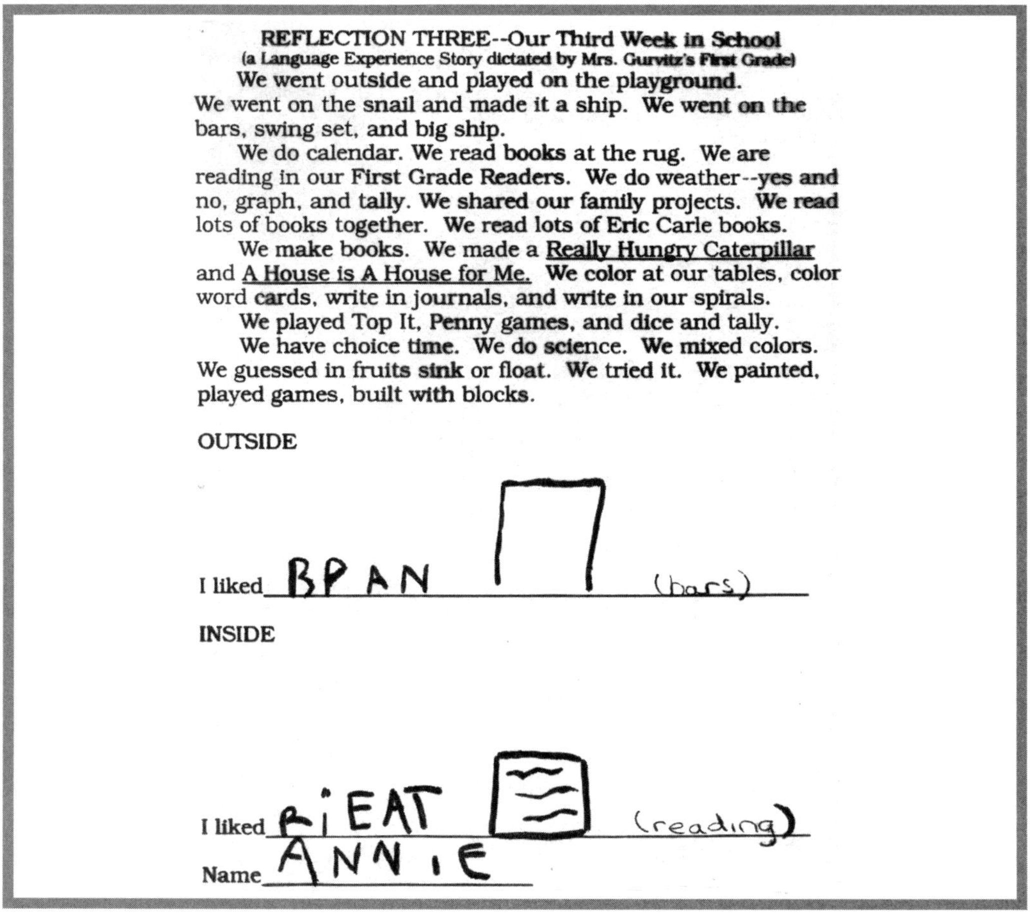

REFLECTION THREE--Our Third Week in School
(a Language Experience Story dictated by Mrs. Gurvitz's First Grade)
We went outside and played on the playground.
We went on the snail and made it a ship. We went on the bars, swing set, and big ship.
We do calendar. We read books at the rug. We are reading in our First Grade Readers. We do weather--yes and no, graph, and tally. We shared our family projects. We read lots of books together. We read lots of Eric Carle books.
We make books. We made a Really Hungry Caterpillar and A House is A House for Me. We color at our tables, color word cards, write in journals, and write in our spirals.
We played Top It, Penny games, and dice and tally.
We have choice time. We do science. We mixed colors. We guessed in fruits sink or float. We tried it. We painted, played games, built with blocks.

OUTSIDE

I liked BP A N _____ (bars)

INSIDE

I liked Pi EAT _____ (reading)
Name ANNIE

FIGURE 9.2. First-grade class reflection and individual student reflection.

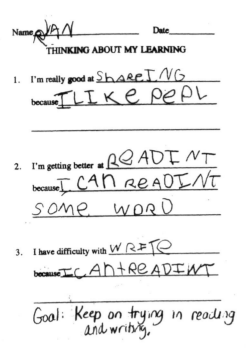

Name __VAN__   Date_____

THINKING ABOUT MY LEARNING

1. I'm really good at __ShAReING__

    because__I LIKe PePL__

    _____

2. I'm getting better at __ReADINT__

    because__I CAN ReADINT__

    __SOMe WORD__

3. I have difficulty with __WRFTe__

    because__I CANt ReADINT__

    _____

Goal: Keep on trying in reading and writing.

FIGURE 9.3. First-grade individual reflection.

and outside. The child adding to the story in Figure 9.2 liked the bars on the playground and liked reading as an inside activity. Although this is a basic kind of reflection, it certainly helps children begin a life-long process of reflection and self-assessment. It also helps children to get in the habit of thinking back on their learning experiences and keeping records of all they do and learn. Figure 9.3 shows an extension of this self-reflection habit that Debbie uses later in the year. Students identify what they are good at, what they are getting better at, and what they have difficulty with. Then each student sets a goal for the next period of time, which is agreed upon and recorded by the student and the teacher.

Debbie also involves parents in the units she teaches. As children build their lists of what they know about the topics under study (using the KWL framework), she helps them identify questions for inquiry. She writes these questions on the chalkboard and then transfers them to large sentence strips. At just the right point she asks each child to select one question he or she wants to research personally. She then puts that question on a "Home Link," a communication sent to each student's home, which has a guide for parents on how to help the child complete the research and bring the findings back to class (see Figure 9.4). As the kindergarten children return with their information, Debbie puts the question-and-answer portion of their sheets on the bulletin board and the class builds its knowledge base (Figure 9.5). At the conclusion of each unit Debbie reviews the work the children have done, and together they assess their accomplishments. Oral summaries of accomplishments can be very powerful as students' discuss the questions they had initially and how much they have learned.

As students engage in research, a major part of the process can be the self-reflection that comes with their description of the process. When teachers and students have developed a rubric for evaluation *before* the projects are begun, the assessment process is much easier. Rubrics also help students to have confidence that what they create meets a class expectation, and the guessing game of how to get a good grade is eliminated. We have seen the power of students sharing in the assessment of their own work.

Individual projects developed with rubrics or clear guidelines provide good evidence of students' learning. So, too, longer-term portfolios make learning concrete and visible to students, teachers, and parents. Each entry in a portfolio should include an explanation of why it is included, what aspect of the student's work it exemplifies, how the piece was completed, and what was learned from the process. Then students can evaluate their own products or their final accomplishments as part of the portfolio process. Because most preservice teachers are now being trained to use portfolios in their own learning, the use of portfolios becomes increasingly evident in classrooms and schools. When the use of portfolios was initially introduced, many teachers had a hard time balancing the time it takes for

---

January

Dear Parents,

The kindergarten children have been studying animals. As part of our animal study, the children have completed the first two steps of our KWL.

First, we listed all the facts that we *KNOW* about animals and individually illustrated one fact.

Second, we listed all of the things that we *WANT* to learn about animals.

Now, we plan to complete our KWL. Your child has chosen one question to answer. Please follow the directions below and complete the assignment with your child.

DIRECTIONS FOR KWL	Question:

1. Discuss the question.
2. Discuss with your child ways in which you could complete your research.
3. Research *together*.
4. Once you find the answer, discuss your answer *together*.
5. Have your child retell the answer in his/her own words.
6. Print your child's response, or if your child prefers he/she may "write" his/her response.
7. Have your child illustrate his/her answer.
8. Return it to school at your earlier convenience. (preferably by Feb. 8th)
 	
          Thank you.
 	
  The Kindergarten Teachers
	I *LEARNED* that:
	
	Name _____

FIGURE 9.4. Home Link.

FIGURE 9.5. Bulletin board contributions from Home Link.

students to assemble their own portfolios and make them attractive, with their value in instruction. More recently we have seen schools streamlining this process as teachers and students become more familiar with what is valuable to collect. The growth in students' ability to engage in reflecting on themselves as learners and see the changes in their observation skills, their reporting of data, the questions they ask, and the kinds of summary papers and reports they create, makes the portfolio process worthwhile.

Primary teachers help students develop this metacognitive or self-reflective stance when they involve students regularly in group and individual reflection. See the example of one student's self-reflection in Figure 9.6. As they were learning

Name: _James_

Name of group: _Types_

Topic I am researching: _Bullfrogs_

_____

The 5 interesting facts I have found out:

1.) _The Bullfrog is the largest frog in north America._

2.) _It takes up to 5 years to become an adult._

3.) _The bullfrog does not like to stalk its prey._

4.) _frogs can be camouflag._

5.) _____

My project might be: _____

FIGURE 9.6. A student's ongoing reflection on learning.

about frogs, the students kept adding to their statements about what they were learning. Their new questions helped shape the direction of the unit.

In a third-grade class, each week the teacher asks students to reflect on their participation and learning. The parents receive these logs and respond. This system keeps a regular communication about learning ongoing in the school. See Figure 9.7 for an example of one exchange.

As sixth-grade students developed their projects on insects, two different teachers involved students in particular forms of self-assessment. The first asked students to put evidence of their learning into their quarterly portfolios. Each step of their research process was to be illustrated and a statement included about how

Weekly Learning Summary

Week_____   Your name:_____

Write about something you enjoyed reading this week: I loved reading Amelia Bedelia!	What reading strategies did you practice this week: We practiced Visualising. I drew ideas from my head.
How did you do in practicing your listening skills this week: I got a little better. I looked right at the speakers.	Explain how you are doing in math: Math subraction was hard.
How is your science team working and what are you learning about frogs: We are still trying to find out why frogs are born deformed.	Parent Response: We enjoy sharing these reflections & are proud of Lesley's work. We all looked for frogs by the lake over the weekend.

FIGURE 9.7. Third-grade home–school reflection.

the student felt about his or her learning and process. The drafts of the report were included in the portfolio with comments from the student. When the final report was shown, the parents, teachers, and other students could clearly see how the student had proceeded with his or her learning.

One of the other teachers decided to use a KWL as a framework for a unit on insects (Ogle, 1994). She had the students begin by listing in their own journals what they thought they knew about insects. This activity was followed by asking them to predict what the table of contents of a book on insects would look like, inasmuch as they would be using several (Figure 9.8). Then the teacher had the students create semantic webs of what they knew. With this information in their notebooks, the students proceeded through the experiences of learning about insects. At the end of the unit each student developed his or her own report on one insect. Finally, the teacher had the students return to the basic questions: What do you know, what is a good table of contents for a book on insects, and how can you organize your knowledge on a semantic map (Figure 9.9). She added questions to help them engage in self-evaluation:

➢ Has your opinion of insects changed from the beginning of this unit to the end? Explain.

➢ When you compare the table of contents you created at the beginning of the unit with the one you created at the end, what do you notice?

➢ How does your knowledge about insects compare with what you knew at the beginning? Be specific.

➢ How does your organization of knowledge into a web reflect your learning? Explain.

By having visible records of what they thought they knew at the beginning of the unit, the students were able, without any prodding, to do some data-based self-evaluation (see Figure 9.10).

In all of these examples the development of students' self-assessment is first modeled and guided by teachers, who make the conditions for good inquiry clear. Setting standards for work is important because elementary school children are clearly novice learners. They need a language to use when describing their own efforts. Rubrics have become a popular means of giving students an indication of what constitutes quality work. When teachers make samples of good student work from previous years available to students, they can build an image of what students at their level are capable of doing. Students often hold erroneous images of what teachers expect and then are disappointed in their grades. If teachers spend more time defining expectations at the outset and students can see samples, the students can feel freer to proceed and focus on their learning.

Some teachers find it useful to make a list of the habits of good scientists. Learning terms like *effort*, *persistent*, *flexible*, *adjusting*, *creative*, *visioning and*

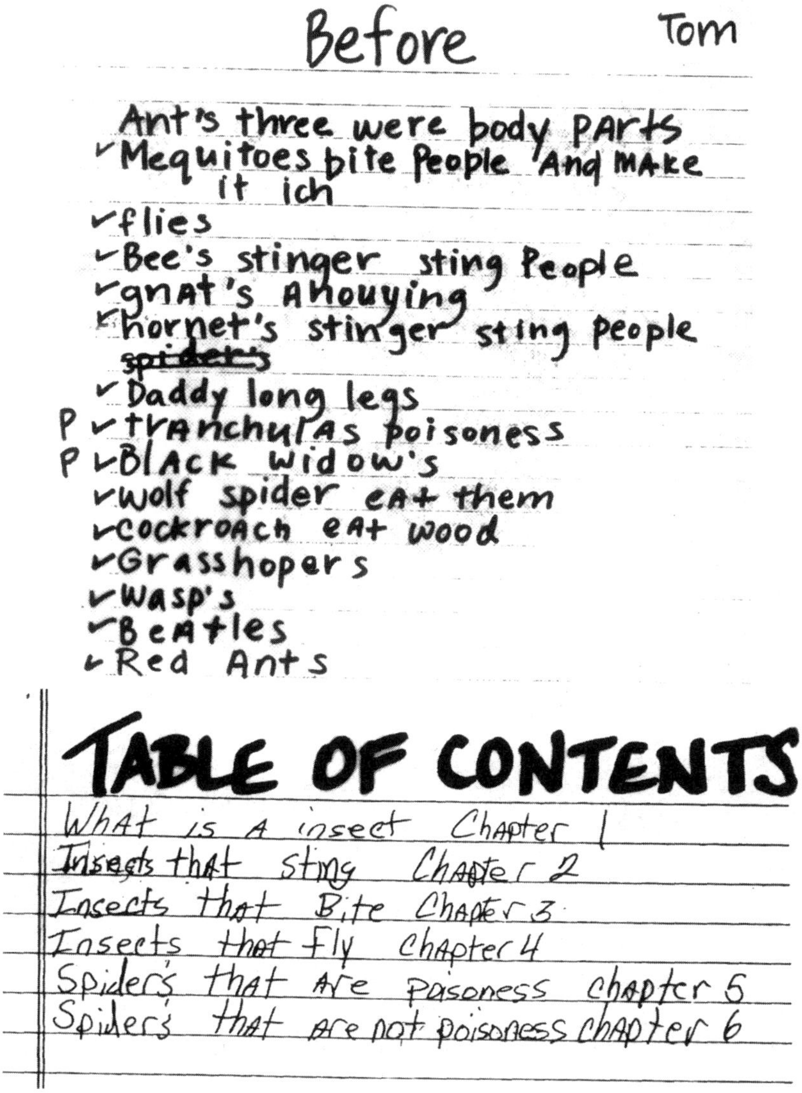

Before   Tom

Ant's three were body PARts
Mequitoes bite People And MAke
        it ich
flies
Bee's stinger sting People
gnat's Ahouying
hornet's stinger sting people
~~spiders~~
Daddy long legs
P tranchulas poisoness
P BlAck widow's
wolf spider eAt them
cockroach eAt wood
Grasshopers
wasp's
BeAtles
Red Ants

TABLE OF CONTENTS

What is A insect Chapter 1
Insects that sting Chapter 2
Insects that Bite Chapter 3
Insects that fly Chapter 4
Spider's that Are pasoness chapter 5
Spider's that Are not poisoness chapter 6

FIGURE 9.8. A sixth-grade student's self-assessment for Insect Unit.

sketching, asking good questions, careful observing, double-checking to prevent mistakes, testing hypotheses, using data correctly, conferring with my partner, making a rough draft/sloppy copy before creating the final product, being neat, cleaning up after my work, and so forth, can help students develop an understanding of what good scientific effort entails. The list varies by grade level, of course, but its use can help in developing a language to describe scientific processes over the elementary years. Hearing students describe their own work using these terms provides evidence of the value of the effort.

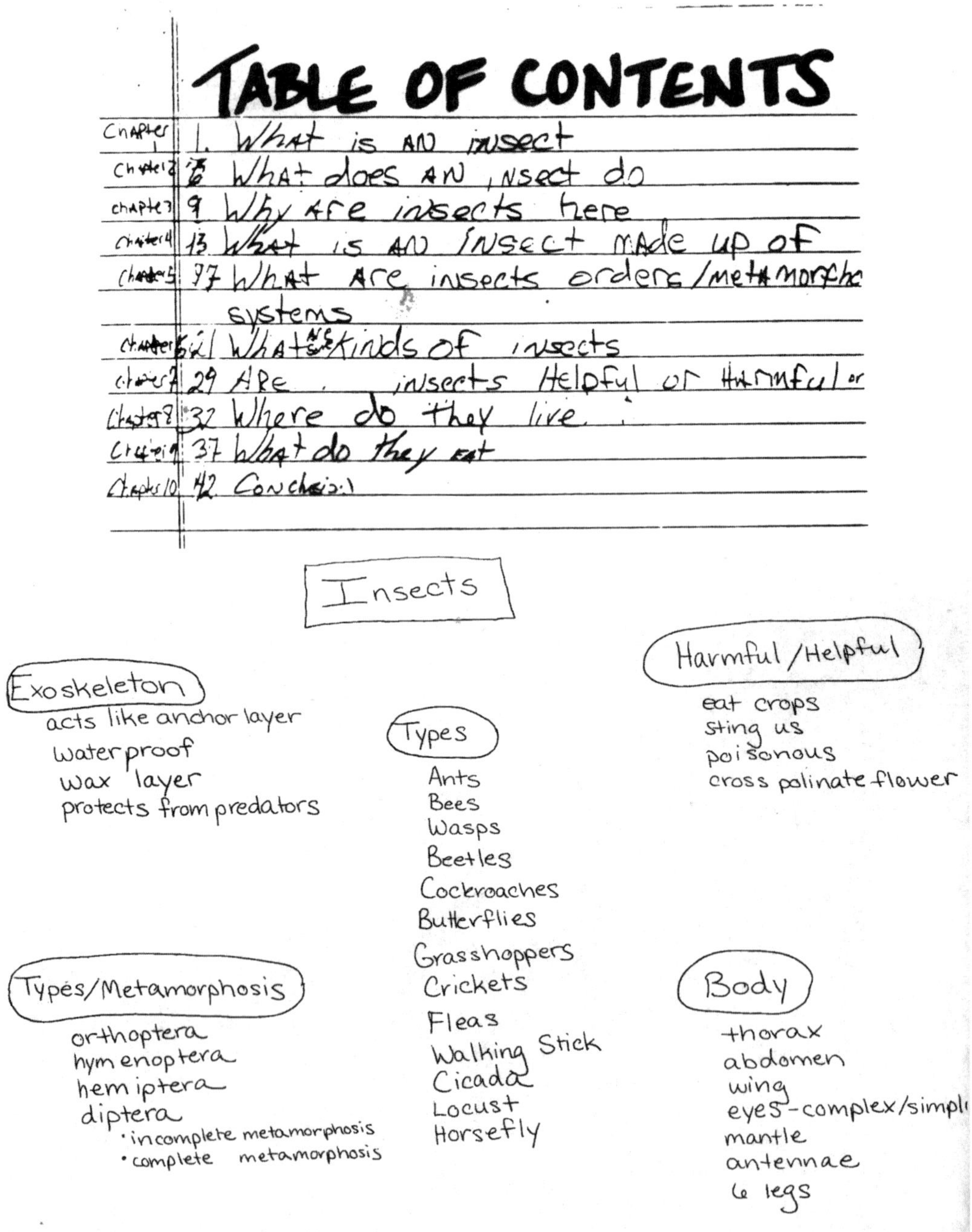

TABLE OF CONTENTS

Chapter 1. What is an insect

Chapter 2. 6 What does an insect do

chapter 3. 9 Why are insects here

chapter 4. 13 What is an insect made up of

chapter 5. 17 What are insects orders/metamorpho systems

chapter 6. 21 What kinds of insects

chapter 7. 29 Are insects Helpful or Harmful or

chapter 8. 32 Where do they live.

chapter 9. 37 What do they eat

chapter 10. 42 Conclusion

Insects

Exoskeleton
acts like anchor layer
waterproof
wax layer
protects from predators

Types
Ants
Bees
Wasps
Beetles
Cockroaches
Butterflies
Grasshoppers
Crickets
Fleas
Walking Stick
Cicada
Locust
Horsefly

Harmful/Helpful
eat crops
sting us
poisonous
cross polinate flower

Types/Metamorphosis
orthoptera
hymenoptera
hemiptera
diptera
· incomplete metamorphosis
· complete metamorphosis

Body
thorax
abdomen
wing
eyes—complex/simple
mantle
antennae
6 legs

FIGURE 9.9. A sixth-grade student's self-assessment at the completion of the Insect Unit.

Comparison of Post and Prior Knowledge
Insect Unit

Has your opinion of insects changed from the beginning to the end of the unit? Explain.
I went from liking insects to being neutral because insects can be very harmful, too. At The beginning I Thought That insects were not that bad, but They are.

When you compare the Table of Contents that you created at the beginning of this unit to the one that you created at the end, what did you notice?
WOW! My first one was very skimpy. It even had spiders in there. My other one (the second) is pretty good. It's long and has accurate information.

How does your knowledge about insects at the beginning of the unit relate to the knowledge you have at the end? Be specific.
I learned that spiders aren't insects. I learned what that crunching noise is when you step on an insect — it's The exoskeleton. I learned about how important insects are!

What else did you learn about yourself as a learner?
I learned that it's good to check my ideas to be sure I'm right.

FIGURE 9.10. Student self-evaluation.

RESEARCH REPORTS

By the time students are in fourth grade and beyond, many schools expect them to learn to do some individual research and produce a written report of their findings. The more the teachers can model the process and provide a clearly defined set of steps for the students, the more likely they will be successful. The TREE (Technology Rich Educational Environment) team of teachers in an area school (Pleasant Ridge, Glenview, Illinois) has developed a clear process for the evaluation of the projects students complete. (See Chapter 7 for a description of the process.) Because the requirements for the project are clearly spelled out in a Project Process Guide, students have a clear idea of how to go about their project research and how to create their final projects. The rubrics also include one for presentation that involves parents, teachers, and the students. (See Figure 9.11 for the Presentation Rubric.) Students do reports twice a year based on the district curriculum's science themes. Among the recent reports are "How Electricity Affects People," "How Do Airplanes Fly?", "Why Are Aeronautical Maps Important?", "The Life of a Humpback Whale," "Chimpanzees," "The American Society for the Prevention of Cruelty against Animals," and "Animal Welfare." When the team of teachers recently chose the theme "Cycles and Change," the students' reports included "The Cheese-Making Cycle," "Arthroscopic Surgery," "The Circulatory System," "Change in Eating Habits," and "Human–Plant Interaction." The products students create are now on PowerPoint, and the presentations are fascinating for everyone (see Figure 9.12 for part of the report on arthroscopy). Students now create both a narrative report and a PowerPoint display, having learned how to use both formats in sharing information. With clear rubrics established, students, parents, and teachers can easily assess students' learning and their ability to share findings with others.

CONCLUSION

Assessing students' learning is an essential part of good teaching. Involving students' in their own assessment creates the most powerful kind of learning because it develops in students an understanding of what it means to learn and grow. When parents also know the expectations and can share in the results of students' efforts, they provide important support for their children's developing independence. In this chapter we have included several examples of teachers' attempts to articulate to students what quality work looks like and to involve them in self-evaluation.

Student: _____ Topic: _____

Parent Signature: _____ Fall Winter Spring _____

Advisor: _____ Year

COMPLETES WORK:

___ INDEPENDENTLY   ___ WITH MINIMAL ASSISTANCE   ___ WITH EXTENSIVE ASSISTANCE

	Exceeds Expectations	Meets Expectations	Working Towards Expectations	Needs Work
USES project time effectively at school	4	3	2	1
PRODUCES work of depth and quality	4	3	2	1
MEETS deadlines	4	3	2	1
CURRENT EVENTS/REAL WORLD APPLICATION				
SELECTS at least three news articles	4	3	2	1
INCLUDES articles *currently* in the news	4	3	2	1
SELECTS articles which are relevant to the project topic	4	3	2	1
CHOOSES articles from a reputable news source	4	3	2	1
SUMMARIZES articles concisely and identifies key points	4	3	2	1
SELECTS an appropriate expert	4	3	2	1
GENERATES pertinent questions	4	3	2	1
COMMUNICATES with expert effectively	4	3	2	1
EXPRESSES thanks to expert in writing	4	3	2	1
POWERPOINT				
ENHANCES audience understanding of topic through information included on slides	4	3	2	1
CREATES attractive slides showing concern for color, design, uniformity and layout	4	3	2	1
USES phrases with bullet points	4	3	2	1
MAKES slides clearly legible	4	3	2	1
INCORPORATES effective and relevant graphics	4	3	2	1
PROOFREADS slides and makes necessary corrections and revisions	4	3	2	1

(continued)

FIGURE 9.11. Presentation Rubric from Pleasant Ridge School.

	Exceeds Expectations	Meets Expectations	Working Towards Expectations	Needs Work
DISPLAY				
CREATES an attractive display showing concern for color, design, uniformity and layout	4	3	2	1
DISPLAYS current events and summaries on a poster(s)	4	3	2	1
EXHIBITS Real World Application results on a poster(s)	4	3	2	1
PRESENTATION				
DRESSES and grooms for a good impression	4	3	2	1
HOOKS audience at beginning of presentation	4	3	2	1
DEMONSTRATES poise through posture, eye contact, and facial expression	4	3	2	1
REFERS to notes: looks at audience and does not read computer screen	4	3	2	1
SPEAKS with expression and proper volume	4	3	2	1
EXPLAINS topic clearly and thoroughly	4	3	2	1
INTEGRATES current events and RWA seamlessly into presentation	4	3	2	1
CONCLUDES presentation effectively	4	3	2	1
DELIVERS 10- to 15-minute presentation	4	3	2	1

TOTAL POINTS: _____ GRADE: _____

120–117	A+	107–105	B+	95–93	C+
116–111	A	104–99	B	92–87	C
110–108	A–	98–96	B–	86–84	C–

FIGURE 9.11. (*continued*).

History

- General History
- —Before 1980's arthroscopy was only used for diagnosing problems
- —Now used for diagnosing and fixing problems
- —Arthroscopy considered one of the most significant advances in past century
- —In 1980's, other joints began to be scoped in addition to knee

Advantages of Arthroscopy

- Advantages
- —Arthroscopy uses 3-5 small incisions, each a quarter of an inch long around joint vs. old way of having surgery on a joint was one large incision and open area
- —Patient recuperation time is usually short
- —Patient can usually go home same day

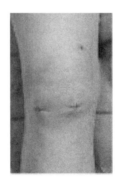

FIGURE 9.12. PowerPoint slides from final report on arthroscopy by a fifth-grade student at Pleasant Ridge School.

REFERENCES

Allington, R. L. (2001). *What really matters for struggling readers: Designing research-based programs*. New York: Addison Wesley.

Allington, R. L., & Johnston, P. H. (2002). *Reading to learn*. New York: Guilford Press.

Alvermann, D. E. (2004). Multiliteracies and self-questioning in the service of science learning. In W. Stahl (Ed.), *Crossing borders in literacy and science instruction* (pp. 226–238). Newark, DE: International Reading Association.

Anderson, C. W. (1987). Teaching science. In V. Koehler (Ed.), *The educators' handbook: A research perspective*. New York: Longman.

Baker, L. (2004). Reading comprehension and science inquiry: Metacognitive connections. In W. Stahl (Ed.), *Crossing borders in literacy and science instruction* (pp. 239–257). Newark, DE: International Reading Association.

Bangert-Downs, R. L. (1993). The word processor as an instructional tool: A meta-analysis of word processing in writing instruction. *Review of Education Research, 63,* 69–93.

Blachowicz, C., & Fisher, P. (2000). Research in vocabulary instruction. In R. Barr, M. L. Kamil, P. B. Mosenthal, & P. D. Pearson (Eds.), *Handbook of reading research* (Vol. 3, pp. 503–524). Mahwah, NJ: Erlbaum.

Blachowicz, C., & Fisher, P. (2002). *Teaching vocabulary in all classrooms* (2nd ed.). Columbus, OH: Merrill-Prentice-Hall.

Blachowicz, C, & Ogle, D. (2001). *Reading comprehension: Strategies for independent learners*. New York: Guilford Press.

Bloom, B. S. (Ed.). (1956). *Taxonomy of educational objectives: The classification of educational goals: Handbook I. Cognitive domain*. New York: Longman.

Buhle, R. (2004, September 16). *Read to Relax Project*. Personal communication.

Casteel, C. P., & Isom, B. A. (1994). Reciprocal processes in science and literacy learning. *The Reading Teacher, 47*(7), 538–544.

Chittenden, E., Salinger, T., & Bussis, A. (2001). *Inquiry into meaning: An investigation of learning to read*. New York: Teachers College Press.

Coffey, J. E. (2003). Involving students in assessment. In J. M. Atkin & J. E. Coffey (Eds.), *Everyday assessment in the science classroom*. Arlington, VA: National Science Teachers Association.

Daiute, C. (1983). *Writing and computers*. Reading, MA: Addison Wesley.

Dickinson, D. K. (1986). Cooperation, collaboration and a computer: Integrating a computer into a first–second grade writing program. *Research in the Teaching of English, 20,* 357–378.

Duke, N. K. (2000). 3.6 minutes per day: The scarcity of informational texts in first grade. *Reading Research Quarterly, 35*(2), 202–224.

Guthrie, J., & Ozgungor, S. (2002). Instructional contexts for reading engagement. In C. C. Block & M. Pressley (Eds.), *Comprehension instruction.* New York: Guilford Press.

Illinois Standards Achievement Test. (2000). Retrieved August 12, 2004, from www.isbe.net/assessment.isat.htm.

Johnson, N., & Giorgis, C. (2001). Children's books: Interacting with the curriculum. *Reading Teacher, 55*(2), 204–213.

Johnson, D. W., & Johnson, R. T. (1999). *Learning together and alone: Cooperative, competitive, and individualistic learning.* Boston: Allyn & Bacon.

Kamil, M. L., Intrator, S. M., & Kim, H. S. (2000). The effects of other technologies on literacy and literacy learning. In R. Barr, M. L. Kamil, P. B. Mosenthal, & P. D. Pearson (Eds.), *Handbook of reading research* (Vol. 3, pp. 771–788). Mahwah, NJ: Erlbaum.

Mayer, D. A. (1995). How can we best use children's literature in teaching science concepts? *Science and Children, 32*(6), 16–19, 43.

McKee, J. (1991). Exploring the tropical rainforest. *Science and Children, 29*(2), 16–29.

McKee, J. (1992). Bat facts and fun. *Science and Children, 30*(2), 26–29.

Moline, S. (1996). *I see what you mean: Children at work with visual information.* Portsmouth, NH: Heinemann.

National Council of Teachers of English and International Reading Association. (1996). *Standards for the English language arts.* Newark, DE: International Reading Association.

National Research Council. (1996). *National Science Education Standards.* Washington, DC: National Academies Press.

National Science Teachers Association. (1999). *Position statement: The use of computers in science education.* Available at www.nsta.org/positionstatement&psid=4.

National Science Teachers Association. (2001). *Position statement: Assessment.* Available at www.nsta.org/positionstatement&psid=40.

Ogle, D. (1986). KWL: A teaching model that develops active reading of expository text. *Reading Teacher, 40*, 564–570.

Ogle, D. (1994). Helping our students see their learning. *Teaching Pre K–8, 25*, 100–101.

Ogle, D. (2000). Make it visual: A picture is worth a thousand words. In M. McLaughlin & M. E. Vogt (Eds.), *Creativity and innovation in content area teaching* (pp. 55–71). Norwood, NJ: Christopher Gordon.

Ogle, D., & McMahon, S. I. (2001). Curriculum integration to promote literate thinking: Dilemmas and possibilities. In J. Flood, D. Lapp, J. Squire, & J. Jensen (Eds.), *Handbook of research on teaching the English language arts* (pp. 1035–1051). New York: Macmillan.

Palincsar, A. M., & Magnussen, S. J. (2001). The interplay of first-hand and second-hand investigations to model and support the development of scientific knowledge and reasoning. In S. M. Carver & D. Klahr (Eds.), *Cognition and instruction: Twenty-five years of progress* (pp. 151–187). Mahwah, NJ: Erlbaum.

Reutzel, D. R., & Cooter, R. B., Jr. (2000). *Teaching children to read: Putting the pieces together* (3rd ed.). Upper Saddle River, NJ: Pearson Education.

Rice, D. C., Dudley, A. P., & Williams, C. S. (2001). How do you choose science trade books? *Science and Children, 38*(6), 18–22.

Roth, K. J., Anderson, C. W., & Smith, E. L. (1987). Curriculum materials, teacher talk, and student learning: Case studies of fifth-grade science teaching. *Journal of Curriculum Studies, 19*(6), 527–548.

Schwartz, R., & Raphael, T. (1985). Concept of definition: A key to improving students' vocabulary. *The Reading Teacher, 39*, 198–205.

Shepard, L. A. (1992). Commentary: What policy makers who mandate tests should know about the new psychology of intellectual ability and learning. In B. R. Gifford & M. C. O'Connor (Eds.), *Changing assessments: Alternative views of aptitude, achievement and instruction*, pp. 301–328). Boston and Dordrecht: Kluwer Academic.

Smith, M. W., & Wilhelm, J. D. (2002). *Reading don't fix no chevys: Literacy in the lives of young men*. Portsmouth, NH: Heinemann.

Thier, M. (2002). *The new science literacy*. Portsmouth, NH: Heinemann.

Thomas, L., & Bitter, G. G. (Eds.). (2000). *National educational technology standards: Connecting curriculum and technology*. Eugene, OR: International Society for Technology in Education.

Tiene, D., & Luft, P. (2002). The technology-rich classroom. *American School Board Journal*. Available at www.asbj.com.

Topping, D. H., & McManus, R. A. (2002). A culture of literacy in science. *Educational Leadership, 60*(3), 30–33.

Waldrip, B. (2001, March). Primary teachers' views about integrating science and literacy: Investigating. *Australian Primary and Junior Science Journal, 17*(1), 38–43.

Wellman, R. T. (1978). Science: A basic language and reading development. In M. B. Rowe (Ed.), *What research says to the science teacher* (Vol. 1). Washington, DC: National Science Teachers Association.

White, B. Y., & Frederiksen, J. R. (1998). Inquiry, modeling and meta-cognition: Making science accessible to all students. *Cognition and Instruction, 16*(1), 3–118.

Woolfolk, A. (2001). *Educational psychology*. Boston: Allyn & Bacon.

Yore, L. D. (2003). Examining the literacy component of science literacy: 25 years of language arts and science research. *International Journal of Science Education, 25*(6), 689–725.

Yore, L., Craig, M., & Maguire, T. (1995). Index of science reading awareness: An interactive-constructive model, test verification, and grades 4–8 results. *Journal of Research in Science Teaching, 35*(1), 27–47.

Zorfass, J., Corley, P., & Remey, A. (1994). Helping students with disabilities become writers. *Educational Leadership, 52*(7), 62–66.

CHILDREN'S LITERATURE

AFRICAN ANIMALS: GRADES K–5

Fiction

Grindley, Sally, and Butler, John, *Little elephant thunderfoot*, Peachtree, Atlanta, Georgia, 1998.—Poachers alter the life of a baby elephant. Grades K–2.—An ultimately heart-warming story that includes much of the research done on elephants' lives in the wild.

Nonfiction

Kulling, Monica, *Elephants: Life in the wild*, Step into Reading, Random House, New York, 2000.—Describes life of elephants in the wild.—Grades K–2.

Lewin, Ted, and Lewin, Betsy, *Elephant quest*, HarperCollins, New York, 2000.—Researchers report on African savannah ecosystem while studying elephants.

Milton, Joyce, *Gorillas: Gentle giants of the forest*, Step into Reading, Random House, New York, 1997.—Describes behavior of gorillas in the wild and how scientists have studied them.

Taylor, Barbara, *Apes and monkeys*, Kingfisher, Boston, 2004.—Recent information from research in Africa is incorporated in this nonfiction resource.

Taylor, Barbara, *Animal giants*, Kingfisher, Boston, 2004.—Features many fascinating facts about the largest animals in the animal kingdom.

ARCTIC ANIMALS: GRADES K–5

Fiction

Grindley, Sally, *Polar star*, Peachtree, Atlanta, 1997.—To learn how a polar bear mother protects her offspring until they can live independently, we follow a mother polar bear and her two cubs from their birth to a dangerous encounter with a hungry male bear.

Nonfiction

Darling, Kathy, *Arctic babies*, Walker, New York, 1996.—Descriptions and photos of some of the young animals that are found in the Arctic.

Patent, Dorothy Hinshaw, *Great ice bear: The polar bear and the Eskimo*, Morrow Junior Books, New York, 1999.—Discusses the relationship of polar bears with humans and gives information about them and where they live in regions of Russia, Denmark, Norway, Canada, the United States, and Greenland.

ASTRONOMY: GRADES 3–6

Fiction

Brooks, Walter R., *Freddy and the men from Mars*, Overlook Press, Woodstock, New York, 1954, copyright renewed 1982.—Something seems suspicious about the capture of the only Martians ever to have visited Earth, so Freddy, the pig detective, goes about his work to expose the hoax with the help of real aliens from Mars.

Brooks, Walter R., *Freddy and the space ship*, Overlook Press, Woodstock, New York, 1953, copyright renewed 1981.—Freddy and some barnyard friends take off for Mars in Mr. Bean's space ship, only to have things go far differently than they had planned, causing them to end up in a stranger place than they ever imagined.

Burkett Kathy, *Out of this world!: Ethan Flask and Professor Von Offel take on space science*, Scholastic, New York, 2001.—An age-old feud between arch-rival families continues as the Von Offels once again try to steal a high-tech solution, threatening to blast Einstein Elementary School into orbit and frustrate the work of good Professor Flask.

Gauthier, Gail, *My life among the aliens*, Putnam, 1996.—Humorous story of an ordinary boy and his ordinary family as they encounter hungry aliens from outer space.

Nonfiction

Couper, Heather, and Henbest, Nigel, *Is anybody out there?* Dorling Kindersley, London, 1998.—Both science and myths of alien life outside our Earth are explored.

Davis, Kenneth C., *Don't know much about space*, HarperCollins, New York, 1994.—Remarkable information about the Sun, stars, planets, and the universe is presented to encourage readers to contemplate interplanetary space travel and living in outer space.

Engelbert, Phillis, and Dupuis, Diane L., *The handy space answer book*, Visible Ink Press, Canton, Michigan, 1998.—Informational resource, good for all ages, to help students understand complicated concepts in astronomy (one of a series of *Handy Answer* books).

Gaff, Jackie, *Superman's guide to the universe*, Dorling Kindersley, London, 2003.—The universe is explained by Superman.

Jefferis, David, *Alien lifesearch*, Crabtree, New York, 1999.—Comprehensive look at our exploration of space, other planets that might support life, and the study of UFOs and aliens.

Kerrod, Robin, *Get a grip on astronomy*, Ivy Press, East Sussex, England, 1999.—The mysteries of the night sky are revealed in this fascinating informational book. It is valuable for teachers as well as for older students.

Pogue, William R., *How do you go to the bathroom in space?* Tom Doherty Associates, New York, 1991.—If students ever wondered what it's really like for an astronaut in outer space, this book answers their questions.

ASTRONOMY: GRADES K–2

Fiction

Asch, Frank, *The sun is my favorite star*, Harcourt, New York, 2000.—Celebrates a child's love of the Sun and its wonder.

Nonfiction

Tomecek, Steve, *Sun*, National Geographic Society, Washington, DC, 2001.—Describes the physics of the Sun. Concepts are presented in an easy-to-understand manner, enhanced by colorful illustrations. It includes historical thought on the relationship of the Earth to the Sun.

BATS: GRADES 2–5

Fiction

Cannon, Janell, *Stellaluna*, Harcourt Brace, New York, 1993.—After she falls headfirst into a bird's nest, a baby bat is raised like a bird until she is reunited with her mother.

Davies, Nicola, *Bat loves the night*, Candlewick Press, Cambridge, Massachusetts, 2001.— Bat wakes up, flies into the night, uses the echoes of her voice to navigate, hunts for her supper, and returns to her roost to feed her baby.

Gilson, Jamie, *It goes eeeeeeeeeeee!*, Clarion Books, New York, 1994.—A new boy who is always causing trouble redeems himself with a science project about bats, which helps him make new friends.

Nonfiction

Cleave, Andrew, *Bats: A portrait of the animal world*, Todtri, New York, 1999.—Excellent nonfiction resource for older students.

Gibbons, Gail, *Bats*, Holiday House, New York, 1999.—Describes different kinds of bats, their physical characteristics, habits, and behavior, and efforts to protect them.

Pringle, Laurence, *Bats: Strange and wonderful*, Caroline House, Honesdale, Pennsylvania, 2000.—Presents the positive attributes of these important creatures.

Sway, Marlene, *Bats: Mammals that fly*, Franklin Watts, New York, 1999.—Provides comprehensive information about bats, including their importance and conservation efforts to protect them.

Teacher Resource

Tuttle, Merlin D. *Educator's activity book: About bats*, Bat Conservation International, Austin, Texas, 1991.—Helpful ideas and information for classroom use, including many activities.

BIOMES: GRADES 3–6

Nonfiction

Kalman, Bobbie, *What is a biome?*, Crabtree, New York, 1998.—Background information on location, climate, and plant and animal life of biomes of the world.

BIRDS: GRADES K–6

Fiction

Arden, Carolyn, *Goose moon*, Boyds Mills Press, Honesdale, Pennsylvania, 2004.—A young girl awaits the goose moon and the return of the geese in the spring of the year.

Bunting, Eve, *Secret place*, Clarion Books, New York, 1996.—A young boy discovers a patch of wilderness in the city where birds find a place to nest. Grades K–3.

Cherry, Lynne, *Flute's journey: The life of a wood thrush*, Harcourt Brace, New York, 1997.—A wood thrush makes his first migration from his home in the eastern United States to his winter home in the tropics.

Nonfiction

Burton, Robert, *Egg*, Dorling Kindersley, New York, 1994.—Comprehensive resource.

Jenkins, Martin, *The emperor's egg*, Candlewick Press, Cambridge, Massachusetts, 1999.—A look at the fatherly duties of the male emperor penguin.

Lerner, Carol, *On the wing: American birds in migration*, HarperCollins, New York, 2001.—Migration of North American birds is presented in detail.

Webb, Sophie, *My season with penguins: An American journal.* Houghton Mifflin, New York, 2000.—A biologist records her research living with penguin colonies.

Poetry

Fleischman, Paul, *I am phoenix: Poems for two voices*, Harper Collins, New York, 1985.—Poems about our fine, feathered friends that can be enjoyed alone or with a partner.

BUTTERFLIES: GRADES 1–3

Fiction

Bunting, Eve, *Butterfly house*, Scholastic, New York, 1999.—A young girl makes a house for a larva with her grandfather, and together they watch it develop before setting it free. The painted lady butterfly comes back to visit her every spring, even as she grows much older.

Coville, Bruce, *The prince of butterflies*, Harcourt Children's Books, 2002.—Fascinated by butterflies, 11-year-old John becomes transformed into one, which changes his life forever.

Johnston, Tony, *Isabel's house of butterflies*, Sierra Club Books for Children, San Francisco, 2003.—In the mountains of Mexico, where the monarch butterflies from the United States winter over, an 8-year-old girl hopes to spare her favorite tree, to which the butterflies come every year, when her impoverished family needs to cut it down and sell it.

Nonfiction

Ehlert, Lois, *Waiting for wings*, Harcourt Children's Books, New York, 2001.—Intriguing nonfiction for young students.

George, Jean Craighead, *The moon of the monarch butterflies*, HarperCollins, New York, 1993.—A monarch butterfly's journey north from Arkansas to Michigan is described in the text for the month of May, which this book represents in George's *Thirteen Moons* series.

Glaser, Linda, *Magnificent monarchs*, Millbrook Press, Brookfield, Connecticut, 2000.— Describes, in simple text and illustrations, the physical characteristics, habits, and life cycle of the monarch butterfly.

Kalman, Bobbie, *The life cycle of a butterfly*, Crabtree, New York, 1997.—Describes the various stages of a monarch butterfly's life, from egg to pupa to caterpillar to butterfly, as well as its migration and the dangers it faces.

Lerner, Carol, *Butterflies in the garden*, HarperCollins, New York, 2002.—Beautiful resource on attracting butterflies to a school butterfly garden.

Rockwell, Anne F., *Becoming butterflies*, Walker, New York, 2002.—The care and keeping of monarch butterfly caterpillars comes alive as students learn about metamorphosis.

Sandved, K. B. *The butterfly alphabet*, Scholastic, New York, 1996.—Glorious photographs of butterflies throughout the world include close-ups of wing designs that seem to depict letters of the alphabet.

Winer, Yvonne, *Butterflies fly*, Charlesbridge, Watertown, Massachusetts, 2000.—A beautifully written and illustrated starter book on the subject.

CENTER OF MASS/CENTER OF GRAVITY/BALANCING: GRADES K–6

Fiction

McCully, Emily Arnold, *Mirette on the high wire*, Putnam & Grossett, New York, 1992.— Mirette learns tightrope walking from a man who has given it up because of his fear. Grades K–3.

Nonfiction

Gerstein, Mordicai, *The man who walked between the towers*, Roaring Brook Press, Brookfield, Connecticut, 2003.—A lyrical telling of Philippe Petit's 1974 tightrope walk between the World Trade Center towers.

ELECTRICITY: GRADES 3–6

Fiction

Lawson, Robert, *Ben and me*, Little, Brown, New York, 1939, copyright renewed 1967 by John W. Boyd.—Benjamin Franklin's companion, Amos the mouse, takes credit for Franklin's inventions and discoveries.

Nonfiction

Bang, Molly, *My light*, Blue Sky Press, Scholastic, New York, 2004.—Depicts, in graphic form, concepts of electricity: how it is created from energy from the Sun and flows into our homes.

Berger, Melvin, *Switch on, switch off*, HarperCollins, New York, 1989.—Explains how electricity is produced and transmitted, how to create electricity using wires and a magnet, how generators supply electricity for cities, and how electricity works in homes.

Cole, Joanna, and Degen, Bruce, *The magic school bus and the electric field trip*, Scholastic, New York, 1997.—Another engaging resource in this outstanding series.

Lunis, Natalie, *Discovering electricity*, Newbridge Educational Publishing, New York, 1997.—Provides reliable background information.

Reuben, Gabriel, *Electricity experiments for children*, Dover Publications, New York, 1966 (reprinted).—Numerous experiments for older elementary students to ground them in necessary concepts for understanding magnetism and electricity.

ENTOMOLOY: GRADES K–3

Fiction

McDonald, Megan, *Insects are my life*, Orchard Books, New York, 1997.—No one at home or at school can understand Amanda's passion for insects until she meets her soul mate.

Nonfiction

Kalman, Bobbie, *The life cycle of a mosquito*, Crabtree, New York, 2004.—High-interest, comprehensive, nonfiction resource.

Poetry

Fleischman, Paul, *Joyful noise: Poems for two voices*, HarperCollins, New York, 1989.—Designed for two children to enjoy together, this book celebrates insects from lice to mayflies.

EPIDEMICS: GRADES 4–6

Fiction

Anderson, Laurie Halse, *Fever 1793*, Aladdin Paperbacks, New York, 2000.—In 1793 Philadelphia, a 16-year-old girl learns about perseverance and self-reliance when she is forced to cope with being separated from her sick mother amid the horrors of a yellow fever epidemic.

Nonfiction

Ward, Brian, R., *Epidemic*, Eyewitness Books, Dorling Kindersley, New York, 2000.—Discusses what an epidemic is, how it evolves, various causes and carriers, and efforts to prevent epidemics. Grades 4 and up.

GEOLOGY: GRADES 3–6

Fiction

Kehret, Peg, *Earthquake terror*, Puffin Books, New York, 1996.—When an earthquake hits the isolated island in northern California where his family has been camping, a 12-year-old boy must somehow keep himself, his partially paralyzed younger sister, and their dog alive until help arrives.

Skurzynski, Gloria, and Ferguson, Alane, *Over the edge*, Mysteries in Our National Parks Series, National Geographic Society, Washington DC, 2002.—While she studies condors in the Grand Canyon, a scientist's life is threatened, and a strange teenage boy may be involved.

Nonfiction

Vieira, Linda, *Grand canyon*, Walker, New York, 1997.—Visitors to the park learn the history and geology of the area, which are depicted with visual drama.

York, Penelope, *Earth*, Eye Wonder Series, Dorling Kindersley, London, 2004.—Offers clear informational text along with powerful photographs of our geological world.

HISTORY OF THE EARTH: GRADES 3–6

Nonfiction

Bailey, Jacqui, and Lilly, Matthew, *A Cartoon History of the Earth* series. Titles include *The birth of the earth*, *The dawn of life*, *The day of the dinosaurs*, *The stick and stone age*, Kids Can Press, Tonawanda, New York, 2001.—Inviting text and pictures turn children on to Earth's fascinating history.

HISTORY OF AFRICAN AMERICANS: GRADES 2–6

Fiction

Williams, Sherley Anne, *Working cotton*, Harcourt Brace Jovanovich, New York, 1992.—An African American girl relates events of a typical day in the life of her migrant family working in the cotton fields of central California.

LIGHT: GRADES K–4

Freeman, Don, *A rainbow of my own*, Puffin Books, New York, 1966.—A child gets a rainbow surprise caused by light refraction. *Note*: This is a delightful book, but a discussion on discerning fact and fantasy is important. This is always an important concept to develop with young children. Grades K–2.

Krupp, Edwin C., *The rainbow and you*, HarperCollins, New York, 2000.—Explains how rainbows are formed by the colors in sunlight shining through raindrops and gives many other fascinating facts. Grades 2–4.

MARINE LIFE: GRADES 3–6

Fiction

Baglio, Ben M., *Dolphin Diaries* series. Titles include *Into the blue*, *Touching the waves*, *Riding the storm*, *Under the stars*, *Chasing the dream*, *Racing the wind*, *Following the rainbow*, *Dancing the seas*, *Leaving the shallows*, *Beyond the sunrise*, Scholastic Press, New York, 1998.—A family travels around the world in a yacht to study and meet the various dolphins that live in the world's oceans and seas.

George, Jean Craighead, *Water sky*, HarperCollins, New York, 1987.—A young boy who is eager to learn about his Ologak ancestry learns the importance of whaling to the Eskimo culture.

Torrey, Michele, *Voyage of ice*, Alfred A. Knopf, New York, 2004.—Two brothers do not realize the harrowing experiences they will face on a whaling boat.

Nonfiction

McNulty, Faith, *How whales walked into the sea*, Scholastic, New York, 1999.—Explains how a large carnivorous land mammal slowly evolved into the sea creatures we know today.

Pick, Christopher, *The Usborne young scientist undersea*, Usborne Publishing, London, 1990.—Comprehensive resource on life under the sea, how it is being studied, and simple experiments that can be done.

Petty, Kate, *I didn't know that whales can sing*, Copper Beech Books, Brookfield, Connecticut, 1998.—Examines the characteristics and life of whales and dolphins.

MATTER: GRADES 1–4

Nonfiction

Beech, Linda, *The magic school bus gets baked in a cake*, Scholastic, New York, 1995.—Presents many kitchen chemistry concepts in an amusing and engaging manner.

Ontario Science Centre, *Solids, liquids and gases*, Kids Can Press, Buffalo, New York, 1998.—Easy-to-follow experiments with helpful explanations.

PRAIRIE: GRADES 3–5

Fiction

George, Jean Craighead, *One day in the prairie*, HarperCollins, New York, 1986.—Animals in a prairie wildlife refuge sense an upcoming tornado and seek to find protection.

Hermes, Patricia, *Calling me home*, Avon Books, New York, 1998.—Abbie moves to an old soddy on the Nebraska prairie to experience the hardships and rewards of living there.

Reynolds, Marilynn, *The prairie fire*, Orca Book Publishers, Custer, Washington, 1999.—A boy takes on a daring responsibility when a prairie fire threatens his family's home and livestock.

Thomas, Joyce Carol, *I have heard of a land*, HarperCollins, New York, 1998.—African American homesteaders leave everything and travel west, attracted by the promise of the 1862 Homestead Act.

Nonfiction

Lerner, Carol, *Seasons of the tallgrass prairie*, William Morrow, New York, 1980.—The plant life of the prairie is described season by season, as well as the role of wildfire.

Warren, Andrea, *Pioneer girl: Growing up on the prairie*, HarperCollins, New York, 1998.—The true story of Grace McCance Snyder, who experienced a hardscrabble life alongside her parents on the Nebraska prairie, surviving fire, blizzards, and other hardships but weathering them with good humor and high spirits.

PREDATORS: GRADES 2–5

Nonfiction

Kenah, Katharine, *Predator attack!* Extreme Readers series, McGraw-Hill, Columbus, Ohio, 2004.—Photography and facts show children how exciting it is to read about life in the wild.

RAINFOREST: GRADES 2–6

Fiction

Cannon, Janell, *Crickwing*, Harcourt Children's Books, New York, 2000.—A lonesome cockroach, Crickwing, has an inspired idea to assist the leaf-cutting ants when their fierce forest enemies attack them.

Cherry, Lynne, *The great kapok tree*, Harcourt Brace Jovanovich, New York, 1990.—This is the rainforest classic. A tree in the Brazilian rainforest is about to be cut down, as described from the animals' point of view.

Cherry, Lynne and Plotkin, Mark, *The shaman's apprentice*, Harcourt Brace Jovanovich, New York, 1998.—A native boy is trained in a shaman's wisdom about the healing properties of plants found in the Amazon rainforest and hopes one day to follow in the wise man's footsteps to become a healer.

Franklin, Kristine, *When the monkeys came back*, Atheneum, New York, 1994.—Always remembering how the monkeys in her Costa Rican valley disappeared when all the trees were cut down, Marta grows ups, plants more trees, and sees the monkeys come back.

George, Jean Craighead, *One day in the tropical rain forest*, HarperCollins, New York, 1990.—A native boy in the Venezuelan rainforest helps a scientist find a newly discovered butterfly in order to save a portion of his rainforest home.

Osborne, Mary Pope, *Afternoon on the Amazon*, Random House, New York, 1995.—Eight-year-old Jack, his seven-year-old sister, and their pet mouse ride in a tree house to the Amazon rainforest, where they encounter many of the wild animals found there.

Nonfiction

Gibbons, Gail, *Nature's green umbrella*, Morrow Junior Books, New York, 1994.—Describes the climate of the rainforest, the layered structure of the plants, and the many animals included in the ecosystem.

Goodman, Susan E., *Ultimate field trip 1: Adventures in the Amazon rain forest*, Aladdin Paperbacks, New York, 1999.—Describes rainforest ecology and depicts a trip down the Amazon with kids.

Kratter, Paul, *The living rain forest*, Charlesbridge, Watertown, Massachusetts, 2004.—An ABC book of rainforest animals, including characteristics and interesting facts.

Osborne, Will, and Osborne, Mary Pope, *Rain forests*, Random House, New York, 2001.—Nonfiction resource, companion to *Afternoon on the Amazon*.

Pratt, Kristin Joy, *A walk in the rainforest*, Dawn Publications, Nevada City, California, 1992.—Excellent nonfiction reference written by a teenager.

Scholastic, *The magic school bus in the rain forest*, Scholastic, New York, 1998, based on *The magic school bus* books written by Joanna Cole.

Yolen, Jane, *Welcome to the greenhouse*, G.P. Putnam's Sons, New York, 1993.—Beautifully illustrated poetic description of a tropical rainforest.

Zak, Monica, *Save my rainforest*, Volcano Press, California, 1992.—A 9-year-old Mexican boy initiates a campaign to save the rainforest in southern Mexico. True story.

Teacher Resource

Malnor, Bruce and Carol, *Teacher's guide, A walk in the rainforest*, Dawn Publications, Nevada City, California, 1997.—Contains lessons to accompany *A walk in the rainforest* by Kristin Joy Pratt.

RODENTS: GRADES 1–4

Nonfiction

Kalman, Bobbie, *Gerbils*, Crabtree, New York, 2004.—Information on the selection, preparation for, and care of gerbils.

Kalman, Bobbie, *What is a rodent?*, Crabtree, New York, 2000.—One of a series of excellent nonfiction resources by Bobbie Kalman.

SNOWFLAKES: GRADES 2–6

Nonfiction/Biography

Martin, Jacqueline Briggs, *Snowflake Bentley*, Houghton Mifflin, Boston, 1998.—Biography of a scientist who photographed thousands of individual snowflakes to study their structure.

WATER CYCLE: GRADES 2–6

Poetry

Locker, Thomas, *Cloud dance*, Harcourt Brace, New York, 2000.—Superb illustrations and lovely lyrical text describe clouds.

Locker, Thomas, *Water dance*, Harcourt Brace, New York, 1997.—Thomas Locker provides lyrical text and glorious painting to describe the various states of water.

Martin, Bill, and Archambault, John, *Listen to the rain*, Holt, New York, 1988.—Wonderful poetry for choral reading.

Nonfiction

Hooper, Meredith, and Coady, Chris, *The drop in my drink: The story of water on our planet*, Viking, New York, 1998.—Examines the amazing story of water, how it is always changing, and the essential role it has played and will continue to play in life on earth.

AN EXTRA: GRADES 2–6

Scieszka, Jon, *Science verse*, Penguin, New York, 2004.—Dynamic cartoons and humorous poetry concerning nearly every science discipline will keep everyone chuckling.

INDEX

"f" following a page number indicates a figure; "t" following a page number indicates a table.

G

Gender issues, 88
Geology unit, 122–124. *See also* Unit
    studies
Glossary, 77
Goals, learning, 15, 18, 56
Graphic information in texts, 87
Graphs, 83–84
Group-work
    environment and, 15
    research and, 95–96
    unit studies and, 35–36, 42–43, 47–49
    vocabulary expansion and, 74

H

Handheld computing devices, 158. *See also*
    Technology
Headings in informational texts, 81–82
Hypotheses creation, 30, 42

I

Index, in informational texts, 77
Informational texts
    basic features of, 79–84, 81*f*
    learning to use, 77–79
    national standards and, 11–12
    organization of science library, 89–91
    overview, 76–77*f*, 103
    during read-aloud time, 91
    reading directions, 102–103, 104*f*
    research and, 91–98, 92*f*, 95*f*
    selecting, 84–89
    teaching students to read, 5–6
Inquiry-based science
    assessment and, 167, 168*f*
    curriculum integration and, 5, 31
    informational texts and, 77
    national standards and, 7, 11
    overview, 2–3
    process skills and, 29–30
    in unit studies, 37, 42
    vocabulary expansion and, 57

Instruction, 27–28, 77–79, 154, 165–166
Integration of language and science
    literacies
    activities, 30–32
    learning centers and, 18
    overview, 26–27
    rationale for, 5–7
    selecting texts and, 84–85
    unit planning and, 27–28, 32–34
International Reading Association (IRA).
    See also National Council of Teachers
    of English (NCTE), standards and
    standards and, 10*t*
    unifying concepts and, 29
    unit studies and, 35, 42, 46–47
International Society for Technology in
    Education (ISTE), 153
Internet. *See* Technology; Websites

J

Journaling. *See also* Writing
    curriculum integration and, 32
    developing, 137–140, 138*f*, 139*f*, 140–
        141*f*, 142*f*, 143*f*, 144*f*–145*f*
    in unit studies, 45*f*, 134–137, 135*f*,
        136*f*
    vocabulary expansion and, 68

K

Knowledge, prior, 31
Knowledge building stage
    overview, 34
    unit studies and, 35, 42, 47, 48–49
KWL chart, 141*f*

L

Language arts activities, 35–36, 42–43, 47–
    48
Language arts center, 18–19. *See also*
    Learning centers
Language arts competencies, 30–32